LABOR, LOYALTY, & REBELLION

LABOR, LOYALTY, REBELLION

SOUTHWESTERN ILLINOIS COAL MINERS AND WORLD WAR I

CARL R. WEINBERG

SOUTHERN ILLINOIS UNIVERSITY PRESS / CARBONDALE

Library of Congress Cataloging-in-Publication Data
Weinberg, Carl R., 1962–
Labor, loyalty, and rebellion : southwestern Illinois coal miners
and World War I / Carl R. Weinberg.
        p. cm.
Includes bibliographical references (p.) and index.
    1. Coal miners—Illinois—History—20th century. 2. Coal
mines and mining—Illinois—History—20th century. 3. Labor
movement—Illinois—History—20th century. 4. Illinois—
Economic conditions—20th century. 5. Illinois—Social
conditions—20th century. 6. World War, 1914–1918—Illinois.
7. World War, 1914–1918—Economic aspects. 8. World War, 1914–
1918—Social aspects. I. Title.
HD8039.M62U676 2005
331.88'122334'09773809041—dc22
ISBN 0-8093-2634-5 (alk. paper)
ISBN 0-8093-2635-3 (pbk. : alk. paper)   2004023654

For my parents, Meyer and Erica Weinberg

CONTENTS

ILLUSTRATIONS

ACKNOWLEDGMENTS

Writing a book is a humbling experience. This project began nearly fifteen years ago and eventually became a sprawling 634-page manuscript. Although I thought that it could be published with little revision, I found out otherwise. With the help of many people, I managed to do the work that enabled this book to be born.

Hats off first to the scholars who read my work at an earlier stage and made valuable suggestions for making it better. They include James Barrett, David Brody, John Demos, David Emmons, Julie Greene, John Laslett, Joseph McCartin, David Montgomery, David Roediger, and Gaddis Smith. I also received encouragement and insight through conversation, e-mail, and otherwise from Steve Clark, Debbie Elkin, Dick Gazley, Yvette Huginnie, Brian Kelly, Daniel Letwin, Jane Levey, Caroline Waldron Merithew, Sylvie Murray, Scott Olsen, Bryan Palmer, Gunther Peck, Shelton Stromquist, Will Wilkin, Lane Witt, and David Zonderman.

I am especially grateful to David Montgomery. It was a pleasure to work closely with someone who shared my deep interest in both the working-class past and the working-class present. In addition to his unparalleled knowledge of social and labor history, always reflected in immensely detailed comments on chapter drafts, he had the rare ability to offer genuinely constructive criticism. Over the past decade, he has continued to provide timely insight, aid, and advice.

One of the most gratifying aspects of my research was talking with retired southwestern Illinois coal miners and their families. I am indebted to the following individuals, nearly all now deceased, for sharing their experiences and perspectives with me: Frances Bauer, Pete Perry, Hawley Canterbury, Jack Canterbury, Vernon Canterbury, Joe Brabec Sr., Leroy

Harris, Tony Hrebik, Peter Magdich, Katherine Mans, Albert "Kites" Meyer, David Thoreau Wieck, and Diva Angostinelli Wieck. A number of local historians, miners, scholars, and librarians helped me locate these individuals and directed me toward other useful sources. They include Regina Agnew of the East St. Louis Public Library, Florence Berkholder of the Collinsville Public Library, Professor Shirley Carlson at Southern Illinois University Edwardsville, ex-miner "Jocko" of Benld, Elda Jones with the Marissa Historical and Genealogical Library, Kathleen Jones of the Glen Carbon Library, Viola Krivi of the Mt. Olive Public Library, Billie Laumbattus of the Marissa Public Library, Delta Barber Masterson of Belleville, Betty Nielsen of Mt. Olive, Lucille Stehman of Collinsville, Virden miner David Yard, Marla Zubal of the Mt. Olive Public Library, and James Hogg at the Museum of Science and Industry in Chicago.

Also of great assistance were the staff in the reading rooms of the National Archives in Washington and the Newberry Library in Chicago; archivist Marie Hackett at Southern Illinois University Edwardsville; Richard Walsh of the Illinois AFL-CIO, who graciously allowed me to look at the Illinois Federation records; Pete Hoefer of the George Meany Memorial Archives, who alerted me to the Illinois collection; the staff of the Illinois State Historical Library; and Dr. John Hoffman of the Illinois Historical Survey, who guided me through the John Walker Collection. In addition, thanks go to miner Dennis Skeldon for a tour of the Monterrey No. 1 mine near Carlinville. In Washington, D.C., Maier Fox, formerly researcher for the United Mine Workers of America, was instrumental in enabling me to gain access to union records. I am thankful to President Richard Trumka of the United Mine Workers for granting me permission to look at this material. Thanks also go to Jane Charles of the current UMWA Archive at Pennsylvania State University.

In my hunt for photos, I had assistance from the following individuals: Gregg Ames of the St. Louis Mercantile Library; Doris Bauer of Caseyville, Illinois; James Cornelius of the Illinois Historical Survey; Rebecca Gedda of the Collinsville *Herald Journal;* Becky Matthews of Collinsville; Gloria Baracks of G. Bradley Publishing; and Mary Wallace at the Reuther Library at Wayne State University.

In recent years, a number of my colleagues at North Georgia College and State University were extremely helpful in the process of making my work suitable for publication. They include Ray Rensi, Stephen Smith, and B. J. Robinson. Special thanks go to fellow historian Christopher

Jespersen, who carefully read and commented on the manuscript, and to geography guru Robert Fuller, who created the initial map. Moreover, students in History 2000, 3160, and 4232, who were forced to read about the Prager lynching, asked me good questions and kept me on my toes.

Editors Karl Kageff and Carol Burns of Southern Illinois University Press did a fine job of guiding me through the review and editorial process, and Barbara Martin gave much needed advice on the technical side of publishing the book. Julie Bush provided expert copyediting, and cartographer Gena Howe created an excellent final map. Readers' reports from Joseph McCartin and Carl Oblinger were invaluable in helping me strengthen the book and get it ready for publication. Thanks also to Jim O'Brien for a fine index.

The book is dedicated to my parents, who have always believed in me, even when I didn't share their confidence. Though my father did not live to see this book published, his encouragement and example helped make it possible.

Finally, my children, Kevin and Anna, have made life such a joy that the difficulties of completing a book are magnificently reduced in comparison. And the greatest thanks go to my wife and lifelong companion, Beth. She has been my best critic and strongest supporter. I can say for certain that without her, this book would never have come to be.

ABBREVIATIONS

AFL	American Federation of Labor
APL	American Protective League
B&C	Journeymen Bakers' and Confectioners' International Union; later Bakery and Confectionery Workers International Union
CFL	Chicago Federation of Labor
CND	Council of National Defense
CPI	Committee on Public Information
FBI	Federal Bureau of Investigation
FMM	Four Minute Men
IBEW	International Brotherhood of Electrical Workers
ICD	Illinois Council of Defense
IFL	Illinois Federation of Labor
IOOF	International Order of Odd Fellows
ISF	Italian Socialist Federation
ITU	Independent Textile Union
IUMMSW	International Union of Mine, Mill and Smelter Workers
IWDL	International Workers Defense League
IWW	Industrial Workers of the World
NAACP	National Association for the Advancement of Colored People
SLP	Socialist Labor Party
SLSR	St. Louis Smelting and Refining
UMWA	United Mine Workers of America
UMWJ	*United Mine Workers Journal*

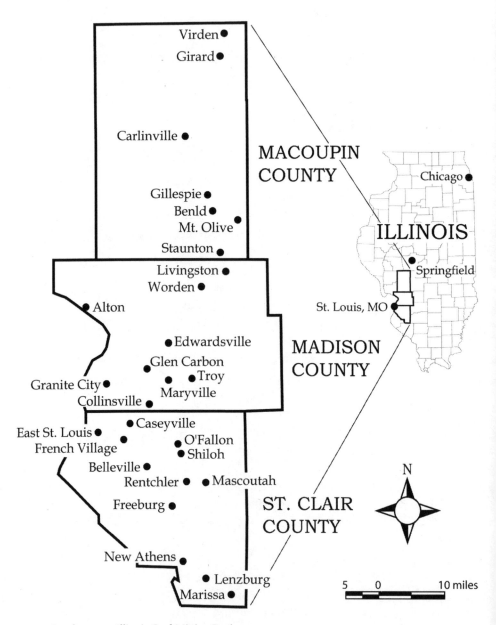

Southwestern Illinois Coal Mining Region

LABOR, LOYALTY, & REBELLION

Introduction

When I was a boy growing up in the suburbs of Chicago, one of my favorite family excursions was a trip to the city's Museum of Science and Industry. Vintage airplanes hung from the ceiling in the main hall. My brother and I whispered long-range conversations in the echo chamber. Baby chicks hatched before our eyes. But the most intriguing exhibit, and the scariest, was the coal mine. After a long wait in line, we entered the mine elevator and headed straight down into what seemed to be the bowels of the earth. We rode on an underground trolley in complete darkness. We jumped in our seats when the tour guide detonated a tiny demonstration gas explosion inside a sealed box. And when it was all over, I was glad to get back to the "surface."

Many years later, I returned to the museum with my own children. The mine was no longer menacing; what struck me now was how fake it seemed. The coal was shellacked. The "miners" were mannequins, frozen in place. By this time, I had learned a bit about coal mining and its history. I had discovered that a century earlier, my home state of Illinois was one of the leading producers of coal and a center of coal mining unionism in the United States. I had spent a good deal of time studying the coalfields of southwestern Illinois, adjacent to St. Louis, Missouri. And I had toured a working deep-shaft coal mine in the area. Somehow, as a child, it had never occurred to me that there were actual coal mines in Illinois.

When I entered the museum's mine elevator, or "cage," as an adult, I happened to look to my right and spied a heavy metal plaque mounted on the wall. This informed visitors that the coal in the museum mine had been retrieved from an abandoned Consolidated Coal Company mine in, of all places, the very region I had been studying. Mine No. 15 was near

Mt. Olive, Illinois, which, I had learned, boasted the resting place of famed labor organizer Mary "Mother" Jones in the Union Miners Cemetery. In her will, she had asked to be buried with the martyrs of the 1898 Battle of Virden.[1] These men had been union coal miners from Mt. Olive who gave their lives to secure Illinois as a stronghold of the United Mine Workers of America (UMWA). Mt. Olive, I also had learned, continued its role as a center of labor radicalism during World War I, when local miner Adolph Germer became the national secretary of the Socialist Party, which opposed U.S. entry into the war. Consolidated Coal Company was one small part of a larger story that I came to know by poring over local newspapers, interviewing retired miners, and delving into government archives and union and company records in countless small Illinois towns, in Washington, D.C., and in my hometown of Chicago.

My newfound knowledge of that museum coal mine and the genesis of this book began in graduate school when, one day, I found myself reading a tattered copy of what, after nearly half a century, is still a standard work in its field: *Opponents of War, 1917–18*, by H. C. Peterson and Gilbert Fite.[2] Like many graduate students, I was desperately searching for a topic for my latest seminar paper assignment. I wanted a topic that could combine my interest in diplomatic history with a growing interest in social and labor history. I had become convinced that one could not understand the big political decisions made in Washington during World War I without getting a feel for what was happening on the ground among ordinary working people. Since Peterson and Fite's book is a virtual encyclopedia of dramatic incidents on the American home front during World War I, there were any number that seemed worthy of further research. One, however, seemed to fit the bill particularly well. On April 5, 1918, about ten miles east of St. Louis, on the outskirts of a southwestern Illinois coal mining town called Collinsville, there was a "patriotic" lynching. The victim was a thirty-year-old immigrant worker from Dresden, Germany, named Robert Paul Prager, who was accused of sabotage and spying for the Germans. This was more than a local story. As soon as Collinsville residents had lynched Prager, they moved Collinsville into the national and international limelight. News of the lynching quickly spread across the nation. In Washington, Prager's death was discussed by the Wilson cabinet. The Collinsville events became part of the debate in the U.S. Senate on the proposed Sedition Act. They spurred a range of popular responses nationwide, expressed in a flurry of letters to top government officials and in public statements of protest. The lynching even made headlines in Berlin.[3]

Published descriptions of the lynching, whether in brief textbook vignettes or in journal articles, tended to suggest that Illinois working people were conservative, hysterically anti-German, and blindly patriotic during World War I. The main scholarly article on the lynching, by Donald Hickey, was entitled "The Prager Affair: A Study in Wartime Hysteria." Paul Boyer's textbook *The Enduring Vision,* for instance, places Prager's story under the heading "Wartime Intolerance," where readers learn that "some Americans became almost hysterical in their hatred of all things German, their hostility to aliens and dissenters, and their strident patriotism."[4] And indeed, as I read issues of the *Collinsville Herald,* it was clear that coal miners contributed to the great patriotic crusade. They bought scads of Liberty Bonds, gave to the Red Cross, participated in local Councils of Defense, registered for the draft, fought overseas, and, in some cases, carried out vigilante attacks on "disloyalists."

But as I continued reading, the picture grew more complicated. In the year following the American entry into World War I in April 1917—that is, in the year preceding the lynching—the miners of southwestern Illinois, since they were key war industry workers, came under intense pressure to support the war effort and, particularly, to stay on the job. But they often refused. Instead, they saw the war as their opportunity to demand higher wages, better working conditions, and a measure of human dignity. In mid- to late 1917, they staged a series of strikes, unauthorized by union officials, which all but shut down war production in the region. They did this in defiance of government authorities, union officials, and employers, who all collaborated closely in forcing the miners back to work.

As for the debate over World War I, many southwestern Illinois miners doubted whether it was in fact a war for democracy. This area of Illinois, as it turns out, was a stronghold of the Socialist Party, which opposed the war on the basis that it was a falling-out among rival capitalist thieves. Miners commonly complained that this was a rich man's war. There were also plenty of German Americans in the area who felt the tug of patriotism for their homeland. Contrary to my initial impression, this region was hardly a bastion of support for the war.

Moreover, after the armistice, the southwestern Illinois coal miners became known for their radicalism. They carried out a political strike in support of the celebrated Tom Mooney, a militant unionist sentenced to death for allegedly throwing a bomb in a patriotic parade in 1915. They helped form the independent Labor Party in Illinois and elected miners on the new party ticket in Collinsville and Maryville, as well as in other coal towns. After being penalized for the Mooney strike, the miners erupted in a rank-and-file rebellion against the conservative state leadership of the UMWA. They not only fought for union democracy but also passed a resolution demanding that their employers turn over the mines to the miners. Then during the national coal strike of November 1919, when union president John L. Lewis complied with a federal injunction by ordering miners back to work, the miners of southwestern Illinois were one group who once again refused. Finally, under the influence of these events and inspired by the Bolshevik revolution in Russia, a very small number of miners from the area even joined the fledgling Communist Party.

Upon digging deeper into the Prager lynching, I was presented with a puzzle: On the one hand, the miners of southwestern Illinois were fiercely patriotic. In complying with the demands of war mobilization, they seemed to outdo themselves in proving their loyalty to the nation. On the other hand, both during the war and after, these same miners earned a reputation for disloyalty. Again and again, they refused to subordinate their common interests as working-class people to the greater interests of the nation. How could I explain this paradox?

One possible solution is to show that different groups of miners were carrying out different and contrasting activities. That is, there was a radical, Socialist faction and a conservative, patriotic faction and therefore no internal contradiction. To some extent, this was true. Frank Farrington, the president of the Illinois miners union, was a relatively conservative labor leader. He had to deal with constant challenges to his policies from Socialist miners like Adolph Germer. Building on research done by John Laslett on the politics of UMWA District 12 (Illinois), my study finds that in places like Collinsville, these political battles between miners were reflected locally, with Socialists and Farrington loyalists vying for control.[5]

In southwestern Illinois, factionalism within the ranks of coal miners also extended to the issue of American entry into the war and support for war mobilization. At union conventions, in barroom conversations, in union meetings, and in street confrontations, coal miners debated the Great War. While historians have recognized the larger debate among labor leaders at this time, few works have focused on working people and World War I in a particular region or locale. The rich potential of this approach has been demonstrated by historian David Emmons in *The Butte Irish*. Emmons found that the war produced intense debate among copper miners in Butte, Montana, the most Irish town in America. Because of their Irish Republican sympathies and their hatred for the British Crown, many miners rooted for the German Army and even formed a local alliance with German American nationalists.[6] In contrast, David Corbin's influential study of the southern West Virginia miners offers several broad generalizations about coal miners' stance toward World War I: "The nation's miners responded enthusiastically to the war for democracy," and, "The miners' union believed that World War I was a fight for American values."[7] The situation in Illinois seems considerably closer in its complexities to the picture presented by Emmons. The apparent paradox is partly resolved, then, by noting that over time, the war boosters in southwestern Illinois coal mining communities managed to silence those miners who questioned the war.

But the picture of factionalism is complicated by the fact that there were miners who seem to have belonged to both factions. For instance, some miners involved in the Prager lynching—and there were far fewer than previously supposed—had been wildcat strikers labeled as subversive the previous fall. One of these was Joseph Riegel, a German American and the ringleader of the Prager lynch mob. The allegedly "anti-German" lynching was, in fact, led by a "German" worker who was himself under scrutiny for his lack of loyalty. It is likely that the depth of class conflict in the region, neglected in previous scholarship on the Prager lynching, made many workers particularly sensitive to charges of disloyalty.[8]

Yet another way that many scholars would resolve the apparent paradox of the southwestern Illinois coal miners is to argue that patriotism and class consciousness are not opposites. When workers staged wartime strikes or embraced radical political ideas, they were simply expressing another variety of patriotism. Indeed, while the older Marxist tradition of labor history viewed patriotism as conservative, social historians in more recent years such as Herbert Gutman, Sean Wilentz, and others have reacted against this interpretation, which they see as imposing on workers an ahistorical standard of political consciousness. Instead, these new labor historians show how workers borrowed the language of the first American revolution and tried to use it for their own class purposes later in the nineteenth century. As Wilentz writes, historians should reconsider "what is usually accepted as a monolithic 'bourgeois' liberalism—with a fuller appreciation of the ways in which American liberal political ideas could acquire distinctly anticapitalist (and not simply entrepreneurial 'anticorporate') connotations, from the late eighteenth century on."[9] Thus, the trend recently has been to regard so-called labor republicanism as a clever appropriation, a kind of turning of the tables on the oppressor.

In his examination of the southern West Virginia miners, David Corbin is similarly impressed by how coal miners used the traditional republican language of American rights, the Constitution, and citizenship in their campaign to unionize the West Virginia coalfields. In trying to recapture an authentic, home-grown radicalism, Corbin is eager to show that even if they did not use Marxist terminology, hidden in their "Americanism was an ideology, containing values, beliefs, principles, and goals, as coherent, radical, and understanding of an exploitative and oppressive system as any ideology announced by Socialists, Communists, or Wobblies." And even though he acknowledges that patriotism could be used against workers, Corbin insists that "the Americanism that the miners espoused was one that promised liberty, equality, and dignity to all people."[10]

It may be historian Gary Gerstle who has taken the argument furthest in favor of what he calls "working-class Americanism." In his finely crafted and provocative study of Rhode Island textile workers in the 1930s and 1940s, Gerstle found that union leaders consciously tried to portray their working-class demands as being in the tradition of patriotic American heroes such as Lincoln, Jefferson, and Washington. Just as Corbin claimed a rough equivalence between Americanism and Marxism, Gerstle wrote of "working-class Americanism" that its "rhetorical assault resembled, in many ways, the socialist critique of capitalism." And he argues that this strategy succeeded in conferring "the respectability of history on the labor movement's aims."[11] This respectability, in turn, convinced the federal government to step in at crucial points in textile strikes and assure the workers' victory.

More recently, historian Joseph McCartin has argued in support of Gerstle's focus on Americanist language. In his study of working people and World War I, McCartin suggests that working-class aspirations and activity during World War I are best viewed through the lens of "industrial democracy," a phrase that workers and middle-class reformers used to dress labor's demands in patriotic garb. According to McCartin, workers made advances during the war through a short-lived but powerful alliance between militant unionists and progressive-minded Wilson administration officials who collaborated on a program to democratize—or in wartime language, "de-kaiserize"—American industry. The National War Labor Board played a key role in promoting shop committees, in the absence of previous strong union organization, which allowed for unexpected and far-reaching gains on the part of workers, though McCartin is careful to note the contradictions and limitations of these gains. In explaining how progress came about, McCartin emphasizes the practical utility of the patriotic demand for "industrial democracy": "[B]ecause it was protectively rooted in what Gerstle calls 'working-class Americanism,' this demand transcended class to appeal to 'American' values, a crucial asset in a political culture that persistently denied the reality of class."[12]

There is no doubt that many southwestern Illinois miners, though not all, would have agreed with the idea that they could be patriotic Americans while they fought for their interests as workers. When they made radical demands on employers and the government, coal miners often spoke in patriotic language. The organizers of the Mooney protest strike, for instance, were careful to schedule it on July 4. In the subsequent rebellion, miners who had served in the war played a leading role, marching in full uniform and bearing the American flag. During the war, union leaders hammered away on the need for miners to demonstrate their patriotism. This would protect miners' reputation, and, after the war, they would be repaid for their service to the nation.

But my study of the southwestern Illinois miners suggests something quite different from this rather benevolent view of "working-class Americanism." In Collinsville, the working-class patriotism that the war unleashed did not guarantee equal rights to all. It divided workers as much as it united them. In a very real sense, it was not patriotism but the willingness of miners to be branded unpatriotic that proved most effective.[13] When miners did make gains in wages and working conditions during the war, it was due to their "disloyal" strike actions rather than a reward for their patriotism. Moreover, miners' patriotism did not pay off as the union hoped it would. Despite the commitment of some in the Wilson administration to "industrial democracy," many coal miners in southwestern Illinois experienced the aftermath of World War I as a bitter betrayal by Wilson. These findings resonate with Brian Kelly's recent study of Alabama coal miners in the World War I era. Like McCartin, Kelly sees the economic and ideological impact of the war as crucial in enabling black and white miners to make major gains in union membership. But he also notes that miners' acceptance of the Wilson administration's rhetoric "undermined labor's potential for mounting a unified resistance." Or, as he puts it at another point, "Organized labor's attempt to match the employers' patriotism exacted a heavy toll on its esprit de corps."[14] Unity with the government and employers on the war question, that is, led to divisiveness among working people.

As I began to reconstruct the rich history of struggle that provided the context for the Prager lynching, it became clear that beyond that one dramatic episode, the response of the southwestern Illinois coal miners to World War I was a story in itself that needed to be investigated. Two intertwined conclusions emerge from this story. First, the war cost coal miners dearly. Not only did some give their lives in Europe and make material sacrifices at home, but the broad working-class solidarity that the UMWA had taken decades to build took some serious blows. By participating in war mobilization, miners inevitably went to war with each other, most fatally in the case of Robert Paul Prager. But the story does not end there. As Karl Marx wrote in 1848, when rival national groups of capitalists are forced to fight each other, as they did in World War I, they are "compelled to appeal to the proletariat, to ask for its help, and thus to drag it into the political arena. The bourgeoisie, itself, therefore, supplies the proletariat with its own elements of political and general education; in other words, it furnishes the proletariat with weapons for fighting the bourgeoisie."[15] Along these dialectical lines, the war also exacted a price on coal mine owners and the government authorities who led working people into war. Miners and other workers nearly ground the war economy to a halt in the fall of 1917. And once fighting ended on the western front, a deep-seated rebellion broke out in the Illinois coalfields as workers sought to cash in on their wartime patriotism. Thus, the price of patriotism was paid twice, first by the coal miners, then by their class adversaries.

The book's first chapter sets the stage for the World War I years. It charts the transformation of southwestern Illinois from a relatively isolated, primitive rural backwater into a more urbanized, industrialized, highly unionized center of the coal industry with a well-deserved reputation for labor radicalism. Chapter 2 chronicles the debate among working people over the war and provides a local and regional view of war mobilization. While the Socialist sympathies of many miners made the war a hard sell in the region, miners over time grudgingly lined up with the war effort. Chapter 3 tells the story of the 1917 wartime strike wave in the region. Chapter 4 charts the upswing in the spy scare and vigilante violence in the spring of 1918—what I call "patriotic pugilism." Chapter 5 provides a detailed narrative of the Prager lynching and its meaning and impact. Finally, Chapter 6 shows how the Wilson administration's wartime rhetoric had unexpected consequences, unleashing a profound working-class upsurge in the same region that had been so loyal to the government the previous spring.

The Southwestern Illinois Coalfields

I n 1842, Charles Dickens visited southwestern Illinois. Touring the young American nation, the great English author wanted a glimpse of the famed Looking-Glass Prairie. When he later recorded his impressions of the countryside surrounding Belleville and Collinsville in *American Notes,* Dickens described a primitive American backwater. Upon crossing the Mississippi River from St. Louis, Missouri, he wrote, we "began to make our way through an ill-favored Black Hollow, called, less expressively, the American Bottom." This was the name for the expanse of extremely rich farmland running along the Mississippi through St. Clair and Madison Counties. Dickens's party of fourteen traveled in several horse-drawn carriages along a country road described by the author as "one unbroken slough of black mud and water." As they rode along, sinking into the mud on occasion almost up to the windows, "the air resounded in all directions with the loud chirping of the frogs, who, with the pigs (a coarse, ugly breed, as unwholesome-looking as though they were the spontaneous growth of the country), had the whole scene to themselves." Here and there, Dickens wrote, "we passed a log-hut; but the wretched cabins were wide apart and thinly scattered, for though the soil is very rich in this place, few people can exist in such a deadly atmosphere." After some more hours of bumping along and being besieged by the infernal "music" of the frogs, Dickens and company arrived in Belleville. This he portrayed as "a small collection of wooden houses, huddled together in the very heart of the bush and swamp." The local criminal court was in session, trying some men accused of horse-stealing. The horses of those engaged in the courtroom were tied to a temporary wooden rack set up in the "road; by which is to be understood a forest path, nearly knee deep in mud and slime."[1]

When Robert Paul Prager encountered the same area three-quarters of a century later, he met a region transformed. A dense network of railroads, along with the automobile, began to edge out the horse-drawn carriage. The few hardy pioneers of the 1840s had multiplied to include tens of thousands from around the globe. They were attracted not only by the rich bottomlands of the Mississippi but also by the growing industry in the periphery of St. Louis. Increasingly, they came to dig coal in large corporate-owned deep-shaft mines. In the wake of these economic and demographic shifts came changes in the workplace, coal mining unionism, politics, and survival strategies. All of these facets of life in the region would shape the circumstances in which Robert Prager and thousands of coal miners found themselves in Collinsville in April 1918. In a variety of ways, this picture of a coal mining region provides essential context for the dramatic conflicts of the World War I years.

Southwestern Illinois is a roughly 1,700-square-mile stretch of land comprising Macoupin, Madison, and St. Clair Counties. By the eve of World War I, this farming region in the hinterlands of St. Louis was home to a growing number of highly capitalized deep-shaft coal mines owned by big railroad companies such as the Illinois Central (Madison Coal Corporation) and Chicago & North Western (Superior Coal). Southwestern Illinois was also the heart of the most solidly organized unit of the United Mine Workers of America in the entire nation (UMWA District 12). UMWA members worked in the big mechanized mines that increasingly employed recent immigrants from southern and eastern Europe as well as in the larger number of small-scale hand-mining operations, some of them owned cooperatively, which depended on highly skilled pick miners.

Just north and east of the metropolis of St. Louis and across the Mississippi River lies Madison County. Population is concentrated on the western edge of the county, adjoining the Mississippi River. That portion includes Granite City and Wood River, both budding industrial towns in the early 1900s. Just northwest of Wood River, on the banks of the Mississippi, is the older river city of Alton, famous for its high bluffs and infamous for the 1837 lynching of abolitionist Elijah Lovejoy. Northeast of Granite City is Edwardsville, the county seat, where Prager's lynchers were tried. And sitting astride the southern Madison County line is Collinsville.[2]

Established for decades as a market center for area farmers, Collinsville underwent substantial growth in these years as big mines and local industry were established by investors in St. Louis.[3] Louis Lumaghi, for instance, operated three mines that supplied a local chemical plant, a lead smelter, and a brickyard and also shipped coal west to St. Louis. Mine Nos. 2 and 3 continued working throughout the World War I years. E. C. Donk, also of St. Louis, owned three Madison County mines: No. 3 in Troy, east of Collinsville; No. 2 in Maryville, a hamlet north of town, where Robert Prager worked; and No. 1 in a section of Collinsville, several miles square, known variously as "Cuba" and "Donkville." In 1906, Consolidated Coal of St. Louis opened Mine No. 17 just south of town, on a spur off the Vandalia Railroad (a proprietary line of the Pennsylvania Railroad). As of 1910, these mines together employed nearly 2,000 mineworkers.[4] From 1900 to 1920, the population of Collinsville more than doubled, jumping from 4,021 to 9,753.[5]

In light of the significance of "anti-German" sentiment during World War I, it is worth noting that Madison County was heavily populated by German Americans. One scholar calculated the percentage of households with close ties to Germany, meaning that either husband or wife was born in Germany or had a parent who had been. The smaller towns tended to have the highest percentage, such as Alhambra, with 79 percent. But even Collinsville, in 1910, had 51 percent of households with close ties to Germany, and Alton had 26 percent.[6] Ties to Germany were reflected in the continuing presence of Evangelical and Lutheran churches where services were still conducted in German.[7] German social clubs (*Turnerverein*) and singing societies (*Liederkranz* and *Mannerchor*) were also common. In Madison County, Alton, Edwardsville, and Highland, among others, had *Turnervereins,* and Glen Carbon had a *Liederkranz.*[8]

In terms of European settlement, the area comprised by St. Clair County dates back further into the eighteenth century, and the names of its major coal mining town, Belleville, and small hamlets like French Village reflect the predominance of French traders and trappers who came to the Illinois country in that early period.[9] The northern portion of St. Clair County lies directly east of St. Louis, and the industrial center and county seat of East St. Louis was its biggest and best known locale. While many "new" immigrants poured into East St. Louis, the largest St. Clair County city, the county's coal mining workforce was predominantly made up of those of German and British heritage. Many of these miners descended from earlier generations who had settled in the Belleville area, fought for the Union in the Civil War, and established mining labor unions in the 1860s. As of 1904, out of 175 immigrant miners in Belleville, 63 were born in England and 90 in Germany.[10] So many Germans had settled in Belleville during the late nineteenth century that it was known as *kleine deutches Athen in Amerika.* The city sported the following German groups: Belleville Turnerverein, Belleville Liederkranz, Germania Bund, Kronthal Liedertafel, Arbeiter Unterstuetzungsverein, Franken Unterstuetzungsverein, West Belleville Arbeiter Bund, and German-American Alliance.[11] In neighboring mining and farming towns in St. Clair County like Freeburg, Lenzburg, and O'Fallon, at least 60 percent of households had close ties to Germany in 1910. In New Athens, the figure was 81 percent.[12]

Since it was the oldest mining field of the three southwestern counties, the Belleville area saw more continuity than the other two in the closing years of the century. A large number of smaller and hand mines continued to operate, some of them cooperatively owned and run by coal miners. Still, the new order was taking shape in St. Clair, as illustrated by the two mines opened in 1899 by St. Louis and O'Fallon Coal Company, a property of the Busch brewing empire. By 1916, St. Louis and O'Fallon Mine No. 2 ("Black Eagle") was the tenth most productive in the state, employing 616 workers. In a cage hoisted by steam engines, workers descended straight down a shaft of some 200 feet and traveled an extensive rail system on cars hauled by five subterranean locomotives. Each skilled pick miner, who formed a small minority in this mine, prepared the wall of coal ("face") in his particular working place ("room") by carving an empty shelf of coal at the bottom of the face ("undercutting"), which would allow the rest of the face coal to fall down and not straight out when blasted. Far more numerous than the pick miners were the 300 relatively unskilled loaders, who shoveled coal after a total of thirty-six electrically powered undercutting machines prepared the coal for blasting. With the help of specialized shot-firers, tracklayers, timbermen, cagers, and trappers, miners raised over 750,000 tons of coal to the surface in 1916. Not one lump of coal was sold to the tiny neighboring community of French Village. Every available ounce poured from the tipple down a chute into rail cars owned by Busch's St. Louis & O'Fallon Railroad and headed for the nearby bottling plant and enormous brewery in St. Louis.[13]

While the St. Louis and O'Fallon mines were major employers in St. Clair County, most area residents knew them by another name—the

"Nigger Hollow" mines. Various theories have been advanced to explain this name, ranging from the 1917 East St. Louis riot to the sight of miners turned black by coal dust traveling on the railroad from the mine, which lacked a washhouse until 1915. But an entry in the 1899 coal report announces the following: "The St. Louis & O'Fallon Coal company has sunk . . . main and escapement shafts. It is located in what is called 'Nigger Hollow,' one and a half miles northeast of Birkner, St. Clair county."[14] The name apparently preceded these coal mines and may have referred to a small African American community outside of Belleville similar to that of Brooklyn, Illinois. In any event, all evidence suggests that if African Americans lived in the vicinity of Busch's mines, none worked in them. Though hardly unique to St. Clair County, the casual racism of the "Nigger Hollow" label was all too common.

The newest of the three counties was Macoupin, a perfect rectangle straight north of Madison County. Compared to the other two, Macoupin was sparsely populated, lacking any industrial towns. Aside from the county seat at Carlinville, population was concentrated on the extreme northern and southern ends of the county. These were nearly all mining towns, including Staunton, Mt. Olive, and Gillespie in the south and Virden and Girard in the north. As in St. Clair and Madison Counties, German immigrants were numerous, particularly in Staunton and Mt. Olive. An investigator for the U.S. Immigration Commission who visited Mt. Olive commented that "Germans are, in a large measure, in control of the business and industrial, as well as the political and administrative, affairs of the community. The mayor, the postmaster, the bankers, and the mine superintendents are Germans." He added that Germans also comprised at least one-fourth of those employed in the mines.[15]

In 1904, Macoupin County residents founded a new town in the name of local landowner and coal dealer Ben L. Dorsey. Oral tradition has it that a sign bearing his name was partially downed in a storm, leaving his first name and middle initial but only the first letter of his last name— hence the town of Benld. By 1910, its growth spurred by Superior Mine No. 2, Benld sported a population of nearly 2,000. Russian and Italian immigrants were particularly numerous in Benld. Russian miners built an onion-domed Russian Orthodox church that still stands today. Young Avinere Toigo, born in Pittsburgh in 1902 of Italian parents, arrived in Benld at the age of three. By 1915, with his coal mining father sick from tuberculosis, he joined hundreds of others down in Superior Mine No.

2, working as a laborer.[16] Frank Bertetti, another young Italian American miner at No. 2, recalled of Benld: "It was like a booming frontier town. Some of the sidewalks were wooden planks. The miners walked to work in all kinds of weather." The town boasted thirty saloons.[17]

Though the southwestern Illinois coalfields were increasingly urban, most coal mining families lived a semirural existence by today's standards. Living just outside of Collinsville, for instance, the family of Frank Nizolek depended largely on his earnings from working at Consolidated Coal, but they did not rely exclusively on coal mining to put food on the table. On a small piece of land that the family owned, the Nizoleks kept chickens, raised a vegetable garden for their own consumption, grew spinach and strawberries for market, and sold their large crop of tomatoes to Brooks Tomato, the local ketchup factory. As daughter Fran recalled, "That's what we survived on, truck farming . . . when those tomatoes was ripe, you picked them, you put them bushel boxes, and you put them in a wagon. Then, you hitched a horse to it or if it was a truck bed, you can take it down there and they'd weigh it and they'd pay you by the ton. And the farmers waited for that check in the fall of the year."[18]

Like the Nizolek family, many mining families also owned their own homes. Out of forty-eight families surveyed in Pana, twenty-six owned a home, eighteen rented, and four indicated a combination of the two (perhaps purchasing a home in the course of the year).[19] In an unnamed southern Illinois mining town studied by the Dillingham Commission, 53 percent of mining families owned their own homes. These included both native-born workers and those born in Italy, Lithuania, and Poland. Though few of these coal mining towns were company towns in the classic sense, rail and mining companies did often build and sell housing to mining families. In Glen Carbon, Illinois, for instance, when the Madison Coal Corporation mine closed down in 1931, many miners were able to purchase, at a low price, homes they had been renting for many years.[20] The most common coal miner's residence in Pana was a single-floor, detached four-room frame house. The family typically got water from a well or pump in the backyard. A privy, or outhouse, served each family though occasionally was shared by two households.

Despite the impressive degree of home ownership among coal mining families, they lived in a state of constant economic insecurity due to one key fact: coal miners experienced chronic underemployment. They rarely worked more than two-thirds of the 300 possible workdays in a year and often worked considerably less. The lack of regular mining work was due to the intense competition and frequent failure of small producers; the inevitable need to close mines periodically for repairs; and the seasonal nature of smaller "local" mines, which produced coal for heating, as opposed to bigger "shipping" mines, which supplied railroads and industry year-round.

The normal unpredictability of work worsened during general economic downturns, such as the depression of 1913–15. It was most severe in St. Clair County. Of the fifty shipping mines operating there in 1913, only thirty-three were producing coal during 1915. In the same period, the total number of working miners dropped more than 30 percent, from 5,707 to 3,950. The number of days worked slipped from an already low average of 160 to 157. Coal production fell by 37 percent.[21]

Coal mining families met the challenge of survival in a variety of ways. Coal miners' wives earned money taking in boarders, doing laundry, providing domestic work, and serving as midwives. Miners' daughters also increasingly joined local industry. In Collinsville, for instance, they commonly worked at the Brooks Ketchup factory or the Chester Knitting Mill. The opportunity for the participation of young women in the industrial workforce in Collinsville is illustrated by a hiring drive initiated by the Chester Knitting Mill in the fall of 1911. Already employing some 100 local young women, the mill sought to double this number. To entice Collinsville's female youth to work at the mill, according to an article boosting the cause, the management was "doing everything in its power to surround the young ladies employed with all the comforts and conveniences that go to make an ideal working place." Collinsville's "industrious daughters," the article concluded, "should take advantage of this opportunity to become useful members of society amid ideal surroundings and desirable associates."[22] For their part, miners' sons, before they joined their fathers working underground, typically labored on local farms. Family members collaborated in raising food. And, during the most desperate times, coal mining women and children supplemented the family fuel supply by "stealing" coal, which had fallen on the local railroad tracks. In the bitter winter of 1914–15, for instance, when work was scarce, Staunton police nabbed several suspects accused of this "crime." A subsequent investigation by the local newspaper revealed how commonly local women applied this survival tactic—"many persons" lived the entire year without purchasing any coal.[23]

Miners and their families also relied on a panoply of fraternal organizations to provide a margin of social security, as well as sociability. Through fraternal groups, mining families "helped each other in sickness and in death," as one Macoupin County historian wrote.[24] Main Street in Collinsville offered a typical conglomeration of secret societies, social clubs, benevolent associations, and immigrant political groups. They included the ever-present Moose, Elks, Odd Fellows—to which Robert Prager belonged—Knights of Pythias, and Masons. At Fulton's Hall—downstairs a saloon and upstairs a large meeting room—the following immigrant-based organizations met: the Polish Society, the Bohemian Benevolent Society and Eliska Krasnohoeska (the women's branch), the Bohemian Taboritu Society, the Czech Slavic Benevolent Society, and the Lithuanian Alliance of America, Branch 159.[25] Fulton's was also the meeting ground for the Lithuanian Socialist Federation and the Lithuanian Workers Literature Society, both under the leadership of Frank Skamarakas, a miner at the Donk No. 2 Maryville mine where Robert Prager worked. Down the street, at Holsweg's Hall, members of the Societa Dogali Fratolanzo came together, an organization of Tyrolese Italian-speaking residents of Collinsville.[26]

Beyond providing a hedge against economic insecurity, the fraternal lodge also served an obvious social and recreational function for its members. For at least one coal miner from St. Clair County remembering his fraternal activities, this seemed to be the main purpose. "Back in those days," recalled Hawley Canterbury, "there wasn't much to do. You know, you didn't get out of town, the way you do now. And I can remember, here in O'Fallon, they had the Redmen and Knight of Pythias and Woodmen and the Masons . . . I belonged to the Redmen and the Knights of Pythias and the Masons. . . . It was just mostly social, visiting. I'm a past master of the local, the lodge here in O'Fallon. Past patron of the Eastern Star, and past associate guardian of the Job's Daughters . . . I think it was just social. Back in those days, it was once a month, or whatever it was, you get together and have this meeting and visit and socialize, have lunch and whatnot. Initiate new members now and then . . ."[27]

Since many working people, including unionized coal miners, belonged to fraternal organizations, and since they often shared meeting places, these types of organizations were in some ways mutually supportive. A coal miner in Collinsville, for example, who wrote to UMWA presidential hopeful John Walker during the 1916 union election penned his letter on Moose lodge stationery.[28] Across the country in Lynn, Massachusetts, electrical workers organizing during World War I met in the local Odd Fellows Hall.[29] And the local saloons, or "halls," which often provided space for fraternal groups to meet, also hosted numerous union meetings. An advertisement in Belleville made the dual nature of the saloon explicit: "Chas. Wasmann, Saloon And Headquarters for Unionists."[30]

Despite the ways in which fraternal groups brought working people together in a relationship of mutual support and friendship, fraternalism also had another side that could work against the cause of working-class solidarity. As Mary Ann Clawson has shown, fraternal organizations were neither simply expressions of a working-class "collectivist counterculture" nor vehicles for "lower-middle-class respectability." Based on her study of fraternal organizations in late-nineteenth-century Belleville, Illinois, and Buffalo, New York, Clawson found that while many working-class men belonged to Masonic-like fraternal organizations—such as the Knights of Pythias and Odd Fellows—this "did not lead to the consolidation of lodges as organs of working-class solidarity."[31] Most fundamentally, the cross-class membership of the lodges and the consequent brotherly bonding between workers and their employers promoted ties based on ethnicity, nationality, and gender as opposed to class. Of all the fraternal orders, the Masonic lodges tended to include a large proportion of the local ruling figures as well as a small proportion of better-paid workers. In Collinsville, the lodge leadership included prominent merchants, manufacturers (a member of the Brooks family, who owned the local ketchup factory), and the mayor, R. Guy Kneedler. In Staunton, one of the more illustrious Masons was F. E. Weisenborn, a longtime mine superintendent. Pete Perry, an Italian American miner, who worked at Madison No. 2 in Glen Carbon, recalled that his British coworkers in the mines—"Johnny Bulls"—belonged disproportionately to the Masonic lodge. "Man, they knew everything and didn't do nothin', but they knew everything," Perry said. "Goddamn, you could have more fun with them guys. Work is out. They wanna boss. Get these Mason rings, you know they wear them. Someone say, 'What the hell you do with that ring there?' 'I'm a Mason.' They get jobs, good jobs, foreman jobs, see. And I says, that ring you got on your finger there, that thing got you in bad. Ever since you put that ring on that finger, you ain't been worth a damn. Just kid him along, see. And he wouldn't work. They always want that money, see."[32]

The gender, racial, and ethnic segregation of the major orders also had a divisive effect. The Odd Fellows and Masons simply excluded blacks from membership. In response, blacks organized their own parallel orders but were not recognized as legitimate by their white "brothers." The Masons made institutional provision for women's participation but always on a rigid, gender-segregated basis. Like African American men, no woman of any race or ethnicity could be a true Mason. As for their ethnic composition, the Masonic-type lodges such as the Knights of Pythias and the Odd Fellows maintained a fairly open attitude toward ethnic diversity until the late nineteenth century. They allowed for foreign-language lodges and for translation of their elaborate rituals into languages other than English. With the rebirth of the nativist movement in the 1880s, however, along with the wave of "new" immigrants in the following decade, "fraternal orders retreated from their previous acceptance of ethnic diversity." During this period, German American lodges of the Knights of Pythias fought a losing battle against the elimination of their right to form other than English-language lodges. One of the last holdouts was the Von Moltke Pythian Lodge of Collinsville, which was "absorbed" in 1915 by its English-speaking counterpart in town.[33]

German Americans in the Odd Fellows fought a similar battle, but they held out longer than their Pythian counterparts. As late as 1917, in St. Louis, German Americans attended the Hormonie Lodge, Number 353, of the Independent Order of Odd Fellows (IOOF), along with Robert Paul Prager. After moving across the Mississippi to Collinsville in fall of that year, Prager attended meetings at the Collinsville IOOF Lodge but continued to attend meetings also of the Hormonie Lodge. Most likely, it was worth the trip to enjoy the camaraderie of fellow German Americans, especially during that trying time.

While coal mining families faced a constant challenge to their financial survival aboveground, coal miners faced the daily fight for physical survival underground. Despite, and sometimes because of, the advances in mining technology, coal mining in southwestern Illinois in the World War I era remained dangerous and deadly work. The three most common sources of death and injury to miners, as they might have described them, were "bad top," "bad roads," and "bad shots." For miners and loaders in southwestern Illinois, by far the most common cause of injury and death was a collapsing roof—"bad top." Falls of coal, slate, soapstone, and clod accounted for a large portion of deaths and maimings of these mine workers. In 1916, for example, 63 percent of the mine deaths and 38 percent of the injuries in the region resulted from some type of roof fall.[34] Most of these incidents occurred in the miners' or loaders' rooms.

If miners and loaders comprised the group of workers in southwestern Illinois who experienced the highest absolute number of accidents and deaths, it was mine transport workers—mule drivers, locomotive drivers ("motormen"), and their assistants ("trip riders")—who had the highest death and accident rate. In Macoupin and Montgomery Counties in 1916, for instance, drivers comprised only 3.9 percent of the underground employees but accounted for 14.4 percent of the recorded injuries. To put it another way, of the miners in the district, 1.8 percent were injured that year. In contrast, 9.6 percent of the drivers sustained a serious injury—an injury rate five times higher than that of miners and loaders.[35]

If the dangers from roof coal and pit cars affected the largest number of mineworkers, the hazards of blasting down the coal at the face—"bad shots"—were the most dramatic. This particular danger is especially relevant here in light of the fact that Robert Paul Prager came under suspicion as an underground bomb plotter whose alleged weapon was blasting powder. To illustrate, consider the case of one Mr. Hanley, the shot-firer in an Odin, Illinois, mine. On a January day in 1897, the men had left the mine after a day's work, and only Hanley and the water bailer remained underground. After firing a shot in a miner's room, Hanley ran to safety in the adjoining room. When it exploded, the shot blew only a bit of coal off the front, "pounding it to dust." "Simultaneously," reports the district mine inspector, "there was a tremendous roar and a stream of fire rushed out of the room, and dividing, passed in and out the entries, threw loaded cars off the track, smashing empty ones and tearing up the track in several places." The force of the explosion was such that it "blew down the timbers along the entry, smashed the trap doors to kindling wood all over the mine, and set fire to timber 1,300 feet from where the shot was fired." Fortunately for Hanley, miners had not yet driven a crosscut between the two adjoining rooms so that when the shot went off, the air around him "served as a cushion instead of being driven before the force of the explosion." For just such explosions, Hanley had been supplied with a wet sponge. Placing it over his mouth and nose, he crawled a long way out the entry before reaching a space where the air could be safely breathed.[36]

Economic insecurity and mining hazards led coal miners to band together into unions as early as the Civil War era. In fact, the Belleville coalfields own the distinction of sparking in 1861 a union that evolved into the first, though short-lived, national miners' union, the American Miners' Association.[37] In the thirty years following the establishment of this organization, southwestern Illinois coal miners took part in a succession of coal mining unions. They included the Miners' Benevolent and Protective Association, the Miners National Association, the Illinois Miners' and Mine Laborers' Protective Association, the Knights of Labor Trade Assembly No. 135, and the National Progressive Union of Coal Miners and Mine Laborers, all of which preceded the formation of the UMWA in 1890.[38]

It took the monumental strike of 1897 to make the promise of the UMWA in southwestern Illinois into a reality. Though only a tiny minority of Illinois coal miners belonged to the union when the strike began, thousands of miners, including many in Macoupin, Madison, and St. Clair Counties, answered the national strike call. The key to the success of the strike in southwestern Illinois was the great march through the region led by "General" Alexander Bradley of Mt. Olive. Hundreds of striking miners tramped through Belleville, Glen Carbon, Collinsville, and many other coal towns, "[g]athering strength like a rolling snowball," as one reporter put it.[39] The march drew support from a number of sources, including local merchants who contributed provisions and local politicians who provided public places to sleep. Women in coal mining communities provided hot coffee and helped keep the wooden commissary truck full. Solidarity between more recent immigrants and older native-born miners also contributed to the success of the strike. At the head of a caravan of Mt. Olive miners, for instance, walked Bradley and a Slavic coworker who bore aloft a huge American flag.[40] This solidarity was not to be taken for granted, considering that immigrants from southern and eastern Europe increasingly were hired as unskilled "loaders" to shovel coal cut by undercutting machines. Experienced miners tended to view these workers as interlopers rather than as fellow miners. As one observer of the industry explained, "By the [undercutting] machines part of the craft has been taken away from coal mining, and there are men—'foreigners' mostly—who do not know how to 'mine' coal by hand."[41]

By January 1898, District 12 UMWA leaders and coal operators signed a statewide union contract that included the eight-hour day, mine-run payment for coal, recognition of the union pit committee, and an automatic checkoff of union dues from the miners' paychecks. But when a number of employers in southwestern Illinois refused to honor the new contract, miners returned to the barricades, this time with guns in hand. Coal companies in Pana and Virden recruited African American miners from Birmingham, Alabama, as a strikebreaking force and sent them on special armed trains to their mines. On October 12, in Virden, armed unionists fought armed mine guards and succeeded in preventing a train carrying strikebreakers from stopping at the mine, forcing it to continue on to Springfield. Five guards were wounded and four killed. None of the black strikebreakers was killed, but several were wounded, at least one seriously. At their own cost of seven dead and thirty wounded, the armed miners assured that the new UMWA contract would be truly statewide. Illinois now joined Indiana, Ohio, and western Pennsylvania in comprising what coal operators and miners called the Central Competitive Field, the heart of union power and soft coal production.[42]

Just as divisions between native-born and immigrant workers were beginning to weaken, however, those separating black and white miners seemed to grow stronger. Despite the fact that black union miners from Springfield and elsewhere took part in defending the union at Virden, it seemed to many Illinois miners that "Negro" and "strikebreaker" were synonymous. Though blacks did toil in many southern Illinois mines, the mines in the southwest corner of the state, from Virden to Belleville, remained almost exclusively white by the outbreak of World War I. Many towns in this period sported unwritten "sunset ordinances," which barred blacks from remaining in town after sunset.[43] Hawley Canterbury, who grew up in St. Clair County in the town of O'Fallon during this time, recalls that "they had a rule around here, no blacks in town after sundown."[44] Although other larger mining towns closer to St. Louis such as Collinsville and Belleville had growing black populations, Virden in 1920 had an official black population of three.[45]

While the events of 1897–98 narrowed the horizons of miners' solidarity on one level, the intensity of the conflict radicalized many young coal mining unionists, such as John Walker, Adolph Germer, and Frank Hayes. They shared an attraction to a more militant stance toward the employers, a willingness to embrace the mass strike as a legitimate weapon against the mine owners, and a rejection of the older class harmony viewpoint that early mining unionists and the Samuel Gompers leadership of the American Federation of Labor (AFL) championed. Shortly after the formation of the Socialist Party of America in 1901, Walker, Germer,

Hayes, and other relatively younger miners' leaders joined the party. Before long, southwestern Illinois, particularly the Belleville area, became a bastion of support for Socialism. By 1905, Adolph Germer regularly corresponded with Eugene and Theodore Debs and reported on the progress of the party's growth among St. Clair County miners. In Staunton, a carpenter's son named Edward Wieck joined the party in these years, influenced by miners there. Working briefly at the local post office, Wieck read miners' Socialist newspapers from cover to cover before they did.[46] By the war, he was a prominent voice for the Socialist Party both in the large Staunton UMWA Local 755 and in the Illinois district at large.[47] By 1908, the party was gaining a steady stream of votes from miners at election time. Running for General Assembly in St. Clair County, for instance, Adolph Germer got 3,656 votes.[48] Though this represented only some 5 percent of the votes cast, it most likely was a much higher percentage of miners' votes. That same year, Frank Hayes nearly won the Collinsville mayor's seat on the Socialist ticket.[49]

The political perspective of the Socialist Party in southwestern Illinois is captured in the 1916 "municipal platform" of the party in Staunton. The Staunton Socialists pledged their loyalty to the party and to "the principles of international socialism." They appealed "to the working class, both men and women, and to all who are in sympathy with these principles enumerated in our platform, to join in this great movement for industrial and social freedom." The Socialist Party, the Staunton members explained, "represents the interest of the working class in antagonism to the interest of the exploiting class, and therefore concerns itself with the welfare of the workers."[50]

In pursuit of these goals, Socialists in the Macoupin, Madison, and St. Clair County coalfields ran for office on a regular basis and established a significant base of support. In Staunton, for instance, in the spring 1915 municipal elections, Socialist candidates captured an average of 25 percent of the votes. Although a majority of Staunton voted Republican, the 1916 presidential elections saw one-fifth of the city vote for Allan Benson, the Socialist candidate. In the spring of 1917, Louis Fickert, a tracklayer at Consolidated Coal Mine No. 14, won election as alderman in Staunton's Second Ward on the Socialist ticket.

In St. Clair County, the Socialists mounted a full electoral slate in a number of towns. In Belleville, Socialist miner Thomas J. Hitchings was elected to the city council in 1914. Also in that year, O'Fallon elected a

Socialist mayor. In the 1916 elections, in the mining town of Mascoutah, south of Belleville, two Socialists joined one of their comrades already serving on the town council. That year the Socialist aldermanic candidates of Belleville were defeated but only by a hair: Edward Welsh lost by only 14 votes out of 460 cast, and fellow Socialist Philip Sauer lost by a mere 8 out of 516. Hitchings was ousted from office by nine percentage points.[51]

In Madison County, as well, the Socialists were active. As noted above, Collinsville had come close to electing UMWA leader Frank Hayes in 1908. That proved to be the high point of the fortunes of the Socialist Party there. Nevertheless, the party continued to be a presence in city elections from 1912 through 1917. Local candidates regularly polled 15 to 30 percent of the vote. Miner R. C. DeLaney won election on the Socialist Party ticket in Collinsville's Fourth Ward in 1915 and was reelected in April 1917, two weeks after the United States entered the war.[52] National Socialist Party candidates also fared respectably before the war. In 1912 in the Collinsville election, Eugene Debs polled over twice the vote gained by Progressive Republican Theodore Roosevelt, with a citywide total of 21.4 percent.[53] Even in tiny Maryville, which consisted almost entirely of the families of miners at the Donk No. 2 mine where Prager worked, Socialists contended for office, electing H. P. Wallace to the board of trustees in 1916. He was the third-highest vote getter with a grand total of 64. County, state, and national candidates also polled respectable totals in the city. For instance, the Socialist slate polled over 40 percent across the board in Collinsville's First Ward, with an average of 22 percent for the city as a whole.[54] The Socialists also drew support from Livingston, a Madison County railroad town organized around the huge New Staunton Coal Company mine. In 1916, the Socialist Party national ticket garnered 20 percent of the vote there.[55] This tiny town of 1,200 became the scene of some intense battles over conflicting loyalties once the United States joined the war.

Not only did Socialists get electoral support in the coalfields, but coal miners played a prominent role in the Socialist Party leadership in southwestern Illinois. Of the twelve candidates in Collinsville elections from 1915 through 1917, for example, at least eight were coal miners, including one mine examiner.[56] In Belleville, which drew on a more varied working class, four of eleven Socialist Party candidates in the 1915 election can be identified as miners.[57] Of the six Staunton Socialists who ran that year, five were miners.

As historians of midwestern Socialism have noted, the main base of support for the party came from the so-called old immigrant groups of workers, particularly German Americans, Finns in the upper Midwest, and those from the British Isles. This is certainly the general pattern in the region. In Belleville, for instance, three Sauer brothers led the 1915 ticket, along with Neuf, Nebgen, Lehr, and Kniepkamp. In Staunton, as well, German Americans were prominent, including John and Edward Wieck, A. C. Schneider, and William Koenigkraemer, among others. Miners such as Adolph Germer of nearby Mt. Olive, whose father was a Socialist in northern Germany, were the "red diaper babies" of their era.[58]

In Collinsville and Maryville, though German Americans were numerous, the composition of the party seems to have been more ethnically diverse. Consider this list of Socialist candidates for the 1915–17 period: Victor Saladin, Sam Britton, Charles Britton, Edward Franek, Robert Bertolero, Joe Chebanoski, Bert Miranda, R. C. DeLaney, R. L. Zvingilas, Frank Hrebenar, Thomas Paul, Harry Ewing, Hoke Wallace, John Kettle, and William Katilus. Though deducing ethnicity from names can be a hazardous enterprise, it seems fair to conclude that in addition to the obvious complement of Italian Americans and those with ancestors from the British Isles, there were also Bohemian, Polish, and perhaps Lithuanian Socialists.

The radical political currents of the southwestern Illinois coalfields were reflected in the broader internal politics of the Illinois district of the UMWA. District 12, with some 90,000 unionized coal miners, was not only the most powerful single unit of the UMWA (Pennsylvania was composed of a number of districts) but possibly the most contentious. The Illinois district featured intense internal conflict between the right and left wing in the years immediately preceding World War I. And due to the weight of the Illinois district in the UMWA as a whole, the affairs of the Illinois miners were often directly tied to power struggles on the national level. In 1914, for instance, Socialist Adolph Germer ran for District 12 UMWA president against Frank Farrington. By 1914, Germer and Farrington had both held elective office in District 12. Germer was the sitting vice president, a post that Farrington had filled under President John Walker. Both men were known throughout the state, and they each seemed to symbolize the respective opposing factions in the UMWA— Farrington, the popular "big, blue-eyed Republican" from Streator, in northern Illinois, with a fanatical devotion to the sanctity of the contract and a flair for businesslike efficiency; Germer, the battle-tested Socialist militant from Mt. Olive, who had run for office and had just returned from a stint as International Organizer with the fighting southern Colorado miners of Ludlow massacre fame.[59] By October, the interest in the election was felt throughout Illinois coalfields. As one Belleville newspaper reported, the contest was "assuming such serious proportions that miners in every local in the state are taking sides and the December election promises to show the largest vote in the history of the mine workers." The "Socialist wing" of the miners stood behind Germer; "many of the miners, opposed to the socialist doctrines, are behind Farrington," the paper noted.[60]

In early November, just weeks before the election, a printed circular letter surfaced in the Illinois coalfields. Entitled "A Traitor Exposed," and signed by three southern Colorado miners, the circular "charged that Germer had betrayed striking miners by turning weapons over to the militia, had been arrested not for his union work but because he had been having illicit relations with the wife of a local merchant, and that he had neglected his organizing duties and spent most of his time writing articles for various newspapers." Miners throughout the state received copies in the mail. Although these accusations were later proven false, investigators appointed by UMWA International president John White initially issued a report, just in time for the election, that confirmed the charges and explicitly denied that Farrington had instigated them. White's announcement was not surprising, considering he was known to sympathize with Farrington and his more conservative brand of unionism.[61] Before the voting commenced, copies of the report appeared in Illinois newspapers and public places and were nailed onto telephone poles. All Illinois UMWA locals received copies. According to one account, some miners even heard it read aloud as they cast their vote. By all accounts, the "Traitor Exposed" circular accomplished its task—Frank Farrington won the election.[62] Farrington's victory and the war within UMWA District 12 were a crucial part of the contested terrain that Robert Paul Prager encountered as he arrived in southwestern Illinois just three years later.

Little is known about the contours of Prager's life before he came to Collinsville. He was born on February 28, 1888, in Dresden, Germany, into the working-class family of Karl and Mary Louise Prager. Robert Paul had six brothers—Max, Henry, Fritz, Carl, Haus, and Kurt—and one sister, Louise. At the age of thirteen, Prager left home. Four years later, he arrived in the United States. For the next seven years, he worked his way through the Midwest. One of the few things we know for sure about these years of Prager's life is that in 1912, the young man was arrested and convicted for theft in Indiana. A week before Christmas in 1912, a Lake County, Indiana, court sentenced Prager to a maximum of eight years in prison.[63]

Though prison records do not indicate what Prager was accused of stealing, authorities at the state reformatory in Jeffersonville, Indiana, recorded a number of facts about Prager that give us a glimpse of the man. He was single at the time; could "read and write readily"; was in "fair" mental and physical condition; smoked cigarettes; did not drink; did not attend the YMCA or Sunday school or church (the record also listed "none" as his parents' church affiliation); had no previous arrests or convictions; and was working as a baker at the time of his arrest. The character of Prager's associates at this time, according to the prison record, was "bad." While in prison, Prager was initially assigned to kitchen detail, no surprise considering his trade. The document also indicates that twice in 1913, Prager was accused of disorderly conduct and that on two other occasions, he visited the prison hospital. Finally, on February 9, 1914, Prager was paroled, after serving some fourteen months behind bars.

Upon getting his freedom, Prager moved west. He briefly lived in Niobara, Nebraska, but left in May 1915, shortly after the sinking of the *Lusitania* raised anti-German feeling nationwide. Prager soon settled in the German American mecca of St. Louis, Missouri, and continued working as a baker. Though we do not know the specifics of Prager's work or union experience in St. Louis, we do know that German immigrant workers were pioneering labor unionists who built the Journeymen Bakers' and Confectioners' International Union (B&C) into a real power after its founding in 1890. Baker and union activist Peter Beisel had come to the United States in 1875, a generation earlier than Prager but at the same age of seventeen. Beisel received his apprenticeship in baking in Hessen, Germany, and apparently imbibed Socialist ideas as well. The fact that Prager left home at the age of thirteen suggests that, like Beisel, he may have done his apprenticeship in Germany, before coming to the United States. After working first in Chicago, then getting blacklisted, Beisel became a leader of Local 15 of the B&C in St. Louis, an all-German local. German Socialists played a key role in union politics, and at their 1891 convention, they convinced delegates to endorse the Socialist Labor Party and reject AFL president Samuel Gompers's conservative program.[64]

Immigrant bakers contended with the worst of conditions that all bakers faced. In St. Louis, young bakers worked seven-day weeks. They typically worked in small "cellar bakeries" and often lived upstairs or in the back with their employer, the master baker. If not, they might live in a "baker's home," which was a neighborhood saloon, whose proprietor got a fee for providing workers for the baker. Workers who did not spend enough at the bar might be fired.[65] These conditions, combined with the growing mechanization of the industry and the growth of baking factories, led to explosive growth for the B&C. By 1916, the union had signed contracts with three of the big baking conglomerates, including Kroger. To celebrate their newly adopted country's birth as well as their union victories, on July 4, 1916, shortly after Prager arrived in St. Louis, some 800 B&C members and their families held a parade, featuring three bands and union leader Peter Beisel mounted on a white horse.[66] If we accept a statement from Prager shortly before his death that "I have been a union man at all times and never once a scab," then he might well have marched with them.

In the half-century since Charles Dickens rode through muddy marshes into the Illinois prairie, the southwestern Illinois coalfields had undergone a profound transformation. The small-scale artisan world of hand-mining was rapidly disappearing. In its place emerged a new order in which the lives of working people were subject to corporate forces reaching far beyond this corner of the Land of Lincoln. Miners and their families came from an ever-greater portion of the globe. As the contest between miners and their employers became a bitter one, working people began to organize on a wider scale. The southwestern Illinois coalfields had become a sophisticated high-stakes battleground of working-class politics.

From the perspective of a young German American labor unionist named Robert Paul Prager, southwestern Illinois probably seemed a fine place to be. As the American war effort heated up, there was plenty of work in the bakeries and mines; unions guaranteed relatively high wages; and Prager enjoyed the company of recent German immigrants who joined him at work, at Odd Fellows meetings, and in political life. But as it turned out, the United States' declaration of war in April 1917 changed everything. How the mobilization for "preparedness" and then intervention began to reshape the lives of Prager and thousands of other working people in southwestern Illinois is the subject of the next chapter.

"Lining Up the People with the Government"
Working People and War Mobilization

On May 31, 1917, nearly two months after America had declared war on Germany, President Woodrow Wilson's private secretary, Joseph Tumulty, sat down to write the president a letter. As he composed his thoughts, Americans across the country were busily preparing for the first draft registration day under the new Selective Service Act, which would feature grand patriotic parades for all the world to see. Publicly, the nation seemed to be pulling together to support the war effort. But on this day, Tumulty was worried, and he confided his private concerns to the president. "It is very distressing," Tumulty wrote, "to find a spirit of indifference abroad with reference to the attitude of the general mass of people toward the war. *Their 'righteous wrath' seems not to have been aroused.*"[1] As applied to the coalfields of southwestern Illinois, Tumulty's observation was more accurate than he could have imagined. The outbreak of World War I and the period of American "preparedness" were subjects of ongoing and occasionally hot debate among coal miners, since many believed that big business stood behind the drive toward war. In the coal towns of the region, including Maryville, where Robert Prager and his coworkers toiled in the Donk No. 2 mine, a number of currents ran freely in these "neutral" years, ranging from anti-war Socialism to Catholic and labor pacifism to German nationalism. After the United States declared war on Germany in April 1917, while pro-war sentiment gathered strength through the year, mobilization met resistance every step of the way, whether it concerned the Selective Service, Committee on Public Information propaganda, Liberty Bonds, the Councils of Defense, or even the hallowed Red Cross. Still, by early 1918, the "righteous wrath"

of the region's working people was expressed in general, if often grudg-
ing, compliance with the war effort.

As Robert Prager may have experienced in his short stay in Nebraska,
the sinking of the *Lusitania* in 1915 intensified pressure for national unity
in the face of potential domestic subversion. In his annual message to
Congress of that year, President Wilson lashed out against naturalized
citizens who "have poured the poison of disloyalty into the very arteries
of our national life." To combat the alleged threat, the president requested
that Congress enact appropriate legislation "at the earliest possible moment and feel that in doing so I am urging you to do nothing less than
save the honor and self-respect of the nation. Such creatures of passion,
disloyalty, and anarchy must be crushed out."[2] Wilson's message was
received loud and clear in southwestern Illinois. Commenting on the
president's speech, the *Collinsville Herald* editorialized that "[e]very loyal
American will agree with President Wilson in that part of his message
relating to disloyalty."[3] Still, what is striking about southwestern Illinois
during the "neutral" period is precisely how difficult it was for the "loyalists" to carry the day.

At coal miners' conventions in early 1916, both the growing possibility of U.S. intervention and anti-war sentiments were much in evidence.
In Indianapolis at the UMWA International meeting, miner Dave Wilson of O'Fallon, Illinois, in St. Clair County, introduced a resolution
explaining that "there exists in this country at the present time a group
of capitalist jingoes, organized by the Morgans of the steel trust whose
sole purpose at this time is to enlist the support of influential men in
every community [to support greater military spending] whereby they
would be empowered to rob the nation 'legally' while the people were
deluded by the cry of patriotism and preparedness. . . . We are opposed
to preparedness as contemplated by the powers that be." But since weapons of war would be manufactured anyhow, Wilson urged the miners to
petition Congress to place the arms industry under government ownership so that any profits would go to "the masses, who in case of war would
be called upon to shed their blood, and pay all taxes."

Another variation on the anti-preparedness theme was offered at the
convention by Socialist Party leader Adolph Germer, who carried credentials as a delegate from his coal mining base of Mt. Olive, Illinois. Pointing to the activities of "the munitions ring and other military madmen,"
Germer declared that "[m]ilitarism and navalism are the inevitable fore-

runners of war, the killing and maiming of countless numbers of human beings, the heart-rending scenes described from Europe and the destruction of property of unlimited value." Linking the drive toward war with assaults on the working class, Germer stated that "[m]ilitarism in any form is the bulwark of the capitalist class when labor revolts against economic exploitation and oppression, besides resulting in enormous profits to those who deal in military munitions." Germer urged coal miners to protest military training in the public schools and lobby against increased military and naval spending.[4]

Two months later, Illinois miners continued this discussion at their district convention where Socialist miner Edward Wieck of Staunton introduced another resolution from Local 755 on preparedness. Like many of their counterparts, the Staunton miners attributed the pressure for higher military spending to "persons connected with great corporations who would profit by larger expenditures for war supplies." "These corporations are the bitterest enemies of organized labor," the resolution said. And just as Dave Wilson of O'Fallon suggested, the Staunton local resolved that miners oppose any increase in military spending "unless the element of profit to private firms and individuals be eliminated, thereby allowing this question to be viewed from an unselfish standpoint." If miners support preparedness, Wieck warned, "we will put more money in the hands of these people to fight organized labor." He urged every miner to "go home to his local union and impress upon the members their duty to study this question, create sentiment and have the matter settled in an unprejudiced way."[5]

As a measure of how uncontroversial this position on preparedness seemed at the time, the resolution committee recommended passage and the delegates agreed without further debate. And while working people did participate in preparedness parades, some also held counterdemonstrations. In Canton, a coal mining town near Peoria that elected a Socialist mayor in 1914, the secretary of the local Trades and Labor Assembly wrote to President John Walker of the Illinois Federation of Labor (IFL) in May 1916, asking him to speak "at an anti-preparedness meeting which we propose to hold June 4."[6]

As part of discussing the preparedness movement, miners' delegates at the 1916 Illinois convention also heard from Agnes Burns, a coal miner's daughter and Women's Trade Union League organizer.[7] A former school-teacher, Burns said that "many of the teachers are realizing that much of the history and literature and even the songs have unconsciously been developing the spirit of militarism." She herself recalled teaching boys and girls patriotic songs, including one in which the boys sing proudly:

We'll be the soldiers then,
Loyal and sturdy men;
We'll play the fife and drum,
Soon in the years to come,
Loudly the bugle blow;
Bravely to meet the foe . . .

"Such a song to teach children in the twentieth century civilization," Burns exclaimed. "We are to hold out nothing but war! war! war! to our children? Is that the future?"

If this brand of anti-preparedness seemed more strictly pacifist than that expressed by Germer or Wieck, Burns also introduced a working-class aspect to it. "[T]he spirit of the workers fighting in the trenches is not dead," she said. Burns quoted an English trade unionist who recently had spoken in Chicago, saying, "The men of England want to say to their brothers in Germany, 'We are not fighting you, we have no quarrel with you. We realize you are our brothers, but we are fighting because we were told to fight, because we were led to believe we were fighting for our country and our liberty.' And the men in Germany want to say to their brothers in England, 'We have no quarrel with you. We are fighting because we were told to fight, because we were led to believe we were fighting for our country, our fatherland and our liberty.'" Burns ended her speech declaring (this time quoting English Romantic poet Robert Lovell) that workers had a "world-wide fatherland."[8]

The relevance of the preparedness controversy to working people nationwide was brought home soon after Illinois miners held their 1916 convention. Thousands of miles away in San Francisco, trade unionists organized an anti-preparedness meeting on the eve of a preparedness parade planned for July 22. They were well aware that the main organizers of the coming parade were anti-union businessmen, promoters of the "open shop." In the days leading up to the parade, a number of mysterious death threats were delivered to parade organizers. Aware that violence during the event could be used to discredit the union movement, the city labor council passed a resolution urging anti-preparedness workers to protest only by "silent non-participation." On July 22, two minutes into the grand parade, a bomb exploded, killing ten people and wounding forty. Four days later, police arrested four trade union militants including Tom Mooney, a Socialist and leader of the International Molders Union.[9] Sentenced to death after a conviction that later proved to be based on fabricated testimony, Mooney became a cause célèbre for the militant section of the labor movement, and his name became known worldwide. Illinois miners would play a key role in winning support for Mooney, whom they viewed as one of their own. Not only was Mooney a union militant, but his father, Bernard, had been a southern Indiana coal miner and an organizer for the Knights of Labor. Mooney spent much of his early childhood around the mines of Washington, Indiana, and later spent time in Chicago.[10]

Working people took part in discussion of preparedness not only in union conventions but also in church. The St. Clair branch of the Federation of Catholic Societies held its 1916 convention in the coal town of O'Fallon. After attending a high mass at St. Clara's Church in O'Fallon, the 200 delegates participated in a public meeting that featured talks on "The Living Wage" and "Settlement Work," subjects that were clearly meant to appeal to a working-class and immigrant audience. Delegates then got down to business and adopted a resolution relating to the European war. "Whereas, Christ, the Savior and the Prince of Peace, came to proclaim and to bring peace to all men," that resolution began, " . . . and Whereas a pagan and false fetish of patriotism is endangering the Christian conception of peace, and Whereas War is frequently unjust and unnecessary and declared by and in the interest of a few who seek to enrich and advance themselves thereby at the people's frightful expense of treasure of blood and life," the Catholic delegates urged the following measures. First, they advocated "every effort and agitation which will resent the bloody and cruel sacrifice of the people to this false fetish of patriotism." Second, they endorsed Senator Robert LaFollette's effort to allow the American people to vote on war.[11] In light of the wave of patriotism that was already rising and would crest following the U.S. entry into the war, it is noteworthy that organized Catholics would paint that phenomenon in such dark colors.

Though anti-war resolutions spoke in general terms about war, for many miners and other working people in southwestern Illinois, especially recent European immigrants, the contending forces were not abstract combatants but relatives and friends they had left behind in Europe. In

November 1915, for instance, Mrs. John Falcetti, an Italian immigrant woman in Belleville, got word from her parents in Turin, Italy, that her brother had died fighting with the Alpine Corps against the Austrian army. A second brother had lost a hand in the fighting, and a third was still at the front.[12]

Given this context, it should not be surprising that in addition to anti-war sentiments, there were a variety of European nationalist currents running in and out of the coal towns of this region. Conflicting allegiances could eerily mirror the war itself. For example, in East St. Louis in early August 1914, just as the fighting began on the eastern front, John Visnic, an "Austrian" subject, and John Soulvick, a Serbian, came to blows, drawing the crowd around them into the fracas. A press report described both men as "warm partisans of their respective countries."[13] One year later in Collinsville, a pair of miners working at Lumaghi Mine No. 2 clashed at a dance hall near the mine. Apparently, Louis Sariano, an Italian-born miner, made an insulting remark about the Austrian flag to Austrian-born Louis Vampa. "I will give you a flag," answered Vampa as he pulled out a revolver and fatally shot Sariano in the stomach. One can only speculate what other conflicts between the two men may have laid the foundation for this quick draw of a pistol, but the incident illustrates the way that the patriotic gore of Europe, thousands of miles distant, might be experienced quite intensely by working people in this corner of Illinois.[14]

The passions stirred by rival nationalisms among miners came up for discussion at the 1916 UMWA International Convention in a revealing exchange between Ed Wieck and International president John White. Wieck explained that during the summer of 1915, shortly after Italy entered the war, some Italian-born members of Local 755 circulated a leaflet urging their compatriots in the mines not to go back and fight. On their behalf, Wieck submitted it to the Italian-language section of the *United Mine Workers Journal (UMWJ)*, but he never received an answer. It should have been published, Wieck said.

At this point, White speculated that a letter he sent Italian editor Joseph Poggiani probably influenced him not to publish the leaflet. While traveling through the anthracite fields of Pennsylvania in the past year, White explained, some miners complained of the anti-war cartoons and statements in the Italian section of the *UMWJ*. "Some of the officers down there told me that unless those things were eliminated it was going to seriously injure our [j]ournal," White recalled. They told him that "bitter factions were developing down there and it would be wise to omit all these things." In response, White instructed the journal editors to exclude anything "that might tend to cause bitterness among our members." In the UMWA, White said, "there are men of every nationality engaged in that war and the sentiments and traditions that have come here with them are pronounced." In conclusion, White cautioned that "[w]e have to be mighty careful not to have our [j]ournal used as an argument."[15]

While the *UMWJ* avoided confronting the effects of the war on union coal miners, the coal employers' journal *Coal Age* spelled it out in black and white. In early 1916, a cartoon appeared that noted how immigrant miners of different nationalities who had worked together as fellow unionists were now pitted against each other on the field of battle. Tucked away in one corner of the frame, labeled "in U.S. before they left," are miners from Russia, Italy, Germany, Austria, and Wales talking amiably at a union meeting. Nearly every miner wears a smile, and one group in the background stands together in a friendly huddle, hands resting on each others' shoulders. The central action in the cartoon, however, takes place "after arriving on European battlefields." Here we witness hand-to-hand combat on the front lines, as a spike-helmeted German soldier is shot with a pistol from point-blank range, while his compatriot sinks his bayonet into the chest of an onrushing Allied soldier. The cartoon's caption reads, "Brothers once, but now——."[16] Regardless of how many immigrant UMWA members actually joined in the fighting at this stage, this cartoon conveyed the predicament the war posed for workers worldwide.

Though European nationalism came in many varieties in southwestern Illinois, the type that gained the most attention during the early years of the war was sympathy with the German cause. As the events of 1914 showed, the avowedly internationalist principles of the German Socialist Party crumbled in the face of war. It is not surprising then that many German American workers lent various degrees of support to the German war effort. Though many German American miners were attracted to the Socialist stand against the war on a class basis, the existence of what we might call "genuine" pro-Germanism is worth noting, since after the United States entered the war, the government tagged any opposition as "pro-German." In his informative study of German Americans and the war, Frederick Luebke surveyed the range of responses they made to the crisis, which included organizing humanitarian aid, selling German war bonds, publishing pro-German propaganda, lobbying to keep the United States out of the war, and urging U.S. newspapers to maintain a neutral stance.[17] Situated next door to the German American mecca of St. Louis, southwestern Illinois witnessed all of these activities.

Starting in 1914, working people in both Staunton and Belleville had ample opportunity to hear the German government's side of the story. In October 1914, for instance, the Belleville local of the German-American Alliance held a mass meeting at the Liederkranz Hall "as an expression of sympathy for the Germans and Austrians who are now at war with five nations."[18] In October 1915, Stauntonites could pay ten or twenty-five cents to see "German War Pictures—showing the German side of the war," taken by a *Chicago Tribune* reporter "by special permission of the Kaiser."[19]

German nationalists also took aim at pro-Allied newspaper coverage. In early 1915, after a big meeting of the American Neutrality League in St. Louis, publicity manager Eugene Vogt came to Belleville to form a local branch. In his speech, he pointed out examples of pro-French or pro-English coverage. Whenever an American made public comments favorable to Germany, he noted, "he is immediately accused of not living up to the spirit of President Wilson's proclamation of neutrality. 'Why doesn't he go back to Germany?' Or, 'Has he no respect for our dear mother country?' I might say, purely parenthetically, that England is not my mother country nor does she stand in relation to a majority of American citizens. To our citizens of Irish extraction she enacts the role, rather, of the cruel stepmother. If every hand in America [were] to reach across the sea, we would find most of them outstretched into other lands than Great Britain."[20]

In 1916, working people in Staunton attended showings of German government war footage. At the Labor Temple in July, *Germany's Fighting Forces* was screened, complete with photos taken "by one hundred and six enlisted soldier camera men who daily risked their lives that the world might know how gloriously the Germany of today is prepared to defend her homes and her people."[21] In September, a "Deutsche Kriegsbilder" was held featuring "sensational moving pictures" of the "European War as It Is," taken by photographers for a leading German newspaper. A quarter of the proceeds from the event, which also included a speech by F. W. Seelig of Emden, Germany, would benefit German war orphans. An advertisement in the *Staunton Star-Times* enthusiastically urged German readers, "Kommt alle und sehet den Kaiser und von Hindenburg an der

Front."[22] Similarly in Belleville in March 1916, German Americans organized a German War Festival at the Liederkranz Hall. Attendees could enjoy a big card party lasting through the afternoon and evening. Proceeds would benefit "German war sufferers."[23]

To what extent German American miners took part in these activities is unclear. Given the predominance of miners in a town like Staunton and the large number of German Americans, it is likely that a significant number might attend such events. At the same time, the perspectives of German Americans on the war were hardly uniform. Some of the miners who were most outspoken in opposing the war from a Socialist standpoint—such as Edward Wieck and Adolph Germer—were German Americans. But just as a rudimentary patriotism was common in "American" workers, no doubt a pride in the fatherland was also common in German American miners. A typical example may have been miner Pat Classen, the son of a German miner who arrived in the United States in the 1890s. During the war, Classen worked in the mines around O'Fallon in St. Clair County. His nephew Vernon Canterbury, who grew up in O'Fallon at that time, described Classen as "an active miner. And he was pretty outspoken all the time" in his support of Germany in the war. As Vernon recalls, the family used tell him, "Pat, you better keep quiet. You're going to cause yourself trouble." But Classen persisted in defending "some of the actions of the German army. In other words, he just more or less bragged on the German army. He didn't think we could defeat them."[24]

While some German American workers cheered on their national team, the major political force in the American working class that refused to root for any nation was the Socialist Party. On August 14, 1914, less than two weeks after the war began, some 2,000 people attended the International Anti-War and Peace Demonstration in St. Louis, organized by the Socialist Party there.[25] If this was like subsequent anti-war meetings, there were plenty of Illinois miners in attendance. In the next three years, prominent Socialist leaders made frequent stops in the southwestern Illinois coalfields. From August 1914 to July 1917, for instance, Staunton hosted major speaking events for the following: Eugene Debs, Allan Benson, Emil Seidel, John C. Kennedy, Janet Fenimore Korngold, and Ella Reeve Bloor.[26] Most of these events drew a mainly working-class audience from many of the surrounding coal towns. Since the Socialist Party included a wide variety of viewpoints, the messages heard by working people in Staunton ranged from Debs's fiery condemnation of capitalist warmakers to Benson's more restrained warnings about the latest developments in the halls of Congress.

In his December 1915 speech at the Staunton Labor Temple, Eugene Debs began by giving his audience a brief history of class society, according to a press report, "going back to ancient history and coming down to the present time showing at different stages the exploitation of labor and the ruling of capital." Debs then "spoke of the terrible carnage in war-ridden European countries and showed how the monarchs exploited the 'patriots' [among] the working man even to the brink of a gory grave." Criticizing the growing clamor for preparedness, Debs "declared we needed no army and showed that preparedness means nothing but war." While "it has been currently reported that socialism is against religion," the article noted, " . . . in his discourse Debs quoted scripture, cited Bible instances and frequently alluded to the 'Divine Being' in some manner or form." Debs's statement that "'it is better to shed light than shed blood' struck a popular chord and called forth cheers from the hundreds of miners, mechanics and their wives and families assembled."[27]

A meeting for Socialist Party presidential candidate Allan Benson on the eve of the 1916 election drew a crowd of 900 men and women who came from Staunton, Mt. Olive, Benld, Hillsboro, Carlinville, and elsewhere.[28] In his speech, Benson "asserted that both leading political parties are strongly drifting towards imperialism." He stressed the little-known Section 79 of the Hay-Chamberlain Army Reorganization Bill, then pending in Congress, which gave President Wilson the power to draft citizens into the army. Benson argued that this would mean "military autocracy" and lamented that few people knew of this sinister plan contained in the bill. Though Benson was neither the orator nor educator Debs was, his presence in the southwestern Illinois coalfields was testimony to the persistent anti-war sentiment there.

In addition to national and local Socialist Party leaders, Italian American Socialists who belonged to the Italian Socialist Federation (ISF) were also active in the region. The ISF, which functioned loosely within the Socialist Party of America, was mainly a party "at-large," with small clumps of members in widely scattered towns. Thanks to the censorship carried out by the U.S. Postmaster's office, government records offer a glimpse of the struggle for the loyalties of Italian American miners, who were numerous in the coal towns of northern Madison County—Livingston, Worden, Williamson—and farther south in the Collinsville area.

In Illinois, Spring Valley in the north and Livingston in the south appear to have been central distribution points for *La Parola Proletaria,* the newspaper of the ISF. In October 1917, J. W. Donaldson, postmaster of Livingston, reported that the paper was being distributed "to numerous towns throughout the state from this office by the Socialist Party here, in bundles." These latter towns included Staunton and Worden.[29] From Spring Valley, papers were distributed to a range of towns in the northern coalfields, as well as to Collinsville subscribers.[30] In relative terms, Livingston seems to have drawn a particularly high number of Italian Socialist miners, considering that in a town of 1,000, there were 30 subscribers.[31]

Like the Socialist Party in Italy, the ISF remained true to its internationalist principles and took a firm stand against the war. As one article in *La Parola Proletaria* stated, "Friendly to the war means solidarity to the bourgeois government either monarchical or democratic and to the capitalists . . . and we poor fellows who must pay with life and purse cannot and must not have any solidarity with our assassins."[32] The paper took aim at the very notion of patriotism. One article declared that "[t]rue civilization will never be until all the flags of separate nationalities are struck down and in their stead floats the red standard of socialistic Internationalism." It then called on readers to form a local branch of the People's Council.[33]

A post office inspector noted that *La Parola Proletaria* "has not encouraged the draft enlistments in the army, or assisted in any way to the success of the government loans."[34] Indeed, one Italian Socialist defined the word "slacker" in the following terms: "It means to refuse oneself to the military calls and to go to [slaughter] and let others butcher ourselves for the private interests of the several parasitic gangs of every country." Given the ISF's stand, it may well be that the disproportionate presence of Italian miners who appeared on the delinquent list for northern Madison County, cited below, is not coincidental.

Despite their modest success in propagating their ideas among Italian American miners, the ISF competed with strong currents of American patriotism, as well as Italian nationalism, in these communities. An ISF resolution noted with alarm that even though the Italian Socialist Party opposed the war, "a good number of [comrades] have let themselves be dragged into this slaughter with the end of defending the national independence."[35] The devastating losses the Italian forces suffered and Italy's longstanding claims to Fiume fueled this Italian patriotic fervor, which was evident in the fight between Italian and "Austrian" miners in a Collinsville dance hall narrated earlier.

Pro-war Italian American Socialists also appealed to miners to support the war. From the western front in France, former Maryville resident John Ricca wrote to his fellow Socialist coal miner Dominick Oberto, who remained on the home front working at Donk No. 2.[36] According to Ricca, Meyer London, the Socialist U.S. congressman who voted against war, "does not represent the true socialists of the country, but only small number of deluded persons who do not realize the present social situation." The idea promoted by the likes of London, "[t]hat we are fighting to save the capital of Wall Street, as many persons in United States supposed, . . . is false, absolutely false," Ricca told his friend. Rather, "[w]e are fighting for an high principle, for a just cause for which we all feel proud."[37]

In considering how the working people of the coalfields responded to the challenge of war and to the Socialist Party, one other aspect of southwestern Illinois Socialism looms large. As alluded to above, the Socialists of the coalfields met opposition not only from the supporters of Frank Farrington in the UMWA but also from activists who owed their primary loyalty to the Catholic Church. On returning from the International Miners Congress in 1912, Adolph Germer wrote to Belgian Socialist leader Henri De Mann explaining that American Socialists faced competition from Catholic activists in the labor movement. Referring to the formation of Catholic miners unions in Germany, Germer wrote that "this element is trying to do in this country what they have already done in various European nations." In the face of the activities of the Militia of Christ and the German Roman Catholic Central Verein, Germer predicted that "[o]pen warfare will break out here just as it has abroad just as the power of the socialists grows in the trades union movement and we will have to prepare to meet the situation."[38]

Germer's prediction came true three years later in Belleville, Illinois, during the 1915 municipal elections. Fending off a full slate of Socialist Party candidates, Mayor R. E. Duvall of the Republican-oriented Citizens Party enlisted the aid of David Goldstein, a Catholic anti-Socialist. Active in the cigar makers union in Massachusetts and a former Socialist, Goldstein hoped to discredit the Socialist movement by painting its views on women as immoral and subversive.[39] He toured the nation spreading the word and had visited Belleville twice before, indicating that his views had at least some local base of support. Although Goldstein's title,

"Christianity versus Socialism," suggested a broad brush, he focused on alleged Socialist views of gender roles to stir up his audience. According to a newspaper report, Goldstein, by way of quoting Marx and Engels, "proved" that Socialists were purveyors of "atheism" and "free love." The speaker, the article continued, "based his arguments upon the works of recognized socialists of world-wide authority within the Socialist movement, maintaining [that] the atheist and free love books, of which he named twenty-five, are officially circulated by the Socialist Party."[40] Goldstein had perfected this method in his widely circulated *Socialism: The Nation of Fatherless Children,* which used the writings of well-known Socialists to reveal the dangers to family, religion, and society allegedly posed by the growing Socialist movement. Goldstein coauthored the book with another former Socialist, Martha Moore Avery. According to Goldstein and Avery, Socialists were guilty of arguing that women should be able to choose freely their relationships with men, including the right to end a failed marriage. In response, wrote the authors, "To be brutally frank, what can prompt a woman, with two children, to leave her home and live with 'somebody else' but mere sex passion." What would become of the human race, particularly women, he asked, if they were "utterly 'free' to accept the matrimonial relationship?—Not to speak of moral degradation—how long would the physical structure stand the strain that would thus be put upon it?"[41] After the United States entered World War I, Goldstein and Avery went on to become enthusiastic boosters for the American war effort and diehard opponents of the Bolshevik revolution.[42]

Only a few months later, Catholic opposition to Socialism merged with the issue of the war when the Macoupin County Catholic Federation met in early June 1915. Meeting in Staunton, the delegates passed a resolution stating that their convention "deplores the existence of the present European War and extends its heartfelt sympathy to all fellow men regardless of nationality and creed who are engaged in this terrible conflict." In contrast to the St. Clair text the next year, the Macoupin resolution took few political chances. It called for no anti-war action and did not attack the concept of patriotism. On the other hand, the Macoupin delegates did take a clear stand against Socialism. A second resolution explained that "[a]s the doctrine of Socialism is finding [its] way into all classes of society, it is the duty of [the] Catholic to inform himself on the teaching of the church in this matter and every Catholic should, inasmuch as he is able, oppose Socialism as generally taught by Socialists."[43] The Macoupin delegates found themselves in a difficult position, since those in the area taking the clearest stand against the war were Socialists.

Undoubtedly the very need to make such a strong anti-Socialist statement reflected the appeal of the party to these working people. Although elements of the Socialist Party, including the prominent Socialist newspaper *Appeal to Reason,* did engage in tirades against the Catholic Church, this did not stop some miners of Catholic faith from joining the party. It appears, for instance, that Socialist Victor Saladin of Collinsville belonged to the SS. Peter and Paul Catholic Church in town.[44] Frank Bertetti of Benld, in Macoupin County, recalled that his father, a Catholic Italian-born miner, read *Appeal to Reason* and convinced him to vote for Eugene Debs in 1920.[45]

The U.S. declaration of war in April 1917 put the working-class movement to a severe test. It was one thing to advocate peace in an officially neutral country but quite another to oppose war once declared. While the Socialist Party proclaimed its opposition to President Wilson's course within days at a St. Louis emergency convention, many current and former Socialist leaders, such as John Walker of Illinois, became prominent boosters for the war effort. Like other major unions, the UMWA quickly declared its support for the "war for democracy." But even the pages of the *UMWJ* in these early months reflected the doubts and hesitations of coal miners about jumping on the patriotic bandwagon.

After the February diplomatic break between the United States and Germany, the miners of the Southern Coal Company Mine No. 8 in New Baden, Illinois, expressed their outrage. Under the influence of German American Socialist miners, the members of the local wrote to their U.S. representative condemning the action of the White House in breaking relations with Germany and calling on the Congress to prevent an outbreak of war. In a resolution printed in the *UMWJ,* the miners denounced President Wilson for making the decision without "the sanction or consent of the people." "We are practically ordered," they protested, "to join in the mad dance of death and destruction and to swell the ghastly river of blood in Europe with the blood of American workers."

Rejecting the official reasons for hostility between Germany and the United States, the New Baden miners stated that "the workers of the United States have no reason and no desire to shed blood for the protection and furtherance of the unholy profits of their masters and will not permit a lying and venal press to stampede them into taking up arms to murder their brothers in Europe." If the United States were drawn into the fighting, they warned, the war would be "an inglorious, senseless sacrifice on the altar of capitalist greed."[46]

While never taking such a radical position, the *UMWJ* editors minimized the supposed German threat as late as March 22, 1917. The real danger to workers, they argued, came from proposals for universal military training in the schools. "We recognize no danger from without so fraught with menace to the people of this land," they wrote, "as the proposal to break the spirit of the youth of the land through a system that involves enforced unquestioning obedience."[47] This view harmonized well with positions taken against militarism in the previous several years.

With the U.S. declaration of war two weeks after these words appeared in print, however, the *UMWJ* reversed course. Despite all the UMWA's admonitions about militarism, miners learned in an editorial entitled "Preserving Democracy" that "[t]his war . . . is to be considered a defense of democracy against the danger of encroachments and offense by the only great countries of the world that are controlled absolutely by the powerful few." For the next eighteen months, UMWA leaders from Frank Hayes to Frank Farrington would cultivate this distinction between the "autocratic" capitalism of Germany and the "democratic" capitalism of America.

The distinction certainly made sense to many UMWA members. Miner Joe Bosone, for instance, wrote to John Walker offering his patriotic services. He was apparently one of the Italian American miners not convinced by the ISF's Socialist anti-war message. "If you need any help to stir-up the Italians for war," Bosone wrote, "let me know and i will do all that is in me for the best of our Nation the good old U.S.A."[48] Several months later, Bosone informed Walker that "I am on my way at last, to the fighting line of freedom and for liberty." Stationed at Fort George Wright in Washington as part of the Twenty-seventh Engineers, Bosone wrote that "today I am more then proud of been one of those fellows that realize the necessity of our force, and wealth to be placed against the autocratic world for the Liberty of all the people whom peoples this earth." Linking his war service with the cause of unionism, the miner declared, "And like I fought in the industrial battle field of our common life I will fight in the battle-field for the same cause but in bigger [field?] for the liberty of all the nations."[49] Bosone's words are striking for their reverential, almost devotional tone and their strength of feeling for his adopted country.

But in rushing to support the war, UMWA leaders still voiced some ongoing doubts. For one, they restated the labor movement's longstanding opposition to forced conscription. UMWA International secretary William Green, for instance, took up this point in a speech to Staunton miners shortly after the United States entered the war but before the Selective Service Act passed in Congress. According to a press account, "Mr. Green, in compliance with a request from one of his auditors, expressed his regret that a Conscription measure had been deemed necessary and stated that while organized labor had always been opposed to anything which smacked of militarism, he hoped that the ultimate result would be to [t]he best interests of democracy and forever destroy autocracy."[50]

The miners' leadership also hesitated on the question of suppression of free speech. Noting that the proposed espionage legislation in Congress included clauses even harsher than workers faced in Germany, the *UMWJ* editors stated, "We do not believe that it is necessary to out-Prussian the Prussians in this country in order that we may destroy autocratic government in Europe." The UMWA helped reelect President Wilson, they noted, "but we hold that there could be no greater injustice to the people of the country than an attempt to abrogate by statute, by threat to imprison, the right to criticise either the President or any leader in the government, the army or the navy."[51]

Working-class hesitation about war mobilization was also reflected in the statements of Illinois public officials, even as they urged working people toward war. At a patriotic rally in Chicago on March 31, for example, Governor Frank Lowden explained why working people should be willing to sacrifice for their country. Invoking Lincoln's words, Lowden asked his audience, "Do we still believe in a government of the people, for the people and by the people? Do we wish still to maintain a democratic form of government? . . . If so," he answered, "if these great principles for which our fathers fought and died are still worth our while, no man within our borders, either rich or poor, of high or low degree, should be exempt from service at this crucial time, but owes his ability to serve his country in time of need. The flag does not protect simply those who fight beneath it, it protects all alike, and all owe a common duty to keep that flag."

Even if war were avoided, Lowden continued, the "burst of patriotism" that would accompany military mobilization would help instill a sense of national loyalty in the "average citizen." A surge of patriotism was necessary, in his view, because "[w]e have become absolutely indifferent to the obligations of citizenship.... We treat our country as if it were some great horn of plenty, scattering among the people from a royal hand her precious gifts, and exacting nothing, not even an ordinary obedience, in return. Think of the importance of this idea, if every man were made to feel that his citizenship was so precious that he himself would pay some price for it." Perhaps Lowden had been thinking along the same lines in February when he ordered the week of February 19–23 set aside for singing patriotic songs in Illinois public and private schools. "One of the great unifying, nationalizing influences is the singing of our national songs," Lowden had proclaimed. "Nothing so arouses and fixes a sound and patriotic sentiment as the teaching of these songs to our children." Consequently, teachers were to reserve a special time each day to sing "America," "The Star Spangled Banner," "Hail, Columbia," "The Battle Hymn of the Republic," and "Illinois."[52]

In any event, Lowden's March 31 speech revealed the uneasiness of the nation's rulers as the country headed into war. Even at a public patriotic rally, the governor openly acknowledged that working people, average "citizens" or not, did not necessarily think they ought to sacrifice for the "nation." He made his meaning clear when he added that "[to unite all] these different classes of citizens, to escape class distinctions along undesirable lines, there is no remedy before you so appropriate as universal military training."[53] Or, as Lowden said later in the year, the war would create a "rebirth of brotherhood."[54]

In the early months of U.S. participation in the war, politicians witnessed plenty of "brotherhood" but not the variety Lowden had in mind. One month after Lowden's patriotic Chicago speech, for example, the St. Louis Socialist Party hosted a mass anti-war rally at the city coliseum featuring Adolph Germer as main speaker. According to a summary of his remarks, Germer argued that "the great war is to serve the material interests of the capitalist classes of all the warring nations. Germany is not fighting for democracy and civilization, nor is England, nor Belgium, France or Japan, but in order to expand their trade and make more money out of commerce." Were Illinois coal miners present at the April anti-war rally? Especially with Germer as speaker, the probability seems high. Later in the summer, when 200 unionists in the St. Louis area formed a branch of the anti-war People's Council for Democracy and Terms of Peace, a newspaper reported that "[m]any of the delegates present were from miners organizations in Illinois."[55]

In an anti-war resolution, the assembled St. Louis–area Socialists extended "greetings of solidarity and peace to the Socialists and workers of all countries." They reaffirmed the anti-war stand of the national St. Louis emergency convention, stating that "our entrance into the world war was instigated by the predatory capitalists who boast of the enormous profits of seven billions of dollars from the manufacture and sale of war supplies, and are, therefore, deeply interested in the continuance of the war for purely business reasons." Finally, they declared that "as capitalist militarism on American soil grows and expands[,] in that same ratio our democracy is weakened and our liberties are taken from us." While the rally denounced the war in the name of international class solidarity, *St. Louis Labor,* the local Socialist Party newspaper, still felt the need to portray it in patriotic terms. In prefacing their report, the editors boasted that "[n]o city in the United States can beat St. Louis in *genuine patriotism*—that is, patriotism the aim and object of which is the welfare of the masses of the people."[56] Socialist Party leaders who continued to oppose the war would also persist in declaring their patriotism in the coming months. Their need to do so undoubtedly reflected the immense efforts by government authorities to portray any opposition to the war as illegitimate.

On a national scale, the Wilson administration sought to curb anti-war sentiment and arouse pro-war "righteous wrath," most notably through the Committee on Public Information (CPI).[57] According to CPI director George Creel, the government sought "no mere surface unity" but a "passionate belief" in America's cause that would "weld" the American people "into one white-hot mass instinct with fraternity, devotion, courage, and deathless determination."[58] To develop this instinct, the CPI used a wide variety of media including films, pamphlets, books, news stories, cartoons, and public speakers. The "Four Minute Men" (FMM) gave an estimated total of a million speeches that reached an audience of 400 million listeners from the spring of 1917 to the armistice.[59] Most commonly, these local spokespeople for the government's war program delivered their talks before movie theater audiences. The CPI changed the topic of these speeches weekly and instructed speakers to respond to audience questions either by pleading ignorance or by ignoring them. Once again, the government's strategy reflected a justifiable lack of confidence in the enthusiasm of working people for war.

In southwestern Illinois, many union officials were drawn into the official machinery of war mobilization, but most of the work of the FMM was carried out by professionals and businessmen.[60] In Madison County, for instance, C. W. Terry, an Alton attorney, and Harry Herb, the president of the Alton Board of Trade, divided up the county territory into five districts. Collinsville and Troy constituted District 3, and the other coal towns comprised District 5. For each town, they noted how many theaters were available, since most propaganda speeches took place there. In Collinsville, FMM included two ministers, a plant manager, and a newspaper editor.[61]

In St. Clair County, Belleville formed a local branch of the FMM in October 1917 and then proceeded to recruit speakers in the surrounding towns. These included the coal towns of O'Fallon, Caseyville, Shiloh, Freeburg, Mascoutah, New Athens, and Marissa. Most of the individuals contacted "expressed themselves as perfectly willing to do all in their power to do all that they possibly can," according to the Belleville chairman, who would send speakers out once every one to four weeks.[62]

Macoupin County was organized in a similar way, though some important coal mining towns such as Benld and Gillespie still lacked any FMM as late as July 1918. The county seat of Carlinville got an FMM branch only as the war came to a close.[63] To what extent this reflects political difficulties or bureaucratic inefficiency is unclear. But certainly the fires of doubt about the war that Eugene Debs had stoked in the Staunton area in 1915 still smoldered.

What was the content of the FMM speeches? Records suggest that the FMM in Illinois pulled no punches in working up a vicious hatred for all things German. For a speech entitled "The Beast at Bay" (also innocently designated as "Lecture No. 1"), the speaker received the following talking points: "The vast majority of Germans naturally cruel and stupid—even in peace time child suicide highest in the world—transformation from law-abiding citizens to blood-thirsty ruffians in a single night . . ." Even without any German-bashing, the four minutes were certainly intended to arouse the emotions. For instance, the text of another "lecture" began, "The kaiser, drunk with the stench of millions of carcasses rotting on the blood soaked battlefields, defied us whom he would conquer." Both talks harmonized with the image viewers saw in such films as *Beast of Berlin*, shown in towns across the region.[64] The speeches also gave the lie to President Wilson's stated intention of whipping up hatred only for the kaiser, not for the German people.

In addition to writing their own material, FMM speakers seem to have relayed key speeches by national leaders to working people in their communities. For instance, FMM reported that they read President Wilson's July 4, 1918, message to good-sized crowds in the southwestern Illinois coalfields: in Collinsville, 5,000 people; in Belleville, 5,800; in Staunton, 2,500, which included some from Livingston; and in Freeburg, 300 (at a Red Cross picnic). A note accompanying this report suggests the difficulties still plaguing the FMM at this late date. In one unnamed town, after addressing 1,200 people, an FMM speaker explained that "two other points were tried but they got no audiences. Those not harvesting went to the river and this is where we *caught* the people we did."[65] But the mere fact that the government went to such lengths to bring Woodrow Wilson's words to ordinary working people is important. President Wilson addressed himself to coal miners a number of times during the war. His need to do so reflected the ongoing challenge of mobilizing miners in support of the war.

Despite the rarity of real German spies, the Wilson administration devoted substantial effort to hunting them down. In February 1917, shortly after the United States broke relations with Germany, Attorney General Thomas Gregory approved a Chicago businessman's plan to create a volunteer citizen spy-hunting agency. By the war's end, over 250,000 members of the American Protective League (APL) had made some one million investigations for the Justice Department.[66] Though the APL worked under the supervision of the attorney general, its activity fit neatly into CPI propaganda. For instance, a CPI poster advertising "The Kaiserite in America" urged readers to "pin down" propagators of "German lies." Someone who repeated the "lie," that "It's a rich man's war" or "Farmers are profiteering" was "hurting your country every day. They are playing the Kaiser's game." Every such "lie," according to the poster, "originated with a German spy." Readers who had located "a disloyal person" were instructed to "give his name to the Department of Justice in Washington and tell them where to find him."[67]

In the climate that the government had helped create by 1917, "spy" could mean anyone who questioned the official government version of the truth. APL operatives, along with agents from the Bureau of Investigation of the Justice Department, infiltrated unions, including the Industrial Workers of the World, and political and social organizations and generally kept their eyes and ears open for "suspicious" behavior and commentary. As Gregory boasted later: "After the first six months of the War, it would have been difficult for 50 persons to have met for any purpose in any place, from a Church to a dance hall in any part of the United States, without at least one representative of the Government being present. *I doubt if any country was ever so thoroughly and intelligently policed in the history of the world.*"[68] Because of the wide net cast by the government, expanded further by the Sedition Act in May 1918, local gossip became the subject of federal investigation.

Conversely, events in localities in southwestern Illinois mirrored national developments. In Collinsville, for instance, in the week following the U.S. declaration of war, Joel Zumwald, an interurban conductor of German descent, received what the *Collinsville Herald* called "[a] lesson in Patriotism." According to the *Herald,* Zumwald had been "more appreciative of the yellow and black of the Kaiser's escutcheon than the red white and blue, so much admired by the other interurban employees." For this "disloyalty," Zumwald received a black eye, thanks to a fellow interurban driver by the name of Blackstock. Luckily for Zumwald, bystanders intervened before Blackstock could inflict any further injury. The *Herald's* comment—"Too bad!"—indicates the level of public intolerance for free speech that existed already in the opening weeks of U.S. participation in the war.[69]

Though a minority of coal miners made the ultimate sacrifice for their country by serving in the military, the Selective Service Act of May 1917 ensured that every coal mining family was touched by the machinery of the draft in some way. For the first registration of June 5, 1917, all men between the ages of twenty-one and thirty were required to sign up. Those who were "alien enemies" were placed in Class 5, which meant they would not serve; however, they were still required to register. So-called non-enemy aliens, who intended to become citizens and had filed their declarations, could be drafted.[70] These last two categories made up a large proportion of the coal mining population.

At the January 1918 UMWA International Convention, union leaders claimed that miners led the nation in military service. "The largest number of men in service of any organization or industry is our proud boast," stated one union official.[71] According to him, 19,135 UMWA members, or 29 percent of those eligible, had answered the call to the colors. In Illinois, the UMWA estimated that 3,269 members, or 23.5 percent of those subject to the law, had either volunteered or were drafted. Though some miners volunteered, the majority were probably draftees. In any case, a quarter to a third of those eligible does seem notable if the arbitrary nature of the draft is considered.

On the other hand, if taken as a percentage of the total UMWA membership, the number of miners who saw service was rather small. In Illinois, for instance, those 3,269 represented only 3.75 percent of the entire state's miners, as compared, for instance, to 7.48 percent of the portion of those West Virginia miners in District 29.[72] This may be partly attributed to the higher proportion of older miners in a state like Illinois. The older midwestern mining states of Indiana, Ohio, and Iowa also had low percentages. It also might reflect the high proportion of recent immigrants, though this would not explain the higher percentage in the Pennsylvania districts.[73]

One thing the Illinois figure of roughly one in four certainly reflects is the high percentage of eligible miners who obtained exemptions from the draft. Young married miners were commonly exempted on the basis of family dependency. Of the 1,072 married men in the Staunton area who registered in 1917, for instance, only 115 were placed in Class 1, which meant they were immediately available.[74] And though the law did not specify miners as an exempt class for reasons of war production until August 1918, local draft boards most likely granted many exemptions on this basis before that date.[75] By July 1918, Illinois UMWA president Frank Farrington wrote to Secretary of Labor William B. Wilson urging him to exempt coal miners from the draft. He explained that "[y]oung men working as 'trip-riders,' motormen and mule drivers are fast becoming exhausted by the draft and a serious shortage of labor in the mines will be the result of further drafts."[76] Coal industry leaders echoed this concern, warning of the threat to production posed by the continuing exodus from the mines.[77]

The high level of exemptions could mean many things. Certainly one hard fact was that young mining families desperately needed the income that mining jobs provided. With the unusually steady work available during the war, miners' wages came in on a regular basis. But no doubt, too, there was a margin of choice that young men had in seeking exemptions. For one thing, draft boards reported a rash of marriages as June 5 approached, and in subsequent amendments to the Selective Service Act, they made provisions to close this loophole.[78]

Of course, not all those eligible to register did so. They resisted out of a variety of motives, including fear, immigrant nationalism, and anti-war feeling. Lawrence Tano of Bunker Hill failed to register on June 5. When he was caught, he first lied about his age but then broke down in tears, explaining that his mother had told him to lie and not register.[79] Pete Perry, who was a young Glen Carbon miner when the war broke out, recalled that most families were opposed to the war in this basic human way. "Everybody around here wanted it over with," he explained. "Well, what the hell, [the army] taking the kids over there and get them killed or shot or going over there and then not come back. If we went over there, me and my two brothers, if I'd-a come back and them two wouldn't, how the hell would I feel about it? I didn't want the damn thing neither."[80]

And even when miners registered, they did not necessarily show up for induction. In February 1918, the Madison County exemption board announced that it was hunting down twenty men—all coal miners—four of whom had failed to show up when called and another sixteen who had failed to file their registration questionnaires. They worked at the big mines in Livingston, Worden, and Williamson in the northern part of the county. Twelve were from Italy, four from Austria-Hungary, two from Greece, and one each born in Germany and the United States.[81]

A particularly dramatic and tragic case of draft resistance engaged the residents of Collinsville in early October, as June registrants began to receive their call to the colors. Among the 1,079 men who had registered in Collinsville on June 5 was a twenty-eight-year-old Lithuanian miner named Joseph Stepon. Employed at the Maryville mine where Robert Prager worked later that year, Stepon quit his job the day after he registered. According to Martha Miller, who knew Stepon, after he quit, "He worried and moped and could not be cheered up. He told us often that if he had to go to the army he would shoot himself, but everyone thought he was joking." On October 2, the young miner learned that he was to report for service to Camp Taylor in Louisville. The next day, Miller recalled, Stepon told his mother he felt sick and did not get out of bed. At dinnertime, Stepon came down and said he wasn't hungry. He then went back upstairs to his room, took out his revolver, and shot himself in the head.[82] While few miners chose this way out of their predicament, Stepon's case reveals the intense inner conflicts that the demands of the draft could arouse in the young miners of Collinsville.

Though one can only speculate about the motives of most accused draft "delinquents" and "slackers," government authorities were quite sure that anti-war agitators were impeding the operation of the Selective Service Act in the region. In an editorial printed in the *Staunton Star-Times,* Edward C. Knotts, U.S. district attorney for southern Illinois, was quoted as follows: "Some of them ["pro-Germans"] have gone so far as to curse the government and make it more difficult for the United States to effectively enforce the draft law. We do not expect to allow these people to continue this agitation."[83]

While the number of alleged "slackers" in the southern half of Illinois whose cases came to court was tiny, perhaps amounting to forty, the public campaign to induce working people to comply with the law was quite visible.[84] For instance, ten days after the first registration day, readers of the *Staunton Star-Times* were presented with a full list of those who had registered. "Examine these lists carefully," the editor urged readers, "and in case you know of any 'slackers' report them to the proper authorities."[85] Similarly, later in the year, the paper announced that miner Robert Bonner of Benld had failed to show up for induction when called. Authorities were offering a fifty-dollar reward for his capture.[86]

Perhaps the most dramatic public demonstrations of patriotism in connection with the draft were the Registration Day parades. On June 5, some 2,000 Collinsville residents marched through town to mark the first Registration Day. Marchers included members of veterans' organizations, Locals 264 and 685 of the UMWA, and nonunion hosiery workers at the Chester Knitting Mill. Amid the latter group flew a banner bearing the names of three German Americans who had registered, Louis Logner, John Hausman, and Hubert Getz. In nearby Maryville, Henry Engelbrecht, an "alien enemy" from Germany, distinguished himself as the hamlet's first draft registrant.[87]

Robert Prager, who still lived in St. Louis that spring, was also obliged to do his patriotic duty. Complying with the president's proclamation on "alien enemies," Prager registered as one, then registered for the draft, took out his first citizenship papers, and tried unsuccessfully to enlist in the United States Navy. Apparently, the navy rejected him because he had one glass eye. In commenting on Prager's actions, historian Frederick Luebke suggests that he "felt a strong sense of loyalty to his adopted country."[88] But given the repressive atmosphere that had developed, it seems unclear whether Prager's actions indicated active loyalty, passive obedience, or something midway between the two.

The ambiguity of these public displays of patriotism in Collinsville is suggested by a resolution passed by the miners at Lumaghi No. 3 at a July

3, 1917, union meeting. Though unionists had participated in the June 5 parade, there apparently was some question as to how many would attend an upcoming patriotic parade later in July. As a result, the miners resolved that "any member who does not March in the Parade July 18, be fined 50c and the proceed go to the Red Cross."[89] Though the use of fines for collective discipline was quite common in union affairs, the mere fact that miners felt the need to impose such a measure at this time is significant. It suggests that some miners' "righteous wrath," as Joseph Tumulty put it, had not been sufficiently aroused.

In addition to meeting the demands of county draft boards and the exhortations of the FMM, miners encountered numerous incarnations of the Councils of Defense. Established by federal law in 1916, the Council of National Defense (CND) was charged with mobilizing the industrial and agricultural resources and labor-power of the nation for the inevitable onset of U.S. involvement in the war.[90] The CND's Committee on Coal Production, headed by Illinois coal baron Francis Peabody, and its successor, the U.S. Fuel Administration, would have a great impact on the situation facing coal miners during the war, as the coal industry was regulated by the federal government. In Illinois, on the state and local level, the CND served as the main clearinghouse for the various facets of war mobilization. These included the marshalling of resources, organizing war relief, popular financing of the war, and surveillance and repression of anti-war sentiment.

The Illinois Council of Defense (ICD) was formed in early May 1917. Its fifteen members, appointed by Governor Lowden, were led by Samuel Insull, the owner of Commonwealth Edison. Others included J. Ogden Armour of meatpacking fame; John Spoor, a railroad and banking magnate; Frederick Upham, a coal and lumber dealer; capitalist Charles Wacker; and a number of prominent politicians and professionals. The two representatives of organized labor were Victor Olander and John Walker, respectively secretary and president of the IFL.[91]

The ICD was the nerve center of pro-war propaganda in Illinois. During the war, its Department of Publicity organized a central news service that fired off over 1,000 ready-made news articles and editorials to weekly and semiweekly papers in the state. The previously cited warning from U.S. District Attorney Knotts about "pro-Germans" disrupting the draft, which appeared in a Staunton editorial column, may well have been supplied from ICD headquarters in Chicago. To complement their written propaganda, the ICD speakers' bureau, working with the FMM, organized 500 speakers who addressed nearly 7,000 meetings around the state. In southern Illinois, the bureau made a point of recruiting pro-war German Americans to speak in communities there.[92]

Not satisfied merely to project a pro-war message, the ICD also employed various means to hunt down "subversives" and bring them to "justice." In doing so, the ICD Intelligence Committee cooperated closely with the APL, which was located in the same Chicago office building. The ICD even provided office space for APL operatives.[93] To facilitate local surveillance activities, the ICD encouraged the formation of county and local councils. The latter, referred to as Neighborhood Councils, were formed in towns like Collinsville, Livingston, Staunton, Virden, and others in southwestern Illinois.[94] By mid-1918, local councils were in full swing, acting with wide authority to force compliance even beyond their strict legal authority. But county councils were not formed until late 1917 and local ones not until early 1918.

One reason for the delay may have been the widespread suspicion among workers about the composition and aims of the councils. In Madison County, for instance, the Neighborhood Councils seem to have been led by local businessmen, politicians, farmers, and professionals. The Collinsville council was headed by merchant J. A. Yates and Superintendent of Schools C. H. Dorris. In Edwardsville, the county seat, L. D. Lawnin, a local factory owner, led the council, with the help of a doctor, an attorney, a druggist, and a florist. The Troy council was also led by the school superintendent, while the Worden postmaster headed up the council there.[95]

The composition of these local councils paralleled the lack of labor participation in the councils statewide and in Washington, where this fact drew the fire of national union officials. The national UMWA leadership, for instance, pointed out that the CND's Committee on Coal Production included some notoriously anti-union operators and not a single representative of labor. In a written protest, the UMWA executive board said that "[w]e are willing to fight for the government of the United States to establish world democracy but we must insist as a matter of sincerity that we be allowed to retain some measure of that democracy of which we so proudly boast, in the mining regions of our nation." The government acceded to this demand, eventually appointing seven labor representatives, including UMWA president John White, John L. Lewis, John Mitchell, William Green, and Frank Hayes to the committee.[96]

Once top labor leaders joined the ranks of the CND, however, this decision also came in for criticism by anti-war workers. In late May 1917, for instance, Staunton Socialist Ed Wieck wrote to John Walker, one of the two labor members of the ICD. Wieck asked Walker if his expenses were being paid by organized labor. If so, Wieck wrote, "I for one object to paying bills of that kind with part of my money as I have always been against war for the reason that I could not recognize anything else in war but a betrayal of the working class for the benefit of the owning class." "The entire affair," he wrote in a second letter to Walker, "is only a quarrel between two different sets of them [capitalists] as to who shall pluck the workers. It is a heads I win tails you lose proposition for the workers and, in addition, he loses all the petty reforms that he has been able to get in peace time, all in the holy name of patriotism."[97]

In defense of his participation on the ICD, Walker took issue with Wieck on the stakes for labor in the war. To Wieck's argument that the war was a falling out among thieves, Walker responded: "If it was only a fight between capitalists and would not affect the workers, I would agree with you, but where it is a fight that corporations are involved in, where there is *a degree of difference between the two capitalists* that are fighting, I say to you, that as a matter of good sense and judgement, without any regard for the capitalist at all, the workers that are employed if they have only concern for their own interests they should assist in defeating the particular corporation that would crush them the worst, if it was to win in that struggle."[98]

Beyond contending over the political character of the ICD, Illinois miners also were faced with one of the major national war campaigns that the ICD coordinated in the state—the sale of Liberty Bonds. During the war, the U.S. Treasury Department issued these bonds to fund a series of four Liberty Loans (May 14 and October 1, 1917; May 9 and October 24, 1918) and a fifth Victory Loan after the armistice (May 20, 1919). Thirty-year bonds were available to the public at 3.5 percent interest and were largely tax-exempt.[99] For two years, working people were inundated with demands to buy bonds and help fund the war effort. Most commonly, local banks bought bonds and then sold them to customers. The act of buying Liberty Bonds, far from being an independent investment decision, became one of the public tests of an individual's loyalty to the war effort. Though there was no official legal obligation to buy bonds, or the lower-priced War Savings Stamps, their essentially forced sale and purchase amounted to a vast system of de facto regressive war taxation.

The amount raised nationwide was considerable, totaling over $23 billion. Perhaps even more important than the money raised, however, was the mobilization of minds that the Liberty Loan campaign attempted. Thus, Liberty Bonds were both a revenue measure and a means of arousing "righteous wrath."

In line with their support of the war, the UMWA International Executive Board promptly bought $50,000 in Liberty Bonds for the first loan.[100] They were followed by the Illinois district leadership, which dug deeply into its enormous treasury and by September 1918 had bought $1 million in bonds.[101] Many local unions did likewise, especially by the issuance of the third Liberty Loan in April 1918. For instance, Local 755 in Staunton bought $2,000 worth and Local 720, which organized miners at the Mt. Olive and Staunton mine in nearby Williamson, bought $650.[102] It was estimated that statewide, some 90 percent of the miners had bought bonds.[103]

On the subject of War Savings Stamps and Thrift Stamps, which were low-cost items designed particularly for working-class families, Illinois UMWA president Frank Farrington addressed a circular to all the miners of the state explaining why they should buy. "Every dollar that can be raised is needed," Farrington wrote, "and it is the bounden duty of every loyal citizen and of everyone who shares in America's bounty to help to the point where it hurts to help and then keep on helping to the limit of personal sacrifice." Miners should consider themselves lucky to be on the home front, Farrington argued. "While we are in the security of our homes these men, our countrymen, will go forth to face every death-dealing invention the ingenuity of man can create for the destruction of man. Their lot will be to suffer disease and hardships, to freeze and to starve and to die, and we can do no less than to furnish the money necessary to enable the Government to equip them in a way that will give them a fighting chance."[104]

With such impassioned words, Farrington sent a steady stream of pro-war propaganda to Illinois miners, urging them to sacrifice their hard-earned money for the nation. His injunction to give until "it hurts" could not have made clearer his determination to wring every last cent out of his membership. And indeed, Farrington's circular drew the attention of top officials in Washington, who considered it a model of how union officials could draw the ranks of workers into the war effort. As Secretary of War Newton Baker wrote to Farrington, "I wish to express to you how distinct a contribution this seems to me, and how thoroughly I believe that such leadership as you are showing at this time contributes to the earlier securing of those ends for which the present war is being waged." And he added that "I wish that such documents as this eminated [*sic*] even more frequently from men wielding such power as you."[105]

It was not for nothing that Newton Baker wished for more Frank Farringtons. For while the Eighth Federal Reserve District, of which southern Illinois was a part, consistently exceeded its Liberty Loan subscription goals, the apparent success of the loan in the region masked some considerable difficulties in convincing many working people to take part in the campaign. For one thing, the great majority of bonds were bought by local banks, and they did not always resell them to customers. "In spite of the intentions of the Treasury," writes Marguerite Jenison, "the first loan was not a 'popular' loan, the county quotas being largely underwritten by banks and sold in part to their customers during the campaign or later."[106] The proportion that bank purchases formed of total bonds bought in southwestern Illinois is suggested by the following figures for the three counties: Madison, 84 percent; Macoupin, 71.3 percent; St. Clair, 60 percent.[107] Furthermore, in all of southern Illinois, only 61 percent of bonds allotted to that region were sold in the first loan.[108]

Second, the purchase of Liberty Bonds was not a transaction free from coercion. In at least two cases, for instance, the Collinsville Council of Defense "fined" allegedly disloyal coal miners by forcing them to buy Liberty Bonds and War Savings Stamps.[109] Similarly, in the mining village of White City, near Mt. Olive, according to an affidavit filed with authorities, one Martin Kobelick "when solicited to buy a 3rd Liberty Loan Bond said in the presence of Witnesses that he would rather give $50.00 to the Kaiser than Buy a Liberty Bond."[110] No punishment is recorded for this "crime," but the very fact that such a statement was grounds for legal action—or perceived as such—suggests the real context of Liberty Bond sales.

Finally, as the second Liberty Loan became available in October 1917, rumors circulated that there was an effort abroad in St. Clair and Washington Counties "to cripple the success of the second Liberty Loan." District Attorney Charles A. Karch of Belleville conducted a "thorough investigation," and "the blame is laid at the door of pro-German influences."[111] Just as U.S. District Attorney Knotts blamed draft resistance on German spies, so did Karch attribute fear of low bond sales to "pro-Germans."

The real threat to Liberty Bond sales lay not with imagined German spies but with the persistence of doubts about the war among the region's working people. In November 1917, Collie Clavin, Mt. Olive mayor and cashier at the First National Bank of Mt. Olive, was busy boosting the second set of Liberty Bonds. For the first loan, the bank had bought the modest sum of $5,000.[112] In a letter to ICD head Samuel Insull, Clavin requested a speaker for a planned December patriotic meeting. Though the mayor did not mention how bond sales were proceeding, one can imagine by his report that he was running into trouble. As he explained to Insull, "This is a labor community and a German community. The attitude of the people is not at all what it should be. We want to hold this meeting for the purpose of lining up the people with the government." According to Clavin, the Socialist Party was influencing popular opinion about the war. "This community has been overrun with socialist agitators," he wrote. "There is a socialist speaking here almost every week, and they have the people going in the wrong direction."[113]

The final piece of war mobilization machinery that sought to keep southwestern Illinois marching in the right direction was the American Red Cross. Founded as an independent charitable and medical relief organization, by World War I the Red Cross, according to one of its leading scholars, "had become a national corporation, behind which stood the power, prestige, and authority of the U.S. government; as the poster proclaimed, 'Loyalty To One Means Loyalty To Both.'"[114] As with Liberty Bonds, supporting the Red Cross was not a purely voluntary act but a coercive test of loyalty to the war effort. The APL, for example, listed as one category of "disloyalists" "Liberty Bond and Red Cross Slackers."[115] In line with this approach, in late 1917, the assistant secretary of state of Wisconsin, Louis Nagler, was arrested and charged with violating the Espionage Act when he refused repeatedly to contribute to the Red Cross.[116] Similarly, in Staunton during the next year, Frank Simmering, a miner at Consolidated Coal Mine No. 15, refused to contribute to the Red Cross, and word of this reached the local Council of Defense. Called in for questioning, Simmering defied the authority of the council and started to walk out of the room. In response, Simmering was fined fifty dollars. Several days later, after his coworkers refused to work if Simmering was allowed into the mine, this Red Cross "disloyalist" was fired from his job. Commented the *Staunton Star-Times,* "Just another instance where plain, pesky 'orneriness' has been properly repaid."[117]

The political nature of the Red Cross is suggested also by leaders of the organization in Collinsville. As recorded by Carolyn Dudley Coit, the official historian of the Collinsville chapter of the American Red Cross, which sprang into existence during World War I, the chapter "came into being with the great wave of patriotism that swept aside all driftwood of pacifist origin with the spirit of a compelling force." By the end of the war, the Collinsville chapter, which included Red Cross members in nearby Maryville, grew to 4,000. Its semi-official status is indicated by the fact that Mayor John H. Siegel of Collinsville allowed the local Red Cross board of trustees to meet in the council room in city hall.[118] Some 1,000 students were also enrolled en masse into the Junior Red Cross, chaired by Superintendent of Schools C. H. Dorris.[119]

The main activity of the Collinsville Red Cross was sewing war supplies, which was directed by a group of women drawn from the middle-class and professional leadership of the community. Chapter historian Coit painted the following portrait of Mrs. J. Bruso, one of the chapter's founding members: "She is well read and a good literary club worker. Perhaps her great success in the Red Cross came through her ability to manage adults, keeping a calm and unruffled mind even though the summer temperature went up to the 90's." For Coit, Mrs. Bruso, Mrs. Peter J. Wilson (wife of a coal operator), and many others, this effort afforded women a high degree of public leadership.[120] And they turned out the work. Mrs. Bruso's Hospital Supplies Committee, for instance, manufactured 212 suits of pajamas. The Surgical Dressing Class made 15,540 gauze compresses. And schoolchildren sewed together 1,250 pairs of baby bootees, 15 quilts, and, not forgetting the sterner needs of war, 8,000 gun wipes. Coit humorously noted that in addition to the thousands of items produced by women and children, there were a few literally man-made articles of clothing. R. Guy Kneedler, as a "shining example to bring up the slackers," knitted a sweater. And Superintendent W. E. Newnam of the local lead smelter "made a scarf and counted up stitches in the millions."[121]

The forty-four-member board of trustees for the Red Cross chapter, headed by Chairman Kneedler, included not only the women leaders but also a wide range of clergymen, politicians, professionals, and businessmen and a sprinkling of UMWA officials as well. The latter group included T. J. Reynolds, Robert Bertolero, Mose Johnson, and Victor Saladin.[122] Referring to the participation of labor, Coit wrote that while "Collinsville is a strongly organized labor center . . . during the war period an entirely harmonious spirit prevailed and general co-operation in the Red Cross merged all organizations, fraternal and church societies, without regard for clique, class or creed."[123]

Though the Red Cross clearly made a material contribution to the war effort, it may be that the "harmonious spirit" it tried to create was at least as important to war mobilization. Whether or not every last baby bootee was employed by war refugees or every gun wipe found its place in the trenches or every pair of pajamas found a wounded soldier, Collinsville's women and children could feel that they had contributed to the defeat of the enemy. They had gained a stake in the great patriotic crusade. As Coit put it, "People were thoroughly aroused for the cause of world democracy. The formative period of uncertainty was passed."[124] Or so the patriots of the region hoped.

The war for the minds, hearts, and bodies of working people in southwestern Illinois surveyed in this chapter is captured well by events in Livingston in early 1918. The mobilization of vigilante patriotism on the streets of that small Madison County mining town indicates how the "white-hot mass instinct" desired by George Creel was beginning to burn in southwestern Illinois. In late February 1918, a local patriot wrote an article boasting that "Livingston is one of the few towns in the country that can truthfully say that 'There are no "Pros" here.'" Almost immediately, though, the writer contradicted himself by admitting that "[t]here may have been some here, but they have all been converted and are now plugging for Uncle Sam." How were they converted? A group of young men formed a "100 percent American Club" and "the change in the attitude of some is largely due to the activities of these young men." Then the author explained their mode of operation: "To bring about the desired results, it was in some cases necessary to resort to a little pugilism but Uncle Sam's boys always come out on top and the fellows who received the medicine in each instance rapidly recovered from their anti-Americanism." As evidence of this, "the Red Cross unit has enrolled a few more members and Livingston has become a 100 per cent true blue city." Apparently, war boosters had beaten up recalcitrant workers to secure donations to a medical relief organization. The incident gave new meaning to Farrington's injunction that miners should give until "it hurts." To solidify these patriotic gains, the American Club planned to sign up every resident who would sign a loyalty oath. "There isn't the least doubt but that every one of our residents will be affiliated with the new organization," the writer happily concluded.[125]

Of course there was plenty of doubt, which explained the need for vigilante violence to "convert" resistant workers. It is clear that Livingston harbored Italian American Socialists and others who voted Socialist in the 1916 elections. Moreover, only one week after Livingston had been declared a 100 percent "true blue city," Postmaster J. W. Donaldson, enforcing President Wilson's executive order on enemy aliens, arrested one Anton Korun, a thirty-one-year-old German-born coal miner, who was accused of obstructing the war effort.[126] His real crime, as it developed, was political. According to U.S. District Attorney Knotts, Korun "has while at Livingston repeatedly interfered with patriotic demonstrations by others there, and on one occasion contempiously [sic] tore down in a Saloon of Martin Jontes a Liberty Loan poster and threw the same in a cuspidor." While "this office is not informed as to his previous activities, character and reputation," Knotts wrote, "I am convinced that he is a turbulent and dangerous alien enemy." Korun "should be interned."[127]

While Korun sat in the Springfield jail awaiting his fate, a special agent for the Department of Justice snuck into Livingston, talked to the right people, and painted the following portrait of "the dangerous alien enemy." Korun, he reported, "is said to be a wrestler of considerable ability and embraces every opportunity to get into personal altercations with soldiers and others who are loyal to the United States." But contrary to the local writer's claim about Livingston's patriotic purity, the special agent further explained that Korun "is reported to be a constant reader of German newspapers and to have affiliated with Socialists and other trouble makers." Far from acting alone, "[h]e is a leader of his gang of about forty members and was accustomed to carry a knife and a pair of brass knuckles."[128] Based on this report, Anton Korun, after sitting in jail for three months, boarded a special train bound for Fort Oglethorpe, Georgia, and was interned there as a dangerous "alien enemy" until June 1919.[129]

The picture of wartime Livingston that emerges from Korun's story both confirms and complicates the one presented by the local patriotic newspaper writer. In contrast to his almost desperate attempt to portray working people as uniformly in support of the war, the Korun case provides obvious signs to the contrary. Rather than proving the success of war mobilization, the need for "100 percent American Clubs," which sprung up in many towns in southwestern Illinois in the spring of 1918, points to the ongoing failure of the Wilson administration to prove its case to working people.

At the same time, the emergence of violent street attacks, as well as legal assaults by the federal government, point to the divisive consequences of the war for working people. Though Anton Korun seems to have had a local following among miners, perhaps explaining why the young patriotic "pugilists" steered clear of him, there is no evidence that his union local stood in his defense. The wholehearted support that the UMWA gave to the Liberty Loan campaign, for instance, clearly isolated Anton Korun and other rebellious workers who dared to question its legitimacy. By early 1918, a suffocating "true blue" atmosphere of enforced loyalty was settling over southwestern Illinois. In this setting, the possibility grew of patriotic pugilism giving way to patriotic murder.

But in order to understand the origins of the "white-hot mass instinct" in Madison County, and particularly in Collinsville, one needs to go beyond the debate over the war abroad and focus on the simultaneous class war that raged in the southwestern Illinois coalfields in the late summer and autumn of 1917. In the series of wildcat strikes that swept the region, miners like Anton Korun were joined by thousands of working-class rebels who refused to abandon their collective fight for a better life in order to serve the national cause. If the government faced a challenge in incurring miners' "righteous wrath" on the specific question of the war, the authorities confronted an even bigger task in convincing workers to stay on the job. It was only after this most effective anti-war action was quashed that the superpatriots had full reign in the region.

"To Scab upon This Great National Union"
Wartime Strikes in the Coalfields

N o sooner did the United States declare war against the Central Powers than thousands of workers declared war on employers at home. In the six months following April 6, 1917, some 283,000 workers walked off the job.[1] Illinois miners made a substantial contribution to that total, as some 25,000 UMWA miners in District 12 went on strike during this same period.[2] These coal mining strikes, which were strongest in central and southwestern Illinois, were politically explosive on several counts: they were unauthorized by state UMWA officials, who mobilized all their resources to force miners back to work; the walkouts shut down war production just as draftees were beginning to head off for service in big numbers; and they coincided with a highly visible campaign against the Industrial Workers of the World (IWW) by the federal government, which labeled every strike IWW- and "pro-German"-inspired.

The strikes that form the focus of this chapter took place over a period of roughly six months, from July 1917 to January 1918. In the Collinsville area, the wave ebbed and flowed in four chronological phases. First, from late July through much of August, there was a series of local walkouts of mine drivers who demanded a cost of living raise. Second, from October 17 to October 21, Collinsville miners joined with tens of thousands of UMWA members in Illinois and the Midwest in a strike to force a national wage hike. They were acting to enforce the tripartite Washington Agreement of October 5, in which the UMWA, coal operators, and the U.S. Fuel Administration—which regulated the coal industry under wartime legislation—had agreed on a wage increase for miners and higher coal prices for operators. Third, in late October, striking smelter workers in Collinsville—who had walked out in August—won the support of many local miners who marched in a solidarity parade and threatened a sympathy strike. And finally, in November through January, a group of Bell telephone operators struck for union recognition, earning the active solidarity of Collinsville miners.

When working people went on strike, they were called unpatriotic. And yet the problems that miners and others confronted only multiplied during the war: rampant inflation outpacing wages, safety problems exacerbated by the intense pace of war production, and persisting problems of health and sanitation, as a number of mine owners refused to build washhouses or improve mine ventilation. This put striking coal miners in a quandary: how could they be loyal Americans and still stand up for what they needed as workers? While they resolved this question in a variety of ways, war mobilization continued to advance, making it harder to justify walking off the job. Conversely, the effective end of the strike wave by early 1918 paved the way for the superpatriotic vigilantism to come.

Although all workers who took part in wartime strikes earned the wrath of the government and employers alike, coal miners received special attention since they played a particularly key role in war production. Coal provided 70 percent of the mechanical energy consumed in the nation.[3] When miners dug no coal, industry soon came to a halt. During the war, no less than President Wilson himself singled out miners as vital war workers. "To the miner let me say that he stands where the farmer does," declared Wilson. "[T]he work of the world waits on him. If he slacks or fails armies and statesmen are helpless."[4] Supported by UMWA officials, politicians implored miners to stay on the job for the good of the nation.

Well before the mass walkouts of late summer and fall of 1917, it was clear to federal government officials that even isolated miners' strikes posed a threat to war mobilization. In May 1917, coal miners in Virden, Illinois, walked off the job in protest when the Royal Mine manager shut off the ventilation fan with men still underground. This early Illinois wartime strike drew the immediate attention of officials in Washington. Learning of the strike, an official of the CND's Committee on Coal Production alerted Assistant Attorney General William Fitts, who in turn notified Assistant Secretary of Labor Louis Post. Fitts noted the "size and importance" of the Royal Mine and explained that the strike was due to "stubbornness on the part of both the employers and employed." He then requested the Department of Labor to "induce peace and bring about the production of coal . . . [since] such a strike will probably spread through the coal producing portions of Central and Southern Illinois."[5]

Wartime strikes not only posed the possibility of interrupting the war effort materially but also were linked to the specter of German spying and sabotage. Indeed, as Secretary of Labor William B. Wilson wrote to the president in June 1917, "One of the annoying features of the situation, and one that I know would lead to a great deal of friction among the workmen if it became generally known, is that whenever any disposition is shown by the workers to demand an increase of wages commensurate with the increased cost of living, the employers immediately assume that the action is inspired by traitors or spies and is therefore treasonable."[6] While the secretary's observation was accurate, it conveniently avoided the fact that not only employers but also conservative trade unionists and even the president himself had played a role in making the connection between spying and striking.

The alleged connection between strikes and disloyalty appeared early in the war, even before America entered it. In President Wilson's 1915 State of the Union address, for instance, he drew the nation's attention to "disloyal" Americans who sought "to destroy our industries wherever they thought it effective for their vindictive purposes to strike at them."[7] While Wilson spoke in general terms, he was most likely thinking of a specific group of "disloyalists": the machinists and ironworkers in munitions plants in Bridgeport, Connecticut, and throughout New England who had gone on strike in the summer of 1915 for the eight-hour day. Bridgeport was the heart of America's munitions industry, producing "two-thirds of all small arms exported to European combatants." When workers shut down the Bridgeport machine shops servicing Remington Arms in July 1915, a newspaper headline declared, "German Influence Behind Munition Strikes!"[8] Supporting the government's "preparedness" effort, AFL president Samuel Gompers publicly lent credibility to the "pro-German" charge, saying that "Germans had found some labor representatives" among the Bridgeport workers.[9]

The connection between rebellious workers, anti-war sentiment, and pro-Germanism was deepened in the public mind in the fall of 1915, when a New York grand jury launched an investigation into the activities of Labor's National Peace Council.[10] Formed in June 1915, the council's leadership included a number of national union officials who were responding to the widespread anti-war and anti-preparedness sentiment among the nation's workers. The council called for a ban on the sale and transport of arms to the European belligerents and demanded strict U.S. neutrality toward the conflict. It quickly drew charges of pro-Germanism.[11]

The ranks of Labor's National Peace Council were filled with trade unionists who felt a genuine desire to avoid the horrors of world war and were determined to link up with other workers who felt similarly. Considering the centrality of spying charges against Robert Prager in 1918, however, it is worth noting that unbeknownst to the vast majority of members, the accusations of pro-Germanism against the council had some basis in fact. The grand jury inquiry centered around the activities of a German naval officer, Franz Rintelen, suspected of ties to the council. It soon developed that Rintelen had indeed played a key role in founding the council and even had taken some measures to encourage strikes among dockworkers with the aim of hindering arms shipments to the Allies. The revelations of Rintelen's activities, for which he was imprisoned along with some council leaders in 1917, lent some credibility to the charge that all strikes and workers' anti-war activity were inspired by the kaiser.[12]

After the U.S. declaration of war on Germany, the main target of pro-German charges was the IWW. During the summer of 1917, AFL officials, employers, and the Wilson administration joined together in a determined campaign against the Wobblies, culminating with the massive raid of September. On August 3, a month before the federal IWW raid, *Collinsville Herald* readers learned that "[a] mass of information in possession of the Government leads to the conclusion that the I.W.W. leaders are being supplied with German money to carry on a war against industry intended to cripple the United States Government and its Allies." The article, reprinted from a St. Louis daily, alleged that where workers had gone on strike, supposedly paid off by the IWW "German agents," "no real causes for striking existed. . . . They have been based in nearly every case on fancied grievances."[13]

By the fall of 1917, a newspaper reader might well have concluded that any worker who went on strike was simply an agent of the kaiser. But in order to understand the reasons coal miners walked off their jobs that fall, we need to go beyond the theory of "fancied grievances" to examine three real sources of discontent for miners and their families. First was the problem of inflation. The high cost of living had dogged mining families in the region for decades, encouraging the formation of cooperative stores in many towns. But even as early as 1914, before the U.S. economy recovered from its slump, the restriction of imports due to the outbreak of war jacked up prices to an unprecedented degree. In Belleville, for instance, only ten days after the war began, the price of sugar jumped from $4.34 per 100 pounds to $7.25, navy beans were up from $2.10 per bushel to $3.25, and the cost of a 100-pound bag of flour rose $.25.[14] Nationwide inflation continued throughout the war years. For example, from 1916 to 1918, food prices rose an astounding 52 percent.[15]

In 1916, UMWA coal miners won a wage increase for tonnage miners and company men, but it barely kept pace with the even broader and higher inflation that accompanied the recovery from the disastrous 1913–15 depression. John Walker's brother Jim, a miner at Donk Brothers No. 1 mine in Collinsville, wrote him in April 1916 that "I am getting all the work I can stand, but I dont smile at the boss very much. . . . [T]he living cost is fierce here."[16] With the rise in coal prices and profits generated by the war-induced recovery, miners opened up contract talks a year early and won a further increase in rates in April 1917.[17] Even with this increase, however, spiraling prices ate away at miners' gains. Only weeks after the agreement, for instance, the union reported that "since the recent increase in wages was secured certain operators are attempting to increase the price paid by our members for house coal."[18]

Inflation weighed most heavily on company men and their families. Whereas pick miners and loaders could try to fill an extra car to bring in extra cash, the flat daily pay rate of drivers, laborers, tracklayers, and other auxiliary workers deprived them of that option. In fact, the August strikes centered around the demand of drivers for a pay hike, phrased as eight hours for nine hours' pay. Drivers who were married tended to be young men with young children to feed at home. And of course, single drivers were precisely the ones who were likely to be drafted.

Second, what fueled the anger of coal miners in the summer of 1917 was not inflation alone but the simultaneous reports of high profits for coal operators. Before the creation of the U.S. Fuel Administration in August, coal prices were regulated on a voluntary basis, and Illinois operators made the most of the increased demand for their precious commodity. One Madison County investor in the New Staunton Coal Company, which ran the huge Livingston mine, bought 500 shares of stock worth $100 each. In the first six months of 1917, his original $50,000 investment yielded $40,000, a 160 percent annual rate of return.[19] Similarly, at an August 1917 hearing on coal prices in St. Louis, Joseph Lumaghi, owner of two Collinsville coal mines, testified that with a capital investment of $7,000, annual net profits were $280,000. Commenting on Lumaghi Coal, the *Staunton Star-Times* asked, "[C]an any fair minded man condemn those doing the work and risking their lives every day, that they would like to have at least a little slice of these immense profits?"[20]

Whether or not these examples were typical, the widespread accusation of profiteering was sustained by an investigation done by the Illinois Council of Defense, which sought to regulate the price of coal for its own purposes. After meeting with coal operators and failing to reach agreement on lowering prices, the ICD concluded that "[t]he price of coal is excessively high. It includes a profit per ton much in excess of a fair and reasonable profit."[21] In publicly pushing coal operators to comply with price regulation, Governor Frank Lowden described them as unpatriotic, labeling unfair profits "blood money." After months of wrangling and threats by the Lowden administration to take control of the state's coal mines, the federal government finally stepped in and imposed a schedule of coal prices. In some areas of Illinois, prices dropped as much as $1.30 per ton.[22]

A third source of discontent that powered the 1917 strikes was the continued hazardous nature of coal mining. Despite the introduction of new technology, and sometimes because of it, the coal mining accident rate rose in the World War I years. In 1913, for instance, an Illinois mine inspector commented that "[o]ne bad feature of the district is the increase in non-fatal accidents." As a new safety measure, some mines had begun to hire "face bosses" who visited working places during the day. These mines reported a decrease in accidents. According to the inspector, "The increase of non-fatal accidents comes wholly from mines where face bosses are not employed."[23]

But during 1917 and 1918, miners everywhere were subjected to a gigantic speedup. Not only did southwestern Illinois miners work much more steadily, with the average days worked rising significantly, but their workday also lengthened, as war production demanded an ever-greater supply of coal. As William Graebner has noted, the demands of war production tended to relegate safety matters to the sidelines. Once the United States entered the war, the U.S. Bureau of Mines shifted its emphasis from explosion prevention to weapons production for the battlefields. In line with its support for uninterrupted production, the UMWA also dropped safety concerns from public statements.[24] And mine owners everywhere put a premium on volume production. Even the industry journal *Coal Age* commented in early 1918, "It is said that the high pressure under which the mines have been operated during the past winter has led to laxness in the matter of safety precautions."[25] Even though overall accident and death rates for southwestern Illinois mines stayed relatively constant in this period, the pressures for miners to produce made an already tense work environment even more so.

Reflecting the increased intensity of work, Pete Perry, who worked at Madison No. 2 in Glen Carbon, recalled the war years this way: "They were over there fightin' and we were over here beatin' our brains out working everyday."[26] Indeed, in the big mines of Madison County, the average days worked rose from 180 in 1915–16 to 219 in 1916–17 to 246 in 1917–18. While the Glen Carbon mine did not work literally every day, the days of operation there jumped from a dismal 172 in 1915–16 to 233 the next year and reached 262 during the 1917–18 period. At this mine, which was known for an excellent safety record, the accident rate actually dropped over the last year of this period.[27]

The same could not be said for Donk Brothers No. 2 mine in Maryville, which became the site of the controversy over an alleged bomb plot by Robert Prager in March 1918. Despite the unusually regular employment Donk provided in Maryville (E. C. Donk owned his own railroad line guaranteeing a market and transport for his coal), working conditions in the mine were perceived as unsafe. According to Ernestine Rissi, whose husband was a machine runner there, No. 2 was "the best working mine in this locality, but considered the most dangerous because it has been on fire for years."[28] How much the smoldering mine fire actually contributed to injuries or deaths is unknown. Though the overall death rate at the Donk mines was generally not above average, the following facts are notable in reconstructing miners' perceptions of the Maryville mine: Of the seven deaths at all three Donk mines from June 1915 through June 1917, five occurred at No. 2. Moreover, three of these deaths at No. 2—all miners in their early thirties—took place in a brief period in 1917 between January and April. Finally, between 1917 and 1918, the nonfatal accident rate at No. 2 jumped up 42 percent.[29]

Just as miners viewed the familiar problem of inflation through the new prism of war, unsafe mine conditions also appeared in a new light.

Although miners rarely went on strike during the war strictly over matters of mine safety, the increased risks that many endured as the pace of war production quickened made them even more willing to demand a share of operators' wartime profits. If this was a war for democracy, miners reasoned, employers could at least compensate them for the risks they took on the home front. Indeed, more than one observer noted that miners endured casualty rates that rivaled or surpassed those of the American Expeditionary Forces.[30] Even before the United States entered the war, Bureau of Mines director Joseph A. Holmes noted that while Americans prided themselves on staying out of the "slaughter in Europe," the number of deaths in the "peaceful industry" of mining was "quite as discreditable."[31] Now with the United States in the war, as one delegate declared at the 1918 Illinois miners' convention, miners were even more at risk than "the boys across the water."[32]

The first Collinsville strike of the season took place at Lumaghi Mine No. 2. On July 26, a dozen miners—Italians and "Austrians"—walked off the job alleging that the company had underweighed their coal. Local union officials, led by Local 685 president Robert Bertolero, promptly declared the strike illegal. This, however, only served to enrage other mine workers, who then joined the strike. Like Dominick Oberto in Maryville, Bertolero was an Italian American pro-war Socialist. Having run for mayor on the Socialist Party ticket in the spring of 1917, he went on to become one of Collinsville's most effective and energetic war boosters. Later, he served on the executive committee of the local Council of Defense. Given his embrace of the war effort, his opposition to the strike was to be expected.

But Bertolero failed to prevail on the miners to go back to work. Five days into the strike, at a union meeting described as "one of the stormiest ever known here," he enlisted the aid of District UMWA Executive Board member Mose Johnson who also tried, and failed, to convince the workers to end their walkout. Before long, the conflict in the union hall spilled into the street. Johnson got into a fight with Joseph Riegel, one of the strikers—or "disturbers," as the *Collinsville Herald* put it. Johnson threw Riegel to the ground and gave him a dislocated elbow, for which the striker spent a night in the local hospital. Johnson, who was a loyal and patriotic ally of Frank Farrington, told the *Herald* that "the disturbers were paid agents of the German government deliberately seeking to tie up the mine."[33]

The Lumaghi No. 2 strike not only pointed to the conflicting loyalties tugging at miners generally but also contained some of the key ingredients that produced the Prager lynching. Like the "disturbers," Prager was accused of being a "German agent" by union officials. In fact, Mose Johnson himself would play a crucial role in pinning this charge on Prager. And just as in April 1918, internal union conflict erupted into street violence, though not yet with lethal results. In both cases, moreover, the local press sided with the "responsible" union officials and cast suspicion on the victims of violence. Finally, both incidents took place in an atmosphere of government-inspired alarm over both labor conflict and the alleged German spy threat.

Yet there is an even more intriguing connection to the lynching in the person of Joseph Riegel. Apparently of German American descent and briefly married, Riegel had served a volunteer stint in the U.S. Army, stationed at Jefferson Barracks around 1915–16. After his honorable discharge, Riegel took a position at Lumaghi Mine No. 2. Around this time, he and his wife, Emma, conceived a child, but before long the couple became estranged and separated. After the incident with Mose Johnson, Riegel changed jobs and worked for several months at Consolidated Coal Company Mine No. 17, just over the Collinsville line in Caseyville. In early 1918, Riegel began working as a cobbler in Collinsville. And the day after Robert Prager's body was found hanging from a tree on April 5, Joseph Riegel confessed to having led the lynch mob.[34]

One can imagine some of the conflicting pressures bearing on Joseph Riegel in August 1917. A German American, he was automatically subject to some suspicion. On the other hand, he may well have considered his military service adequate proof of his loyalty to the United States. At the same time, he was swept up in the No. 2 strike, which saw a majority of the mine workers stand in class solidarity with a minority of immigrant workers, some of them presumably "alien enemies." Despite his record of national loyalty, he found himself at odds with a superpatriotic union official bent on impugning his patriotism and classing him as a German agent. Like many working people, Riegel may have wanted nothing more than to be viewed as a loyal American, but the class battles breaking out in August 1917 complicated this task. His union leaders, rather than affirm his act of class solidarity, labeled it treason. So where was Riegel to turn for patriotic affirmation? How could he fight for his class interests and not let down his country?

For their part, Riegel's fellow strikers were willing to hold their class interests in check temporarily. After two weeks, on the advice of union officials, the 400 Lumaghi No. 2 strikers agreed to return to work on August 10, the scale problem still unresolved. The following day, however, workers across town in "Cuba" at Donk No. 1 walked off the job and were joined by their counterparts at Lumaghi No. 3 several days later. In both cases, drivers demanded a one-dollar cost of living raise, and miners walked out in support. Most likely, the fact that many drivers were the sons or younger brothers of pick miners and loaders magnified their solidarity. At Consolidated No. 17, miners kept digging and hauling coal but threatened to join the walkout if drivers there were deprived of a pay hike.[35]

The "epidemic" of drivers' strikes, as the *Herald* termed it, encompassed the entire central and southwestern portion of the state. Its spread seems to have been sparked by the capitulation farther north of a Virden mine manager to drivers' demands for a raise. As Collinsville miners brought production to a halt, then, they were joined also by over 6,000 UMWA members who emptied the big Macoupin County mines around Staunton, Mt. Olive, Gillespie, and Benld.[36] Miners were out in St. Clair County as well. South of Belleville in Mascoutah, miners who belonged to UMWA Local 1285 took an active part in spreading the strike. In a resolution sent to all other locals statewide, they urged top union officials to secure an interstate joint conference with coal operators as soon as possible in order to obtain a raise in tonnage rates and in day wages. "We are on strike until our demands are met, and hope each local union will follow our lead," explained the miners in Mascoutah.[37]

Despite widespread recognition that miners needed a wage increase, the *Collinsville Herald* once again speculated that these strikes—involving thousands of mine workers—were the result of sabotage. Among the "theories" to which editor J. O. Monroe lent credence was that "German agents were stirring up the faction and allowing them to use any pretext that was available. . . . This latter theory was credited by one prominent mine local official here."[38] Monroe's explanation for the strikes dovetailed with the publicity he had given, just weeks before, to the government's alleged case against the IWW, which argued that "no real causes for striking existed."

Although weeks after these strikes broke out, top UMWA officials claimed that they had been negotiating with coal operators for just such a pay increase, President Farrington was anything but pleased by the unauthorized actions of the rank and file. Farrington worked closely with federal authorities to force them back to work. On August 11, as Lumaghi No. 3 and Donk No. 1 miners stayed at home, Farrington sent a panicked telegram to Francis Peabody, the Illinois coal baron, who headed the Committee on Coal Production of the CND. "There are twenty five mines idle in Illinois this morning in violation of agreement all because drivers and motormen are demanding wage increases over that specified in joint agreement," he informed Peabody. In response to the illegal walkout, Farrington explained, he had "ordered men back to work, threatened to expel drivers and motormen from our organization, and notified mine committees that by reason of our joint agreement they are obliged to supply men to fill places of drivers and motormen."

Why had the strikes occurred? Farrington offered two explanations. First, he claimed that the publicity devoted by the ICD to "extortionate" coal profits had influenced miners who "have decided they are going to share in the alleged loot." This suggested either that reports of high profits were inaccurate or that, if such profits did exist, miners had no right to demand their fair share. More important, however, just as Mose Johnson had argued, Farrington offered that he had "reason to believe that agents of Governmental enemies are working among men to curtail production of coal." As a result, he confided to Peabody, he had held a "long conference with Department of Justice, Chicago. That Department has promised to send Secret Service men out to arrest agitators."[39]

In response to Farrington's appeal, Peabody contacted Hugh Kerwin, who served as the private secretary for Secretary of Labor Wilson. By this simple act, Peabody shed light on the real contradictory role of the Labor Department during the war: to advocate for but also to discipline the labor movement. Learning of the Illinois situation from Peabody, Kerwin informed his boss of Farrington's telegram and stressed the urgency of ending the strikes. "Three large railroad systems, Illinois, have sufficient coal not to exceed two to five days," he warned. Kerwin also explained that the strikes had drawn the notice of top government officials: "Secretary of War, Mr. Peabody and Mr. Colver, of Federal Trade Commission, request that matter be referred to you, believing that telegram or telephone message from you to Farrington would assist in resumption of work," he informed Wilson.[40]

The labor secretary also heard from manufacturers in southwestern Illinois who explained that the strike had nearly brought war production to a halt. In a letter written to President Wilson, who passed the letter on to the secretary, Harry Herb, manager of the Alton Board of Trade, painted a dire portrait. "At a meeting today of manufacturers in this district," Herb told the president, "we were directed to call your attention to conditions here which will shut down practically all industries in a few days for lack of coal. Few of the mines in this vicinity are at work and no definite prospects of strike being settled. Manufacturers include foodstuffs and munitions and affect thirty thousand workmen. To close some plants would cause irreparable loss. We ask that positive action be taken for immediate resumption of coal mining operation."[41] Though he may have indulged in some slight exaggeration, Herb's letter graphically conveyed the enormous impact that the August coal strikes made on war production. The Alton businessman dealt coal miners a backhanded compliment by acknowledging the power they wielded. For this very reason, employers and the federal government kept relentless pressure on coal miners to stay on the job.

On August 17, rising to the challenge of forcing the Illinois miners back into the mines, Secretary of Labor Wilson fired off an extended telegram to Farrington, addressed to the strikers, which would serve as the ideological bludgeon to end the August walkouts. Since Farrington's iron fist approach had failed, Wilson tried the velvet glove. For its cleverness, originality, and the light it sheds on larger issues, Wilson's telegram is worth quoting at length. Instead of tarring the miners as pro-Germans, he first tried to establish common ground. He played on his former working-class status by acknowledging that miners acted out of "a laudable desire . . . for higher standards of living than now exist." But in order to maintain standards and even improve them, Wilson explained, miners needed to support the war effort by staying on the job.

The war in Europe was labor's war, argued Wilson. "The American workingman has more at stake in this great war crisis than any other portion of our people," he wrote. If the Central Powers are victorious, he warned, the high wages and living standards that miners had won "are in danger of being lowered to suit the wishes of the German Autocracy." "Labor unions cannot exist and operate freely if liberty is destroyed," Wilson told miners. Their "first duty, not only as patriotic American citizens but as wage-workers, having the future welfare and freedom of the toiling masses at heart," was to safeguard "republican institutions."

If this line of fire was not convincing, Wilson tried another angle. The war not only was labor's war but could be likened to a strike. "Every one of us belongs to a great union," the former UMWA official told the Illinois strikers, "the United States of America." This union "has declared a strike against the tyranny of the German Government." Now appealing to miners' sense of union democracy, Wilson added, "It has declared the strike by an overwhelming vote of the representatives of the union authorized by its laws to act for it," presumably referring to members of Congress. "No greater strike has ever been ordered." And then Wilson came to the clincher: "It would be a serious blunder for any man to scab upon this great national union or do anything that will impair its chances for success." Thus, Wilson argued, strikers against coal companies were the real scabs, whereas miners who returned to work were the real strikers.

At this point in his long telegram to Illinois, Wilson had still one more card to play: he appealed to the miners' "honor" and here raised the specter of pro-Germanism. "The American labor movement has reached its present position of influence," Wilson claimed, "because it has built up a reputation for living up to its contracts." Now, he recalled, "the world has condemned the German Chancellor because of his remark that the treaty with Belgium was but a scrap of paper." In this light, miners "cannot afford to express the thought that the contracts for wages, solemnly made by him, are simply scraps of paper." Do you want to put yourself in the same boat as the evil German autocrats? Wilson implicitly asked the strikers. "The most valuable thing that a workingman has is his honor. If he loses that he is poor indeed."[42]

Wilson's portrayal of the war as a miners' strike offers a fascinating twist on what historian Gary Gerstle calls "working-class Americanism." Gerstle studied Rhode Island textile union leaders who believed that they could harmonize their class interests with those of the nation. Similarly, Wilson urged miners to tie their fortunes to the "republic." But rather than miners presenting their struggles in nationalist terms, the government couched a patriotic crusade in the rhetoric of militant unionism. To a large extent, the need for Wilson to argue in such a way revealed the depth of anti-war sentiment among the Illinois miners. In describing the carnage in Europe as a war for the interests of the working class, Wilson implicitly confronted the view, widely accepted among miners, that this was indeed a rich man's war.

Moreover, William B. Wilson's open strikebreaking during the 1917 strike wave suggests a revision of Melvyn Dubofsky's claim that "the UMW had a warm friend in the secretary of labor."[43] Certainly, Frank

Farrington and the patriotic UMWA officials had an ally in Washington. But for thousands of strikers in southwestern Illinois who defied the government, employers, and union officials by staying out of the mines in August 1917, Wilson's alleged friendship was barely lukewarm. As Joseph McCartin notes, Wilson's labor policy encouraged a degree of unionization on the one hand while it discouraged labor militancy on the other. He writes that "there was a glaring irony here, for labor's most successful radical-led efforts—including the Stockyards Labor Council, the Electrical Manufacturing Industry Labor Federation, and IAM District 55—were profoundly dependent on the same federal labor program that also destroyed the IWW and accommodated the demands of a conservative AFL hierarchy."[44] We might add that the Wilson administration's embrace of the AFL-affiliated hierarchy in the Illinois coalfields pit the Wilsonians against not only the IWW but also rank-and-file UMWA members. And for the moment, this alliance paid dividends. Several days after receiving Wilson's telegram, Frank Farrington informed the secretary that "I can use it effectively. Mining situation in this state is gradually improving."[45] For the moment, strikers in Collinsville and elsewhere deferred to Wilson and returned to work.

At Donk No. 1, in the Cuba neighborhood of Collinsville, miners had stayed on the job, but they conducted an active campaign for a wage increase. On August 23, just as the striking drivers and their supporters were returning to work, members of Local 848 passed a resolution blasting coal operators for excessive profits, demanding a cost of living raise, and requesting that state UMWA officials immediately call a special convention of the miners to launch this fight. In calling for a wage hike, the miners pointed to war inflation and "the fact that the coal operators . . . have admitted under oath the profits that they are now filching from the public [range] in some instances to 150 percent." The Donk No. 1 miners sent copies of their resolution to UMWA locals throughout the region. By the following day, miners at St. Louis and O'Fallon No. 2 had already approved it.[46] Within eight weeks, this trickle of dissent would grow into a torrent of rebellion. In early October, the question of a miners' national wage hike—which the Donk miners had demanded—came to a head and produced a strike in Illinois even larger than the one in August.

The context for the October strikes was the decision made by the Wilson administration to regulate the coal industry for the duration of the war. Based on the August 1917 Lever Act, Wilson established the U.S.

Fuel Administration and put Dr. Harry A. Garfield in charge. By this date, the unrest in the coalfields of Illinois and elsewhere convinced Garfield to support a reopening of wage negotiations in the Central Competitive Field in the interests of labor peace and uninterrupted production for the remainder of the war. The result, in early October, was the tripartite Washington Agreement.[47] Signed by representatives of the UMWA and Central Competitive Field coal operators and approved by Garfield, the agreement essentially aimed to secure continued coal production in return for concessions to the union.

Three features of the agreement are most relevant to this story. First, and most important for organized districts like Illinois, the Washington Agreement of October 5 granted a wage increase for tonnage and company men tied to a corresponding coal price increase for operators. The wage hike, that is, would "become effective only on the condition that the selling price of coal shall be advanced by the United States Government sufficient to cover the increased cost in the different districts affected."[48] In light of the public outrage over high coal prices during the summer, including the protests of miners, the support that UMWA officials offered here for even higher prices is significant. No doubt they believed that miners could not obtain a raise by any other means.

Second, the wage increase was contingent not only on a price increase for operators but also on the adoption of firmer strike penalty clauses in each district to discourage miners from walking off the job. In justifying this, the Washington Agreement stated that "[s]toppage of work in violation of the agreement . . . has become so serious as to menace the success and perpetuity of the U.M.W. of A. and our joint relations."[49] Illinois miners already labored under the shadow of a strike penalty. The relevant provisions of the 1916 agreement, for instance, specified three types of strikes that could be penalized. In the event that miners struck to demand changes that would violate the contract or struck to force a decision in a grievance that had not been resolved, each miner would be fined five dollars each. If miners walked out around an issue that stood outside the realm of the contract—demands to build a washhouse, for example—they were subject to fines of one dollar per day per miner for the duration of the strike. Another provision imposed fines on mine owners if they locked out miners to enforce a condition that violated the contract. Finally, any fines collected would be split evenly by the District UMWA and the Illinois Coal Operators Association.[50]

For the U.S. Fuel Administration, however, these penalties were not sufficiently high to discourage miners from walking off the job. Consequently, the UMWA agreed to make the strike penalty more severe. In the revised Illinois penalty clause, effective November 1, 1917, a number of new features appeared. Instead of separating out the strikes related to the contract and imposing a one-time $5 fine, the wartime clause lumped all miners' strikes together and provided a fine of $3 for the first day and $1 per each additional day per miner. Moreover, it gave employers wide latitude in spotting "slackers" by stipulating that "[t]his penalty shall also apply to men who though not formally striking shall, without notice, quit work as a subterfuge." The clause also instructed that miners' fines were to be automatically deducted from their paychecks, implying that such had not uniformly been the previous practice. Finally, to discourage lockouts, coal operators now paid $1 per day per miner instead of a $100 flat fee.[51]

A third feature of the Washington Agreement was the matter of timing. The agreement was to remain in force for the "continuation of the war" or until April 1, 1920, whichever came first. This seemingly innocuous provision became crucially important after the war, when miners sought to reopen wage negotiations. Aiming to rid themselves of the wartime penalty clause in 1919, months after armistice celebrations, they found themselves presented with the absurd position by employers and government officials that, for the purposes of their contract, the war was still "continuing." After all, the Wilson administration explained, a peace treaty had yet to be signed.

On October 12, 1917, one week after the UMWA signed the Washington Agreement, Frank Farrington visited Collinsville. The occasion was twofold. Local miners were laying the cornerstone of the new Miners' Institute, which would finally provide mining unionists their own meeting place. Introduced by Robert Bertolero, who presided, Farrington reviewed the achievements of the UMWA and paid tribute to the Collinsville miners' newfound home. The day also marked the nineteenth anniversary of the Virden Massacre, which was memorialized each year by miners in the region. On this day that celebrated a militant expression of miners' rank-and-file solidarity, Farrington chose to launch a scathing attack on the recent strikes sweeping the area. The terms he used to condemn them help us understand the odds that local miners faced when they went on strike. "Men who start illegal strikes, bodies that adopt immature and unwarranted resolutions, agitators who go about seeking to call special conventions, stirring up the men and creating a distrust of their officials, are the miners['] worst enemies," Farrington declared. To make his point crystal clear, he explained that "[i]ndividual action is a bigger menace to the organization than all the employers in the country." In terming the August strikes "individual action," Farrington cleverly counterposed the virtue of united, statewide, officially authorized strikes with "anarchical" scattered, smaller local strikes that allegedly dissipated the strength of the organization.

After lambasting the Collinsville rebels, Farrington called on his local allies to do their part in preventing such action in the future. "I would call on the conservative and thinking men of Collinsville to come to the front and put down any such agitations when they arise here," he told the crowd.[52] This remark points to two important things. First, it recognizes the real divisions that existed among miners. Despite the wave of strikes, Farrington did have strong local supporters. Second, like his invocation of the Justice Department weeks earlier, the District 12 president's call for action against "agitations" in a political context that equated strikes with German spies would have unexpected consequences. In giving a beating to "disturber" Joseph Riegel in August, for instance, Mose Johnson had set an example for the "conservative and thinking men" of Collinsville. The distance between such street action and a sturdy tree on the outskirts of town was not far to travel.

The October 5 Washington Agreement officially granted miners a wage increase, but when Farrington spoke to the Collinsville miners one week later, they had not seen one penny of it. The extra money depended on the coal price increase, and negotiations between Garfield and the coal operators were stalled. Throughout Illinois and the Midwest, miners devised their own solution to this dilemma. Despite Farrington's stricture against "individual action," starting October 16, some 15,000 "individuals" walked out of the Illinois mines in protest.

Collinsville was a bastion of the strike. "Every coal mine in Collinsville and vicinity is idle," reported the *Herald* on October 19. Even Robert Bertolero of Lumaghi No. 2, who had opposed the August walkouts, stood with the strikers this time. "They've been promising us a raise for weeks," he explained. "In September they told us to wait until October 1. When October came they told us to wait until the conference at Washington. At that time they promised us the raise on October 16. When that day came they told us they couldn't give us the raise because they hadn't been able to get a raise in coal prices. We simply decided to quit until they gave us what we want."

Here again was an "illegal" action by the miners. Actually, Mose Johnson, Farrington's lieutenant on the scene, was "non-committal" when asked about the mass walkout. "He rather indicated he doubted the legality of the strike, but he did not order the men back to work," the *Herald* reported. Farrington, however, was sure on this score and wired union locals, warning that "[i]f the miners do not return to work I have every reason to believe the strike will resolve itself into a fight with the Federal Government, which I am sure will not temporize with such a serious condition while the nation is at war."[53] Here Farrington anticipated by two years the identical argument used by John L. Lewis to force the miners back to work in the 1919 strike—"We are Americans. We cannot fight our government."

But as they would in 1919, many miners stayed on strike. On October 20, four days into the walkout, 100 delegates, representing some 10,000 striking miners in Macoupin, Madison, Montgomery, Bond, and St. Clair Counties, met at Edwardsville to discuss their next step. The previous day, newspapers had carried a declaration from Garfield of the Fuel Administration that "[w]hatever powers necessary will be employed by the federal government to stop the strike of coal miners in the middle west and prevent interruption to the nation's fuel production." Made acutely aware by Farrington's telegram that their "leader" stood with the government, the miners were backed into a corner.

Still, they used the meeting to launch a campaign against Farrington's course. They circulated petitions for a special state convention—a right under the union constitution but one Farrington was loath to see exercised. They objected to the strike penalty clause, particularly since there was no appeal process for them in case of a strike fine. Striking miners wanted to subject the clause to a referendum vote of all UMWA members. Finally, they passed a resolution that called for the following: accept the new contract; submit the package, with the penalty clause, to the next International Convention, under protest; and oppose any price increase for the coal operators. The UMWA officials' support for higher prices, the delegates declared, "we consider an outrage as we know that the operators robbed the public of hundreds of millions of dollars the past year and are proposing to do the same thing this year, with the miners being used as a catspaw."[54]

Having made a show of strength, the miners voted to return to work.

Within ten days, the government announced that the miners would receive their promised pay hike.[55] The miners had once again "scabbed" on the nation. But rather than jeopardize the UMWA's legitimacy and weaken the union, the October strike ensured that Garfield would settle with the operators and that the wage increase would be implemented. Far from carrying out disorganized individual action, the Illinois "wildcat" strikers were united and disciplined in their conduct. The mass action of the miners' rank and file had forced the government's hand. It was not the patriotism of the coal miners but their willingness to be branded unpatriotic that secured this wage gain.

By late October, except for scattered local strikes over the course of the next year, southwestern Illinois miners were back in the mines for the duration of the war. But the story of miners' conflicting loyalties during the 1917 strikes in Collinsville would not be complete without an account of the miners' relationship to the walkout at St. Louis Smelting and Refining (SLSR), which began on August 4 and continued into November. The local solidarity won by this strike at a key war production facility illustrated the stubborn persistence of class loyalty among a broad range of working people in the area. The company's decision to bring in largely African American strikebreakers threw a spotlight—in the immediate aftermath of the anti-black pogrom in East St. Louis—on the divisive and violent consequences for working people of an enduring racism. Finally, the Wilson administration's participation in breaking the strike through a court injunction put yet another obstacle in the way of convincing workers that the "war for democracy" was their war as well.

A subsidiary of National Lead, the largest lead company in the nation, SLSR came to Collinsville, attracted by plentiful access to fuel, good rail transportation, and relatively close proximity to the Lead Belt of southeastern Missouri.[56] Starting up production in 1904, the Collinsville plant employed 300 to 400 workers.[57] Like other lead smelters that used the Scotch Hearth method, the SLSR plant in Collinsville had death, injury, and illness rates that rivaled coal mining.[58] Faced with mounting discontent among workers at the plant, the company in 1914 sent a new plant manager to supervise a rebuilding of the plant with an eye to improving safety conditions as well as to creating "better feeling between the company and its employees."

During 1916, SLSR saw a similar zinc smelter in Collinsville face a union drive led by organizers from the International Union of Mine, Mill and Smelter Workers (IUMMSW). At the same time, Collinsville Zinc faced a raft of lawsuits from farmers, miners, and other residents who lived in the "Little Italy" section of town who charged that the plant was polluting the air and soil and ruining gardens and crops. SLSR itself faced twenty-one similar lawsuits.[59] As a result, smelter workers' attempts to unionize were welcomed not only by UMWA miners but also by a wider section of the community who already viewed the smelting companies as rapacious outsiders.

While Superintendent W. E. Newnam of the SLSR plant granted workers a cost of living raise in April 1917, aimed at heading off a new union organization drive, and boasted of a perfect safety record the following month, the ongoing conflict over wages, working conditions, and union rights only deepened. After the company fired four union activists in July, some 400 workers walked out on August 4 in a strike that would shut down production for nearly two months.[60]

Coming at a time when miners themselves were beginning to walk off the job for a variety of reasons, the smelter strike quickly drew the support of working people. Within a week of the walkout, the Collinsville Trades Council voted to support the strike. Miners at Donk No. 2 in Maryville announced that they were donating 1 percent of their union dues checkoff to the smelter's strike fund. At Lumaghi No. 3, which had a contract to supply coal to the smelter, miners voted to give the strikers aid.[61] And in the face of SLSR's threat to move production from Collinsville permanently unless the strikers returned to work, the Collinsville City Council adopted the Trades Council's resolution of protest.[62]

In September, former smelter office worker H. L. "Tubby" Evatt wrote a letter to the *Collinsville Herald* that helps explain the broader meaning of this strike. "I was very sorry indeed to hear of the trouble at the smelter," he wrote. "It seems that troubles never come singly tho and that must have been the case with them. It is very unfortunate too, coming at a time when all internal trouble should be forgotten for the common cause. I am afraid the war has not yet been brought home to the people." Evatt echoed Joseph Tumulty's lament months earlier that workers' "righteous wrath" had not yet been fully aroused. This is not to say that because workers went on strike, they must have opposed the war. But Evatt correctly sensed that workers' willingness to walk out, in spite of patriotic exhortations to stay in, reflected a degree of class solidarity that could not help but conflict with war mobilization. Sadly, Evatt's insight into the "trouble" in Collinsville was to be one of his last. He wrote his letter from the western front and weeks later became the first Collinsville man to die fighting in France.[63]

Like the miners, however, the smelter workers found it difficult to forget their "internal trouble" with their employer. At the Masonic Temple, Superintendent Newnam had spent hours that summer knitting a scarf, setting new standards for patriotic sacrifice. In late September, the smelter workers faced a new challenge from Newnam when SLSR decided to make an attempt to restart production with a force of strikebreakers and armed guards. On September 25, the company served a temporary federal injunction against the strikers, which a U.S. marshal posted at the plant gates. Reflecting the support given by miners to the strike, the injunction named not only IUMMSW officers but local UMWA officials as well, including Robert Bertolero and Mose Johnson. The following day, for the first time in weeks, the lead smelter began to operate, though with a reduced crew of seventy-five.[64]

The strikers fought back four days later on September 30 as 1,000 unionists, flanked by thousands more onlookers, marched down Main Street in Collinsville to protest the company's action. Robert Bertolero of UMWA Local 685 led the parade, which included also the Maryville Donk No. 2 miners, who arrived on two special interurban cars. Using the Wilson administration's anti-autocratic rhetoric against SLSR, speakers denounced Newnam as the "czar of labor" and called on all working people to support the smelter workers' democratic right to organize.[65]

Facing this strong show of support in Collinsville, SLSR began to bring in larger numbers of replacement workers from outside of town. On October 15, County Sheriff Jenkin Jenkins, who sympathized with the strikers, began ordering his deputies to arrest strikebreakers—nearly all African Americans—trying to enter the plant. Several days later, Jenkins was cited for contempt under the terms of the company's injunction and was ordered to appear in court. The arrest of Jenkins prompted a firestorm among unionists in Collinsville and beyond. In town, there was talk of a general strike in sympathy with the smelter workers. At the Illinois Federation of Labor convention, which happened to be in session in Joliet, the delegates went on record in support of the smelter strikers and specifically in support of Sheriff Jenkins.[66]

The possibility of a general strike was heightened by events in Springfield the previous month. Striking streetcar workers had held a protest parade early in September, which was attacked by state militia and police. In response, some 4,200 area coal miners closed down eighteen of thirty-one mines and were joined by all the organized crafts in a general protest strike. The strike ensured that a subsequent protest march went unhindered.[67] In both cases, the outrage of working people was sparked by the actions of allegedly neutral government authorities. The supposed democratic promise of the war accentuated this contradiction between rhetoric and reality.

In Collinsville, however, the picture of class solidarity displayed in the wake of Jenkins's indictment is complicated by the role that racial divisions may have played. According to the *Herald,* for instance, unionists resented SLSR's "importation of the negroes. They feared that the negroes would be of the disorderly sort which would endanger the peace of the community." Furthermore, in an interview, Sheriff Jenkins explained that he had arrested the men because he feared that their presence "would cause trouble." To some extent, then, these events provided an echo of the Virden struggle, in which the white "community" mobilizes to defend itself against the black "invaders." Unfortunately, Jenkins's arrest of the strikebreakers encouraged miners to view them as criminals rather than as fellow working people who could be convinced to respect the smelter workers' strike.

This point is important not only for understanding the dynamics of the wartime strike wave but also in looking toward the street violence of the Prager lynching, for the agitation around black strikebreakers in Collinsville occurred only months after the anti-black pogrom in East St. Louis, just a few miles away.[68] There, too, a focus of anti-black sentiment was a union struggle at a smelter, operated there by the Aluminum Ore Company. While the union leadership in East St. Louis did not organize the actual violence of July 2, the prevailing racist sentiments of many workers provided fertile ground for fears generated by the Wilson campaign's charges that Republicans had "imported" black voters during the 1916 elections. Like Robert Prager, the blacks who were killed and terrorized in July were essentially scapegoats. They served as a socially sanctioned target for the anxiety and anger that white workers had accumulated around grievances ranging from employment insecurity to political corruption.[69]

Moreover, the racist violence in East St. Louis not only logically paralleled some of the developments in Collinsville but also physically spilled into the area. In the first night of rioting that preceded the July events, Nelson Cooper, an African American from Collinsville, was riding a train into East St. Louis when he was beaten "into insensibility" by three assailants. On the terrible night of July 2, blacks fleeing the violence rode through Collinsville to Edwardsville. And finally, a saloon porter named Wesley Beaver, who police allege took part in the violent attacks, escaped their jurisdiction into Collinsville during July. The following April, he was arrested and charged along with Joseph Riegel and others in the lynching of Robert Prager.[70]

If the Collinsville miners' solidarity with the smelter strikers was not a simple matter, it still continued to gather force. A week after Jenkins was cited on the federal injunction, the miners at Lumaghi No. 3 raised the stakes in the fight by threatening a strike to prevent their mine from supplying coal to the smelter, which was now running almost at full blast. On behalf of the miners of Collinsville, President William Brockmeier of UMWA Local 826 informed the mine superintendent of their intention.[71]

During the next week, however, Lumaghi called the miners' bluff and their threat unraveled. Other locals denied giving Brockmeier sanction to include them in his statement. The Local 826 president himself denied to the *Herald* that he had threatened a general strike. Still, he insisted that other unionists would back the Lumaghi miners in their demand. According to Brockmeier, every UMWA local in town had agreed to strike if necessary to enforce this demand. Nevertheless, William Brockmeier was left holding the bag. To make matters worse, the Lumaghi No. 3 superintendent gave a deposition to SLSR, documenting the miners' warning and laying the basis for prosecution on the grounds of violating the federal injunction.[72]

This particular series of events is significant because six months hence, Brockmeier would join Riegel and Beaver, charged with hanging Robert Prager. Though Brockmeier seems to have played no role in the actual lynching, his appearance in the defendants list is intriguing. Like Riegel, Brockmeier was a German-American unionist who had publicly distinguished himself by his apparent militancy in the course of a class battle. At the same time, the patriotism of both men was publicly challenged. Though there were no recorded charges of pro-Germanism against Brockmeier, his central role in threatening to shut down a key war protduction facility could not but help raise that question.

A final aspect of the smelter strike that enriches our larger story is the trial of the men charged with violating the federal injunction obtained by SLSR. During the last days of October, twelve strikers, Sheriff Jenkins, and his six deputies stood trial in Springfield on charges that they had impeded production at the plant. Reflecting the close ties between the smelter workers and miners, the strikers were assisted by UMWA attorneys. Since the company had obtained a federal injunction, lawyers for SLSR received aid from U.S. District Attorney Edward C. Knotts, who played an active role for the prosecution. After hearing testimony mainly from strikebreakers, whose rights the defendants were accused of violating, Judge Humphries, and in some cases a jury, convicted Jenkins and his six deputies, as well as nine of the strikers. These included Z. S. Lockhart, the IUMMSW local union president, who was sentenced to ninety days in the county jail.[73]

If working people were angry at the arrest of Jenkins two weeks earlier, they were incensed at the conviction of the sheriff and the strikers. UMWA board member Mose Johnson remarked that the guilty verdicts were sure to cause a storm of protest among unionists all over the state.[74] In Collinsville, the *Herald* reported, "[P]lans and rumours included impeachment of federal judge Humphrey *[sic]* . . . sympathetic strikes of one kind and another and threats to start union controlled business enterprises, including a newspaper."[75]

What seemed to anger working people the most was the open role of the federal government on the side of the company during the trial in the person of Edward C. Knotts. Born on a Sangamon County farm, Knotts served brief stints as a journalist and teacher before starting his legal career. After holding a number of appointed and elective offices in Macoupin County as a loyal Democrat, the talented Knotts, known for his courtroom ability, attracted the attention of Superior Coal, whose administration hired him to represent their interests in the area.[76] As late as 1915, he represented Superior in a series of lawsuits filed by Macoupin County farmers contesting the coal company's right to drill for oil on their land. Commenting on a visit by Knotts to Gillespie, the *Staunton Star-Times* referred to his employer, Superior Coal, as a "large and grabbing corporation" and noted that Knotts "is making no friends in the south end of the county."[77] By the U.S. entry into the war, Knotts had been appointed district attorney for southern Illinois and was the chief enforcer of the federal Espionage Act in the region.

The role of Knotts in the SLSR trial and its political repercussions emerge from a remarkable letter penned by Victor Olander, secretary of the IFL, to AFL president Samuel Gompers in the days following the conviction of the strikers. Olander, who attended the trial, began by spelling out the role that Knotts played in the proceedings. After the testimony was given in the case of union president Lockhart, Olander explained, the SLSR attorney made a brief statement, and attorneys for Lockhart and the allegedly wronged strikebreaker spoke on behalf of their clients. "Then to our utter astonishment," he told Gompers, "United States District Attorney Knotts arose and made the closing plea as prosecutor, urging conviction of the defendant as a necessary measure to uphold the courts and the government in these times of war!" Moreover, in two subsequent cases heard by a jury, Olander witnessed "Mr. Knotts making his appearance in each instance to make the closing address, and in each instance the jury brought in a verdict of guilty, clearly influence[d] to do so by a plea of United States District Attorney Knotts, urging such action as a patriotic necessity."

Olander then explained the problems that Knotts's actions had created. The IFL had been working hard in Illinois to spread the "spirit of loyalty and patriotism," Olander told the AFL chief. For example, in the case of labor disputes, "we have pointed out that the government is seeking to play fair with the workers, that President Wilson has taken a stand for a square deal." Just as the IFL had been making progress on this front, he wrote, "now comes the 'government' through a representative of the Department of Justice, to give aid and comfort to the friends of the enemy in this case by conveying the impression that the government has no further interest in the very serious situation existing at Collinsville other than to send a few lead-poisoned, underpaid and overworked but nevertheless loyal and patriotic citizens to jail." As a result of the district attorney's behavior, Olander added, "Mr. Knotts succeeded in conveying the impression to every one in the court with whom I talked that the United States Government—*I mean the government as represented by President Wilson*—was interested in the conviction of these men."[78] Therefore, Knotts has made "more difficult the work of patriotic citizens who are seeking to uphold the hands of the President to support the real government of the country and arouse to the highest possible pitch the spirit of true loyalty necessary to win the war."

If the perception among working people were to grow that the Wilson administration was indeed not a friend of labor, then the problem of boosting the war would be compounded. Olander knew quite well, he told Gompers, that Edward C. Knotts did not represent the "real government." "I can see the difference between a real representative of our government in these times and a representative of corporations who happens to hold a government job," he wrote. But, he implied, workers in Collinsville and elsewhere did not recognize this fine distinction. Those thousands of miners, smelter workers, and others might come to the "misguided" conclusion that the government was not on their side. What then?

Olander's letter pointedly reveals the ongoing difficulties for the government in mobilizing working people for war in this region. It also indicates that even seven months into the patriotic crusade, ongoing class struggle in the southwestern Illinois coalfields and the government's contradictory role continued to raise questions in the minds of working people about whether the government was indeed theirs. A footnote to the trial provides a powerful illustration of these interrelated points. In December, a Collinsville UMWA official wrote to Victor Olander reporting on the latest developments in the smelter strike. In explaining that three additional strikers had been arrested, the UMWA official could not help noting the irony provided by the case of Frank Rossman, one of the strikers convicted in October. Rossman, he informed Olander, "has a stepson over in France who has won a medal for bravery fighting for worldwide democracy, yet his father lies in jail when he attempted to assert his rights as a citizen of this country."[79] Here, crystallized in a single family, is the political problem that patriotic union officials confronted.

In late 1917, there was one more strike that drew upon the solidarity of Collinsville coal miners and can help us understand the crosscurrents surrounding the Prager lynching. In November, five young women who worked as operators at the local Bell telephone exchange quit in protest. For weeks, Lola Higgs, Mary Killian, Lillian Walker, a "Miss Baehler," and "Miss Higgins" had been trying to organize a local branch of the telephone operators union, a unit of the International Brotherhood of Electrical Workers (IBEW). Unlike other industrial work available to women in the area, telephone operating carried with it an image of cleanliness, respectability, and vital importance to the community. Women who did this work tended to have a high school education and were overwhelmingly drawn from the better-off sections of the working class, particularly native-born Irish Americans. At the same time, the push for scientific management created in the telephone industry a contradiction between this image and the deadening pace and conditions of operating work. Like workers in other AFL affiliates, the nation's telephone operators took advantage of the war boom to press for better wages, better working conditions, and union recognition from the Pacific to the Midwest to their traditional stronghold of New England.[80]

In Collinsville, the Bell managers responded to their union organizing by harassing the five activists until they quit in disgust and declared themselves on strike, sometime in November. Over the next few months, these women waged a fight to regain their jobs under a union contract. In response to offers by Bell to hire them as individuals, the women refused, demanding that the company recognize the IBEW and rehire them as a group. By January, the striking operators succeeded in winning the cooperation of many local unionists. At a mass meeting, presided over by Mose Johnson and Alfred Bailey, a local miners' official at Consolidated No. 17, miners and other working people endorsed a citywide boycott of the Bell telephone service. It was announced that some fifty local merchants had agreed to participate in the boycott. One of the speakers at the meeting was Notley Shoulders, a Collinsville alderman and chairman of the IBEW local. Another speaker was John Hallworth, a Maryville miner and longtime UMWA activist, who "spoke in favor of stronger action, urging that a [boycott] list be sent to each local union in the city with instructions that their members not patronize any of the firms listed as unfair."[81] After a month of boycotting and negotiations, the telephone operators won their jobs back with a wage increase.[82]

As 1917 came to a close, miners and coal operators had reached an uneasy truce. Miners had received their wage increase, operators were making profits, and a temporary calm prevailed on the industrial battlefield. At the same time, the problems that sparked strikes had hardly disappeared. Inflation continued to eat away at miners' earnings. In Gillespie, for instance, three UMWA locals filed a joint resolution with U.S. Food Commissioner Herbert Hoover protesting high food prices. They charged local merchants with "systematic filching." After the November 1 wage hike, that is, retailers simply raised prices. When a committee of miners visited a Gillespie butcher and requested a list of meat prices, he refused to provide one.[83]

Similarly, problems of mine safety and health remained. In the late fall through the spring, a series of mine explosions from Virden to Christopher, in southern Illinois, rocked the Illinois coalfields. Even the forced compliance of employers with washhouse legislation did not guarantee that facilities were adequate. In December 1917, for instance, miners at one Illinois mine refused to change for work when they discovered that the washhouse had no heat.[84] Moreover, in the spring, several mines were closed by state inspectors for poor ventilation.

Because of the pressure to resolve ongoing problems, the proven propensity of miners to go on strike, and the link between striking and national disloyalty, the strike penalty clause became a subject of intense debate at the UMWA national convention in January 1918. As one scholar writes, "[T]he penalty clause set off a virtual civil war within the UMW."[85] The convention discussion clearly revealed the resentment that many miners felt toward the penalty clause. Though few openly championed the miners' right to strike during the war, many of these delegates pointed to the double message the government had sent to the miners about their patriotism.

Their comments were remarkably uniform. As one delegate put it, "I don't want men to say in one breath that the mine workers of this country are patriotic and that they are going to do their full duty in this time of war and then in the next breath say it is necessary to have an automatic penalty clause hanging over them to make them do that work."[86] Similarly, James McLeish of Rendville, Illinois, explained that "[m]y reason for objecting to the penalty clause is this: If they thought we were patriotic why did they put a shackle around our necks in the Washington Agreement? . . . There is no man in the rank and file of this great organization of ours that is not patriotic," he declared, "but we don't want to be led by a halter."[87] Another Illinois delegate used the same language: "[W]e can be patriotic without having a halter around our neck."[88] In describing the penalty clause in these terms, coal miners drew on the language of the movement against slavery, hearkening back to UMWA president Michael Ratchford's denunciation in 1897 of "industrial servitude."[89] The miners of 1918 also accurately perceived—perhaps more than they wanted to admit—that behind the paeans by employers, government, and union officials to their great contribution to the war effort lay a great fear of their lack of commitment to the war, a fear, ultimately, of the class solidarity that so many in southwestern Illinois had harnessed just months earlier.

In defending the penalty clause, which was adopted by a large majority, top union officials employed the same logic that William B. Wilson had used the previous August. While recognizing the anger of many miners at the seeming impeachment of their patriotism, they continued to argue that miners would be repaid for complying with the government's wishes. For his part, Frank Farrington once again explained that miners needed to stay on the job to demonstrate their honor. "If a labor organization demonstrates that it is willing to discharge its obligations to everyone, fulfill every duty imposed upon it by membership in the organization, do the right thing . . . that organization will command the respect of the community at large—and the community at large in our case is the great American public."[90]

Acknowledging the opposition to the penalty clause, John Walker reminded delegates that once the current contract expired, then miners could dispose of the penalty clause as they wished. For now, their highest duty was to the war effort. That meant staying on the job. If miners went on strike, he argued, they would be stabbing American soldiers in the back. In that event, what was a patriotic miner to do? "Why," Walker explained, "you would get that coal rather than see those men killed, *if you had to kill the men that stood in the way of getting it.*"[91]

Finally, William Green, UMWA International secretary-treasurer, echoed Farrington and, if possible, surpassed him in the heights of patriotic rhetoric. By staying on the job, he reminded delegates, miners were protecting the union's reputation. Do not allow yourselves, he warned, "to place upon the banner of this great union one little spot of dishonor." Then continuing the metaphor, he added that "I am willing to wrap Old Glory around my body any time it is necessary to appeal to the reason of my fellow men."[92]

The combined remarks of these three patriotic unionists provide a useful way both to end this examination of the 1917 strike wave and to anticipate key elements of the patriotic violence of the following spring. Frank Farrington doggedly insisted that miners can solve their problems only by proving to the nation how devoted and loyal they are. John Walker, who invoked the specter of striker as spy and saboteur, offered a fitting solution—murder—to that supposed problem. And William Green provided a graphic symbol of respectable unionism as well as militant patriotism by unabashedly wrapping himself in the red, white, and blue. If only coal miners would "do their part," union leaders argued, their government would repay the favor.

Between January and April 1918, as the crisis for the Allies deepened on the battlefield, more and more miners were to take this advice to heart.

An epidemic of forced flag-kissing, flag-saluting, and physical attacks on suspected disloyalists swept through the region. Though miners were hardly content that their collective grievances had been met, the strong current of class solidarity that ran freely through the region from August through October had been largely forced underground. Miners were not to dishonor the patriotic banner of the UMWA. Dogged by questions about their own patriotism fueled by the 1917 strike wave, miners felt the pressure to demonstrate their patriotism like never before.

Miners at the Taylor Mine in O'Fallon, Illinois, in St. Clair County.
Courtesy O'Fallon Historical Society.

Consolidated Coal Company of St. Louis Mine No. 17 in Caseyville, Illinois, in St. Clair County. Miners stand inside the cage, preparing to come up to the surface from the mine bottom. Hoisting engineer William Lepp Sr. stands at left. Courtesy Doris M. Bauer and Jane Bouril.

Arthur, seated, and Leona Thorpe, at left, tie the knot in 1920. Arthur worked at the St. Louis and O'Fallon Black Eagle mine in French Village during World War I. Leona worked in a Collinsville textile mill. Courtesy Becky Matthews.

Mine No. 2 (Black Eagle)—also known historically as "Nigger Hollow No. 2"—was owned by the St. Louis and O'Fallon Coal Company, a proprietary enterprise of the Busch brewing empire of St. Louis. In 1916, this mine employed over 600 workers. Courtesy O'Fallon Historical Society.

This spacious home belonged to Italian immigrant mine owner Louis Lumaghi in Collinsville, Illinois. Lumaghi's three coal mines contributed to the area war economy and were the scene of labor conflict. Courtesy G. Bradley Publishing, St. Louis.

BROTHERS ONCE, BUT NOW—

This cartoon from *Coal Age* illustrated how coal miners' class solidarity suffered under the impact of World War I. Source: *Coal Age*.

Raised in Mt. Olive, Illinois, Adolph Germer mined coal and was a leading voice for the Socialist wing of the UMWA. He served as the Socialist Party's national secretary during World War I. WHi-25280, Wisconsin Historical Society.

A native of the northern Illinois coalfields who disdained the Socialist wing of the UMWA, Frank Farrington presided over the Illinois district of the union during World War I. *Literary Digest*

John Walker—northern Illinois miner, one-time Socialist, and Illinois UMWA official who led the Illinois Federation of Labor during World War I—speaks to a coal miners' mass meeting in Coal City, Illinois, in 1911. Walker is standing at right. IX.B. (2), John Hunter Walker Papers, Illinois Historical Survey, University of Illinois Library, Urbana.

Republican Frank Lowden was the
governor of Illinois from 1917 to 1921.
St. Louis Globe-Democrat Archives, St. Louis Mercantile
Library at the University of Missouri-St. Louis.
Photo by International Film Service Co., Inc./UPI.

Former coal miner and UMWA official William B. Wilson served as President Wilson's
secretary of labor during World War I. National Archives.

Democratic President Woodrow Wilson led the United States through the ordeal of World War I. National Archives.

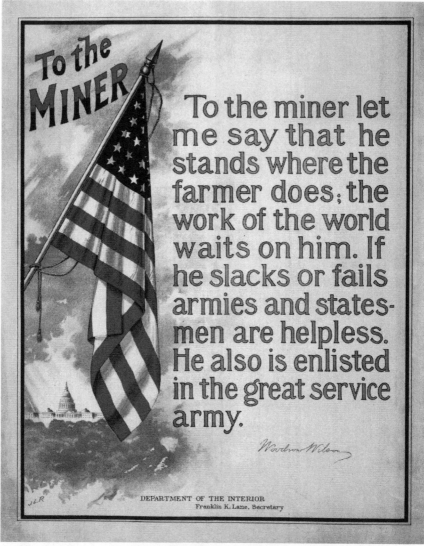

President Wilson's appeal, reproduced for mass circulation by the Bureau of Mines, highlighted the key role of coal miners in war mobilization. National Archives.

James O. Monroe was the editor of the
Collinsville Herald during World War I.
Monroe's articles and editorials were influential
in whipping up Collinsville's patriotic fervor.

Courtesy G. Bradley Publishing, St. Louis.

German-born Matt Sova Jr., at left, lived in Collinsville
and worked in Consolidated Coal Company Mine
No. 17 in St. Clair County starting at the age of fifteen.
He served in the American Expeditionary Forces in
World War I as a cook. Courtesy G. Bradley Publishing, St. Louis.

H. Leighton "Tubby" Evatt was the first Collinsville man in uniform to die overseas in World War I. Before the war, he had studied medicine and worked in the office of the local lead smelter. Courtesy G. Bradley Publishing, St. Louis.

These Collinsville schoolchildren and their patriotic dog belonged to a Junior Red Cross chapter. Courtesy G. Bradley Publishing, St. Louis.

Annabelle Lathrop Woods was a World War I–era telephone operator in Collinsville. Her fellow operators in Collinsville went on strike for union recognition during World War I, earning the active solidarity of coal miners and other working people in the area.

Courtesy G. Bradley Publishing, St. Louis.

A German American coal miner and skilled baker, Robert Paul Prager was accused of spying for Germany. He was lynched on the outskirts of Collinsville, Illinois, on April 5, 1918. *St. Louis Post-Dispatch* Archives, photo by International Film Service Co., Inc.

Robert Prager briefly occupied this cell in the Collinsville city jail before he was seized by a mob of area residents.
Courtesy G. Bradley Publishing, St. Louis.

The lynching of Robert Prager prompted leading African American educator Leslie Pinckney Hill to write President Wilson about the lynching of African Americans during World War I. Wilson declined to answer Hill's letter. University Archives, Cheyney University of Pennsylvania.

Prager lynching defendants during the trial. All were acquitted. *Top row, left to right:* William Brockmeier, Joseph Riegel, John Hallworth, Charles Cranmer, Richard Dukes Jr., and Deputy Sheriff Vernon Coons, keeping custody of the men. *Bottom row, left to right:* Wesley Beaver, Frank Flannery, Cecil Larremore, James DeMatties, Enid Elmore, and Calvin Gilmore. *St. Louis Post-Dispatch* Archives.

The body of Robert Prager lies in St. Matthew's Cemetery in St. Louis. Prager's Odd Fellows brethren paid for the burial. Note the Odd Fellows chain carved into the top of his grave. Photo by author.

"The Spanish Inquisition Has Reached the State of Illinois"
The Rising Tide of Vigilantism

Though the United States declared war on Germany in April 1917, the full impact of this decision was not felt on the home front until early the next year. Only then did American soldiers finish their training in large numbers and begin to fight in the bloody battles, to which their European counterparts had long become accustomed. In conjunction with the higher military and political stakes raised by the Bolshevik revolution in November 1917, the new situation brought on a crisis atmosphere in towns and cities throughout the United States. For the first time, working people in southwestern Illinois were directly confronted with the human cost of the war, as news filtered home of loved ones maimed and killed on the battlefield. Such news could deepen a visceral patriotism but also inevitably raised questions of whether these sacrifices were worth making. As working people continued to question the justification for war, pressure mounted for a Sedition Act, which became law in May 1918. At the same time, the trickle of patriotic street actions of the previous fall in the region became a flood. Rumors of German spy activity mounted, including allegations that the kaiser's agents planned to dynamite coal mines. In this constricted atmosphere, southwestern Illinois miners tried their best to maintain their traditions of class solidarity while simultaneously affirming their patriotism. The case of Severino Oberdan, a miner accused of sedition, challenged their ability to pull off this balancing act. Oberdan's tar and feathering in Staunton in February 1918 at the hands of a mob revealed the divisions among coal miners that had developed and warned of more fatal encounters to come.

While the Wilson administration mobilized "the mental forces of America" at home through the Committee on Public Information, American military commanders began to lead thousands of young American men into the European conflagration. After months of training and waiting, the first American shots were fired on October 17. A total of 4.8 million Americans would serve in the war, some 5 percent of the total U.S. population.[1] As the first casualty reports filtered back into Collinsville, an event took place that decisively shaped the remaining course of the war. In the early hours of November 7, forces of the Bolshevik faction of the Russian Social Democratic Labor Party took state power in Russia. Just as they promised, their first act was to proclaim an immediate end to Russian participation in the European war. It took months for American workers to begin to absorb the political impact of the Bolshevik victory, but the effect on the battlefield was more immediate. With the signing of the Brest-Litovsk Treaty in March 1918, German forces moved west and launched a crushing offensive against Allied troops. With the bombarding of Paris that month, the Germans seemed closer to victory than ever.[2]

As the year 1918 opened, working people in Collinsville began to hear from their sons and nephews and friends stationed in France. Largely due to military censorship, the letters that servicemen sent home revealed little of the grim reality of war. Rather, they tended to focus on the cheerier aspects of camp life and had an optimistic tone. William Turner, who served in the Fifth Field Artillery along with several other local men, wrote on January 16 to thank his family for their latest package. "I am going to give all of the Collinsville boys their tobacco this afternoon as I will have plenty of time to get over to Jim Dukes and Claude Fitzpatrick," he wrote. "All of the Collinsville boys are in the best of health," he continued. "The sun is shining today and it is as clear as a crystal outside and about 6 inches of snow still covers the ground."[3]

Similarly, Ray Cox, with the Twenty-first Engineers, wrote home to Collinsville on February 7 that "there is no use worrying about me being over here, as I am just as good as there. I am well and feeling fine. And eating heartily, so what more can one expect." Cox was busy digging trenches "with shovel and pick," he told his mother. But he added that "[w]e are in no danger at all. So don't worry. We don't even hear a shot, so you know how safe we are." Finally, Cox wished that his "pop could take the trip over here, as it would do him good."[4]

Based on their letters, it seemed that the young workers of Collinsville were on an extended vacation overseas that happened to involve lots of healthy exercise and plenty of food. Despite the seeming incongruity of this picture, it is worth recognizing that the time served by American soldiers was multifaceted and not uniformly grim. Indeed, many of them, like Collinsville coal miner Jim Dukes, had volunteered for service, relishing the opportunity to serve their country.[5] And when dreams of glory ran up against the harsh reality of "no man's land," between battles, soldiers made the best of their situation. Even soldiers in the trenches might find time to go swimming, play football, or visit a nearby farmhouse for a hot meal.[6]

In addition to receiving lighthearted letters, Collinsville residents also began to hear tales of military glory as their native sons confronted the evil Hun. In November, Private Charles Massa of Collinsville took part in one of the first pitched battles fought by American troops in France. Despite the close presence of the opposing armies near the Artois salient, the area had been quiet for some time, and the fresh American troops used this sector for the last phase of their battle training. On November 2, in the dead of night, some 210 German troops launched a raid on the area, held jointly by American and French troops. German artillery laid down a barrage of shells, hemming in the Allied troops, and the infantry then advanced on the trenches with grenades, rifles, revolvers, and trench knives.

As recounted in the *Saturday Evening Post,* Private Massa, along with two others, was caught out at a listening post by the artillery barrage. "Unable to penetrate it," the article explained, "they threw barbed wire into the trenches, kept up a stiff rifle fire and beat the raiders back from that point." All told, the Germans captured twelve Americans, ten privates and two officers. Three Americans died, as well as two French soldiers, and two Americans were wounded. Commenting on the performance of the American troops, the *Post* war correspondent wrote, "Young, inexperienced soldiers went into positions they had never seen in daylight; it was their first time under fire. Despite the elements of surprise and uncertainty, of darkness and the necessity of each group going it alone—despite hard punishment—they did not break, but came back for more. If the history of battles were faithfully written it would be found that many a fine regiment could not say the same."[7]

But if the exploits of Charles Massa may have cheered Collinsville residents, perhaps what made the deepest impact on working people in southwestern Illinois was the bad news from the front. As it happened, the first Collinsville serviceman to die never made it to Europe. Born into a family with American military heritage, Eugene Kohler was a third-generation German American whose grandfather had served in the U.S. Army during the Mexican-American War. In November 1917, during training drills at Camp Taylor in Louisville, Kohler developed a respiratory illness and died on New Year's Day 1918. His death prefigured the toll that influenza would take on American soldiers and civilians alike by the end of the year.[8]

A glimpse of the reality of trench warfare emerges from letters sent by George Ganninger, a twenty-six-year-old Collinsville worker who served in Belgium later in the year in a company of "shock troops" of the 148th Infantry. After a battle near Verdun, Ganninger and a fellow soldier were the only survivors of their squad, which numbered twenty-six when the fighting started. "His rifle and mess kit were shot away and he considered it a miracle that he escaped." In another incident, a group of soldiers including Ganninger were ordered to dig a trench in a stretch of "no man's land." "He said that just as they completed this work a German shell fell among them killing three of the party outright, and the body of one of his companions falling directly upon him after it had been hurled high in the air." Having survived these scrapes, Ganninger was subsequently wounded and died in late 1918.[9] In a sense, Ganninger might have been luckier had he joined his comrades in instant death. The advent of modern weaponry, including large explosive shells that sent shrapnel ripping through human flesh, deadly poison gases, and the highly efficient machine gun, multiplied the variety of new wounds that soldiers suffered. Improved medical technique could reduce the fatality rate but in some cases simply prolonged the agony of the wounded.[10]

Though news from the front had been arriving for nearly a year, it was word from France that twenty-six-year-old Private James C. Dukes had died of pneumonia, reported publicly on March 1, 1918, that brought the war home to Collinsville. The circumstances of his death were not reported. Whether the illness developed in connection with battle wounds is unknown. Most likely, wet, cold, and fatigue dealt him the fatal blow. In any event, the impact of his death seemed to derive from a feeling that one of the town's best had been struck down. Born in nearby O'Fallon and living in Collinsville for most of his life, Dukes worked at Donk Bros. No. 1 mine, as did his younger brother, Richard.[11] According to the

Collinsville Herald, "He was a big strong fellow, much admired by his friends both for his fine physique and his manly ways." He seems to have been a popular and sociable young man, belonging to the local Eagles lodge. In a letter he sent January 9 from "somewhere in France," Jim Dukes seemed well and happy, thanking his parents for "his Christmas box containing good things to eat, sweaters, wristlets," as well as cigars sent by his fellow Eagles. This picture meshed with Turner's letter of a week later, which had reported that the Collinsville crowd was in good health. And now Jim Dukes was dead.

"I cannot [believe] it," said his grieving mother, Jessie, three days after his death. "Not to have his body and to see that he is dead makes it seem like a terrible dream." Her grief may have been accentuated by the knowledge that her only remaining son, Richard, had recently registered for the draft himself.[12] The stunned reaction of Jessie Dukes to her son's death indicates the human impact that the casualties of war were beginning to make on coal mining families.

It was not only news of individual cases that produced a feeling of crisis in the spring of 1918 but also the German offensive that struck the Allied armies. Crisis on the battlefield translated into crisis at home. As Attorney General Thomas Gregory wrote five days after the Amiens disaster in late March, "[T]he hour looks pretty dark but I am confident that the British lines will hold." He believed that the war would continue "almost a year." In the meantime, Gregory wrote, "the grim spirit of this country which is rapidly developing must ossify and there must be no talk about anything except a finish fight, cost what it may in lives and treasure."[13] The perilous situation for the Allies meant that dissent at home could be tolerated even less than before.

Even before the spring offensive, however, the Justice Department had pushed for tougher legislation to deal with opposition to the war. On January 16, the U.S. House of Representatives began debate on amendments—drafted in the Justice Department—to the Espionage Act, which collectively became known as the Sedition Act. The House approved the measure on March 4; after relatively more debate, the Senate passed a similar version on April 10; and on May 16, President Wilson signed it into law.

Two aspects of the Sedition Act are notable here. First, unlike the original Espionage Act, the sedition amendments included a section that explicitly forbade free speech on the war. The list of new legal offenses included the following:

Uttering, printing, writing, or publishing any disloyal, profane, scurrilous, or abusive language intended to cause contempt, scorn, contumely or disrepute as regards the form of government of the United States, or the Constitution, or the flag, or the uniform of the Army or Navy, or any language intended to incite resistance to the United States or to promote the cause of its enemies; urging any curtailment of production of any thing necessary to the prosecution of the war with intent to hinder its prosecution; advocating, teaching, defending, or suggesting the doing of any of these acts; and words or acts supporting or favoring the cause of any country at war with the United States, or opposing the cause of the United States therein.[14]

Though local authorities had not hesitated to use the more restricted Espionage Act for this broader purpose—in prosecuting Anton Korun, for instance, for allegedly tearing down a Liberty Loan poster—the new legislation gave a far wider scope to the government in cracking down on any kind of resistance.

Second, the timing of the Sedition Act is important. The Prager lynching took place after the House passed the bill but before the Senate approved it. One of the main arguments made for its passage was that it would serve to discourage mob violence against "disloyalists." In fact, it probably served to encourage such violence by labeling anti-war speech as criminal. But in the crescendo of vigilante violence that led up to the Prager lynching, a common refrain was that the government was not doing enough to silence "pro-Germans." As in many other lynchings, it was popularly claimed that the "people" were forced to deliver the punishment that the government was unwilling or unable to give.

By late 1917, the "grim spirit" desired by the attorney general was rapidly developing in the southwestern Illinois coalfields. In December, Mayor John H. Siegel of Collinsville publicized an appeal from the American Defense Society that urged residents to form a local vigilance corps. In its form letter, evidently sent nationwide, the American Defense Society recommended that "loyal Americans" organize an American Vigilance Corps that would classify all residents as "Loyal," "Disloyal," "Doubtful," or "Unknown." In addition, another set of classifications would designate those who were "Alien enemy," "Pro-German," or "Anti-Government."[15] Siegel, who doubled as Lumaghi Coal's company doctor, did not succeed immediately in forming the organization.

But as the new year opened, small, informal vigilance bands began to do their work in Madison County. In late January, a few miles to the north in Glen Carbon, miners were relaxing in a local saloon when a group began to sing "The Star-Spangled Banner." Apparently, a number of other miners—allegedly German Americans—refused to join in the fun, which also included the tunes "Good-bye Broadway, Hello France" and "Stars and Stripes Forever," preferring "Deutschland, Deutschland Uber Alles" instead. Hearing of the affront given by these "Prussian vocalists," a dozen "young patriots" arrived at the saloon and insisted that the German Americans join them in the national anthem. When they still refused, fighting broke out. According to a newspaper report, "Barren fists were the main weapon of encounter, intermingled occasionally with a well aimed bar-room chair. Just how long the riot lasted was not devulged [sic], but it was said that the patriots were victorious and caused others to leave hurriedly for their homes, suffering from bruises and cuts."[16] Just as the patriotic pugilists of Livingston beat Red Cross donations out of recalcitrant workers, so the Glen Carbon patriots used their fists to enforce politically correct singing. In doing so, they had carried Governor Frank Lowden's February 1917 patriotic song campaign to its logical extreme.

If patriotic music was one focal point of attacks on disloyalists, another commonly used national symbol was the American flag. On a night in late February, in Curtis's Saloon in Collinsville, in the first reported such incident that spring, a crowd forced Jake Kramer Sr. to kiss the flag. In nearby Maryville, the saloon customers forced Theodore Schuster, a local miner and coworker of Robert Prager, to kiss the flag. When Maryville mayor Fred Neubauer came to Schuster's defense, the crowd asked him to kiss the flag as well, which "he did good naturedly," according to a news report. Subsequently, Schuster's coworkers asked the mine manager to fire him, fearing he would do some damage to the mine.[17]

In an editorial entitled "A Little Tar Might Help," the *Collinsville Herald* editor speculated that news of the local flag-kissings might "be sufficient to quiet" "disloyalists." If not, he continued, "we're satisfied we know a lot of folks who would be glad to join the party." So that no one could mistake his meaning, he added that "there'll be a lot of tar and feathers when the ceremonies begin."[18] In the Schuster incident, Prager's lynching was once again foreshadowed. The miners forced a coworker of German descent to demonstrate his loyalty, fearing that he might be a German spy. And they made explicit their suspicion that he might be plotting to blow up the Maryville mine.

Just as the spring of 1918 saw an upsurge in patriotic mob violence, so did it witness a heightened fear of German spies. Widely circulated press stories alleged that they had started fires, poisoned and put ground glass in food, and blown up ships, mines, and factories, all to cripple the American war effort. In his 1917 Flag Day speech, President Wilson had drawn the nation's attention to this alleged threat, claiming that "vicious spies and conspirators" had "spread sedition amongst us" and "sought by violence to destroy our industries and arrest our commerce."[19] Since the press normally reported Wilson's speeches prominently, his words carried weight. But with the creation of the CPI, Wilson's words reached a much wider audience. The CPI printed almost seven million copies of his Flag Day speech.[20]

In making sense of the hysteria over German spies manifested in southwestern Illinois, it is important to note that a small number of spies and saboteurs did actually exist. Just as the "pro-German" charges against Labor's National Peace Council contained an element of truth, the spy scare drew strength from the well-publicized fact that real German espionage and sabotage had taken place in the years leading to America's entry into the war. In 1915, Dr. Bernard Denburg, reporting to German ambassador Count Johann von Bernstorff, directed a small team of German government agents who carried out legal propaganda aimed at keeping the United States out of the war. Dr. Heinrich Albert ran an operation that spent millions buying up munitions badly needed by the Allies and shipping them to neutral countries, or to Germany when possible, and set up companies, under false pretenses, that won government munitions contracts and then deliberately failed to deliver the goods. Finally, under the direction of Franz Rintelen, German government agents planted incendiary bombs that succeeded in damaging or destroying dozens of ships leaving New York harbor with war materiel for the Allies.[21]

As the result of counterespionage by the Secret Service of the British Admiralty as well as by the U.S. Secret Service, the U.S. and British governments learned of Albert's and Rintelen's activities by mid-1915, and soon they were public knowledge. Seeking any opportunity to stir up pro-intervention sentiment in the United States, the British Admiralty fed information about German espionage and sabotage to the *New York Times* and the *Providence Journal.* Publisher John Rathom of the *Journal* often embellished these true stories with inventions of his own, leading Wilson's first attorney general Thomas Gregory later to comment that many of Rathom's stories were "pure and unadulterated fabrications."[22] Still, the damage had been done. More than a year before the United States entered the war, many Americans were prepared to believe that German spies were everywhere.

Public fears of German sabotage—specifically bomb plotters—were heightened also by a series of explosions at munitions supply dumps and factories, which were inevitably blamed on the German war machine. These included an explosion in Seattle Harbor in May 1915; one at DuPont facilities in November; the gigantic blast at the main loading docks for munitions in New York Harbor, on Black Tom Island in Jersey City, New Jersey, in July 1916; and the destruction of a munitions plant in Kingsland, New Jersey, in January 1917. In the Seattle case, a court later convicted five men, including the German consul in San Francisco.[23]

Despite the existence of a tiny number of real German spies, accusations of spying were often the product of overheated imaginations. In March 1918, for instance, President Wilson took a strong interest in a case of alleged spy activity at the United States Gas Mask plant in Queens, New York. He had heard from Malcolm Ross McAddoo that the company had fired 143 workers for deliberately puncturing gas masks with pins. "I am wondering whether no criminal action lies against such rascals? Is dismissal all that they must undergo?" Wilson asked his attorney general.[24] Gregory informed him that with the right evidence, the workers could be "indicted for treason." After checking with army and naval intelligence and with the gas mask company, however, the attorney general found out the story was a fabrication. A handful of employees had been fired from day to day for "incompetency," and "no one . . . has been discharged for any deliberate injury to the masks." In fact, the rejection rate had dropped from 7 to 4 percent; the few rejections resulted from holes made by air bubbles created in the manufacturing process.[25] The fact that Wilson believed the story on faith and merely asked how the workers could be further punished illustrates the state of the spy scare in March 1918.

Similarly, the rumor of ground glass in food received considerable press attention in early 1918. Consumers claimed to see ground glass or glass splinters particularly in bakery products and believed that German agents had placed them there. But when one congressman inquired at the Justice Department about this problem for his constituents, Attorney General Gregory answered, "The department has received numerous complaints of the presence of broken glass in food substances, but a most thorough investigation has failed to establish a single case in which glass had been maliciously placed therein."[26]

The Justice Department's conclusions received confirmation from a separate investigation done by Robert Paul Prager's former union brothers and sisters in the renamed Bakery and Confectionery Workers International Union. Because of its heavy German composition, Socialist proclivities, and direct hand in the production of food, the "ground glass" charges put the B&C "on the defensive," according to the union's historian. In response, experts hired by the union guessed that the source of the rumors was the wartime substitution of corn and bran flour for wheat. "Corn flour, the experts explained, had many flinty pieces of endosperm that were glasslike in appearance, and bran flours contained particles of the hard outer husk that were slimy in appearance."[27] This simple analysis may well have explained the reports of German sabotage of the nation's food supply.

In response to the publicity surrounding alleged and real German sabotage, the federal government moved to clamp down on access to explosives, with President Wilson signing a new law in December 1917. In a provision ostensibly aimed at spies but affecting thousands of immigrant coal miners, the law stipulated that explosives could be handled only by native-born or naturalized citizens. Since miners handled explosives daily, they needed such a license. Just after the new law went into effect, John Bertuleit, a German-born "alien enemy" coal miner, applied for his license at Collinsville City Hall. Presented with this request, city clerk James Bailey noted the restriction on the likes of Bertuleit and balked. Did the new law mean that unnaturalized miners would have to quit their trade? After consulting with the Federal Bureau of Mines, Bailey announced that Bertuleit and other "alien enemies" could work without a license as long as they bought their powder from a magazine on the mine premises.[28] Though German-born miners could continue mining, the implication of the law was that such workers were not to be trusted.[29]

In southwestern Illinois, charges began to circulate that "pro-Germans" planned to dynamite Lumaghi No. 2 mine, though the stories were later proved false.[30] Similarly, miners in Edgemont, at St. Louis and O'Fallon No. 2, who found a bottle of "mysterious liquid" in the mine shaft believed it to contain explosives planted by a German spy. As it turned out, the "mysterious liquid" was a chemical the miners used to oil their lamps. Rather than dampen the spy scare, however, the case made the miners realize "the ease with which a German agent might entomb them in the caverns of the shaft and of their patriotic duty to their country." Accordingly, the miners' pit committee ordered American flags and a guard placed at the mine entrance to ensure that every miner saluted "with due decorum."[31]

Miners' fears of German bomb plotters were rooted not only in the rumors of spy activity but also in the real ongoing hazards of mining underground in the spring of 1918. The alleged mining bomb plots centered on blasting powder. In order to place miners' anxieties in proper context, it is worth briefly examining three powder explosions that occurred in the region's mines during early 1918. Spanning the month immediately before Robert Prager began working at the Maryville mine, these kind of events—which provide an eerie parallel to the horrors of trench warfare—are crucial in understanding the way that miners "heard" popular warnings of industrial sabotage.

A Russian-born miner with the distinctly un-Russian name of William Matthews arrived for work at the Oak Hill mine near Belleville one day in early February. Upon reaching his room, Matthews found that one of the shots from the previous afternoon had not been fired, thereby reducing the amount of coal he could load that day. With the full crew of miners in the mine and in violation of state mining law, Matthews fired the remaining shot. Though the explosion was confined to his room and no one was hurt, Matthews was promptly arrested. In county court, the miner pled guilty and was fined the maximum penalty of $200.[32]

On February 22 in Virden at the Royal mine, twenty-six kegs of powder exploded, killing four coal miners. The blast was set off by electrical current passing into the mine car holding the powder. The results of the coroner's jury inquest, made public shortly after the explosion, suggested that the company was liable. A subsequent investigation by state mine inspectors confirmed that the Chicago, Wilmington and Franklin Coal Company had been routinely violating the mining code by transporting powder in the mine while the electric current was still running. In this case, the company had also illegally stored a number of kegs in a "manway refuge place," that is, along the rail track in an area mandated by law for miners' safe travel through the mine.[33]

Finally, on March 3, Mike Downing, an experienced shot-firer working in the St. Louis and O'Fallon No. 2, had a terrifying experience. After preparing two shots, he lit the fuses, whereupon they began to sputter.

Knowing he was in danger, he began heading out of his room to the entry. Then, suddenly, his headlamp went out, leaving him in pitch black. "In his confusion," the *Collinsville Herald* reported, "he approached the shots and at this moment both went off with a terrific roar and a blinding glare of light. He shrieked his fear and sank to the ground with bleeding head unconscious." Fellow miners found Downing and got him to a doctor, who treated his severe burns and head injuries resulting from flying coal and debris. Luckily, he lived, "in spite of his nerve wracking and harrowing moment inside the death chamber."[34]

These vignettes convey the variety of real hazards and their causes that the use of blasting powder posed to miners in the months leading up to the Prager lynching. In the first case, the prototypical "new immigrant" miner carelessly and illegally set off a shot at the beginning of a workday. In the second, four miners died because the coal company management cut corners, also in violation of the law. Finally, an experienced miner, having fired hundreds if not thousands of shots, came near death through a fluke. Reacting to these myriad dangers, miners could draw a corresponding variety of conclusions about the cause of powder explosions underground. "Foreigners," bosses, and plain fate were all possible culprits. Given the yearlong campaign by government authorities that associated "alien enemies," spies, and sabotage, however, the first choice became a highly favored one for miners to make in the spring of 1918.

Before we examine the suspicions surrounding Robert Prager that surfaced in late March and proved fatal in early April, it will be helpful to look at a parallel case of a miner accused of sedition that took a different course. On September 21, 1917, federal marshals placed Severino Oberdan under arrest. Oberdan, a coal miner from Nokomis, Illinois, in Montgomery County, was charged with making seditious statements that violated the Espionage Act. In the coming months, he was further accused of belonging to the IWW and terrorizing other coal miners. Documents related to the case suggest that Oberdan, a union militant and elected pit committeeman but probably not an IWW member, was the victim of a campaign led by the Nokomis Coal Company in collaboration with a conservative local union president and District Attorney Edward C. Knotts. His main "crime" seems to have been defending his fellow miners in cases relating to unsafe working conditions and company underweighing of coal.[35]

The most dramatic events of the Oberdan affair took place, however, not in Nokomis but in Staunton, some forty miles to the southwest by rail. It was there, five months after Oberdan's arrest, that the controversy surrounding his case erupted into violence. After a heated debate at a UMWA Local 755 union meeting on February 12, 1918, both Oberdan and his attorney, John Metzen, were beaten, tarred, and feathered; local miners suspected of disloyalty were attacked; and a number were run out of town.[36] Writing to President Wilson, Metzen commented with bitter irony on the date of the attack. "Lincoln the emancipator must have wept at this demonstration of patriotism at Staunton, Illinois, in celebration of his birthday," he wrote.[37]

The attack on Oberdan became the occasion for a more widespread attack on alleged disloyal workers in Staunton. An angry crowd visited a number of homes in town that night, forcing various individuals to salute the flag and sing the national anthem. They also chased a number of radical miners out of town. Ed Wieck saw a group of vigilantes, led by a former mine foreman carrying a rope, enter his boarding house looking for him. He managed to escape, eventually moving to California.[38]

Who took part in this vigilante activity? Wieck reported that the leaders of the mob were all businessmen, lawyers, and other professionals. He also claimed that officials of the Nokomis Coal Company were present that night. At the same time, he believed that it was only with the help of what he called "a few traitors in our organization" that the attacks were carried out.[39] His phrase clearly brings out the internal divisions among working people that had developed. Most likely, some Staunton miners, perhaps more than a few, were part of the attacks on Oberdan, Metzen, and unionists like Wieck.

Though the violence against Oberdan anticipated the Prager lynching in a number of ways, there were also some marked differences in the events leading to the attack. First, unlike Prager, who failed to rally his local union behind him, Oberdan succeeded in winning the support of the two Nokomis UMWA locals, which formed a Severino Oberdan General Defense Committee in early January 1918. In early February, Oberdan's local resolved that his attorney be given the floor at the upcoming district UMWA convention to state the accused miner's case. Moreover, they proposed that the UMWA form a "General Defense Committee" for all members of the union charged with crimes.

Second, the Defense Committee, along with Oberdan and his attorney, John Metzen, carried out an active solidarity campaign around the state. After sending out a letter to all UMWA locals, they toured the coalfields, raising funds and garnering statements of support from other miners. Just days before the Staunton meeting broke up in violence, in fact, Local 755 had voted to donate $100 to Oberdan's defense. What seemed to turn the tide against Oberdan in Staunton was the accusation, in a letter sent by District Attorney Knotts to all UMWA locals, that the miner was a dangerous IWW member. On learning of this letter, Oberdan wrote to his attorney, "The Spanish Inquisition has reached the State of Illinois." He then ominously warned his attorney, "I think you could find a remedy to this[;] otherwise the case of Frank Little may be repeated."[40] An outspoken opponent of the war, Little had been an IWW leader working to unionize Montana copper miners. Company-hired thugs had lynched Little in Montana the previous August.[41]

It is notable that as late as February 1918, a miner accused of sedition could openly fight for and win a degree of solidarity from other coal miners. To be sure, Oberdan had some advantages that Prager would not possess. He had worked in the Nokomis mines for a number of years. He had been elected pit committeeman several times by fellow miners, which suggests a certain degree of popularity. If he was accused of IWW-ism, he at least could not be labeled "German." Still, he was charged with speaking against President Wilson (it appears he actually denounced *Peter* Wilson of the Illinois Coal Operators Association) during a time when forced flag-kissings were carried out on mere suspicion of disloyalty. Thus, even as the spring of 1918 approached, in the face of massive pressure to put their class demands on hold, many miners still were capable of responding to an appeal for class solidarity.

Three days after the attack on Oberdan and Metzen, District 12 UMWA delegates assembled for their biennial convention. Though much of the debate centered around the strike penalty clause, ongoing problems of health and safety, and the recent wage increase, delegates did address themselves briefly to the Oberdan case and the rising tide of vigilante activity. Given the willingness of some miners to rally to Oberdan's cause, the role of union leadership became crucial in forestalling further mob violence. If UMWA officials were to take a clear stand against such attacks, the convention, which ran from February 19 to March 3, would be their best chance. In response to three local resolutions in support of Oberdan, however, the Resolutions Committee proposed that "no action be taken" on Oberdan's case since the charges against him were related to the war and not to his union activity. In discussion, the local chairman of Oberdan's Defense Committee presented evidence that the IWW might have had some role in producing Defense Committee literature. When one delegate called for Metzen to speak on the floor, Farrington ruled the miner out of order.

In summing up the case for the "hands-off" policy, Chairman George Mercer explained the committee's logic. The committee made the proposal "out of a feeling of charity more than anything else. We felt if we could not help the poor devil we did not want to hurt him." In any event, Mercer added, "it is a case that does not affect our organization."[42] Thus, just days after Oberdan, a UMWA member, had been tarred and feathered by other UMWA members in the violent aftermath of a stormy union meeting, Mercer insisted that miners were not affected by the case.

For his part, John Walker, who attended the convention in his capacity as president of the IFL, did take note of the Staunton events. Both in the convention and in a public statement to Illinois unionists issued on March 8, Walker explained his position "in light of recent happenings within our state." On one hand, Walker condemned the vigilante violence sweeping the coalfields. On the other hand, Walker's fervent support for the war worked to undercut his own position. Clearly concerned about the danger posed to the labor movement by the violence taking place between working people, Walker's written statement pointed out how employers had used the same methods against labor activists that superpatriots were now using against "disloyalists." The "labor oppressing interests," he noted, "have . . . organized gangs in the different communities, and hired thugs, gunmen and murderers to go along with them, labeled themselves 'Law and Order Organizations,' paraded themselves as patriots, and ran honest men out of town, sometimes beating them up and murdering them when the working man's only offense was that they were trying to compel unjust employers to give them honest treatment, decent wages, hours and conditions of employment." Working people who used these methods now in the name of patriotism, Walker wrote, were "establishing precedents which the enemies of common humanity and particularly the Trade Union movement will take advantage of to use against us and our movement in the future."[43]

Especially in light of the direct participation of business and professional elements in the Staunton mob, Walker's point is important. In Mt. Olive, as well, Mayor Collie Clavin defended the forced flag-kissings carried out by the local American Club by pointing to their social composition. They were not a "mob," he insisted. "The Club is comprised of our best citizens," he said. Although "best citizens" could well mean working-class residents in the coal towns of the region, it is important to note that just as anti-black lynch mobs often included local notables, patriotic vigilantism encompassed the entire community.

The connection that Walker made between mob violence and attacks on the unions is also worth noting. The generation of miners who listened to Walker at the convention had lived through a series of armed battles between workers and the agents of employers. From Virden in 1898 to the recent Ludlow massacre of 1914 to the lynching of Frank Little, it was highly plausible to southwestern Illinois coal miners in the World War I era that mob violence could be turned against them.[44]

While Walker did condemn mob violence to a point, the way he used his support for the war to get his point across created a highly contradictory message. At the convention, for instance, he cautioned UMWA delegates that "because a man disagrees with you, or even if he does wrong and commits a crime, don't . . . let mob law govern." This tended to suggest that victims of mob violence were guilty and only had to be punished in a proper manner. This point came through more glaringly in his public statement: "Do not under any circumstances participate with any others, no matter who they are, in the name of patriotism, forming mobs and taking the law in their own hands and running people out of town or beating them up or killing them, *without giving them a trial according to due process of law.*" By including the last phrase, Walker again emphasized the question of innocence or guilt of the victim rather than the very legitimacy of superpatriotic attacks.

Moreover, after first pointing out the dangers of mob violence and then complicating his opposition, Walker went on to present his own patriotic credentials in a way that seriously undermined his antiviolence argument. "I have absolutely no sympathy with any man or woman in our country," he declared, "who is either actively *or passively* opposed to our Government in this war or who is assisting in any way the military clique headed by the kaiser that are fighting our nation at this time." Walker boasted that "[t]here is no citizen in our nation that would go any farther towards preventing these people from wielding any influence that would injure our government in this crisis, or to penalize them where it was proven that they had done it, than I would." But it should be done legally, he concluded.[45] This argument, however, was indistinguishable from the pro-war rhetoric, spouted by top government officials in countless public speeches, which had spurred patriotic pugilism in the first place.

If UMWA officials offered confusing guidance on the dangers of mob violence, they provided a clear message on the subject of strikes. In a speech that the Wilson administration reprinted as a pro-war pamphlet, Frank Farrington instructed miners to stay on the job. "Our immediate and fundamental problem," said the District 12 president, "is to win the war. Commonplaces must be set aside for the time being." By the bland term "commonplaces," Farrington meant the variety of grievances that had spurred miners to walk out the previous year—the high cost of living, lack of washhouses, and unsafe working conditions. And, indeed, all of these were discussed by delegates in detail during the convention. "When the war is over and democracy is saved to mankind," Farrington continued, "we shall again take up the commonplace, strengthened and helped by our devotion to duty and fight . . . to the end that industrial justice shall prevail among men."[46] Simply put, miners would show their patriotism and then reap the benefits.

But the relationship between strikes and patriotism in the spring of 1918 proved more complicated than Farrington or anyone else might have imagined. For in March, southwestern Illinois miners added an intriguing piece to their patriotic repertoire: the flag strike. Miners made it known that they would work only at mines that displayed the American flag. When some employers failed to comply, mainly at some mines in the Belleville area, miners refused to work. At the Muren mine of the Southern Coal, Coke and Mining Company, for instance, the company had made arrangements for a flag pole, but there was a delay. Only "[a]fter a 40-foot pole was erected and a 4 x 6–foot flag unfurled" did the miners return to work. To complicate matters further, after this display of patriotism, miners were told they were subject to fines under the penalty clause.[47]

An examination of these intense bouts of patriotism in February and March suggests that more than simple love of country lay under the surface. At St. Louis and O'Fallon No. 2, for instance, where miners had found the "mysterious liquid," their decision to place a flag at the entrance apparently came after recognizing that "their loyalty was brought into question, and that it was their duty to demonstrate that they were loyal." In addition to saluting the flag, each miner was also required to buy at least one Liberty Bond. Similarly, at the big Southern mine at Shiloh, in

St. Clair County, miners offered to work one day without pay if the mine superintendent would turn over the receipts for the coal shipped to the Community War Camp Recreation Fund. An article explained that "[t]he mine workers resent being regarded as disloyal and are determined by this effort to lift the imputation from their shoulders."[48]

Miner Luke Coffey, who worked for Southern Coal in the Belleville area, recalled how a flag strike came about at his mine. One of the local coal operators, according to Coffey, "tried to place the rank and file of this movement in a bad light with the public." In the Belleville newspapers, "[t]hey started it, pro and con, that there were men who were disloyal during the war among the Belleville men." In response, Coffey said, "[e]very local union in Belleville took exception to that, and they had a right to. They had just finished a Liberty Bond drive, and 100 per cent of us bought bonds." The miners' locals sent delegations to the Belleville newspaper that had raised the charge of disloyalty, but "we did not have any luck." "I took the position," explained Coffey, "that if there were any damn pro-Germans in that part of the country they were among the coal operators and not among the miners. We came to the conclusion that if these other industries could afford to hoist Old Glory over their buildings, the coal operators had a right to float it over their tipples." When the owner of Coffey's mine refused to comply immediately with this request, the miners there walked out. Three days later, they returned to work when Southern's general manager agreed to consider their proposal.[49]

Viewing these events, the editors of *Coal Age* were struck by the intensity of Illinois miners' patriotism. "Illinois mine workers do nothing by halves," they noted. "Their loyalty seemed at a low ebb when the war started. Now it is at such a high tide that it sets the nation wondering."[50] The upswing of patriotic activity certainly owed much to the course of the war in Europe and the beginnings of American participation in battle. There had been a change over time. And yet, what *Coal Age* perceived as lack of loyalty—class consciousness—and then the presence of patriotic loyalty in March 1918 may have never been mutually exclusive. In fact, the flag strikes and related activity suggest that, to some extent, miners insisted on showcasing their patriotism because they were aware that it was seriously in question. In other words, fierce patriotism ("loyalty") and strong class solidarity ("disloyalty") fed upon each other.

By early April, the "white-hot mass instinct" sought by the Wilson administration was glowing brightly in Collinsville. In the year since the country had declared war, coal miners had marched in patriotic parades, bought Liberty Bonds, and saluted the flag. At the same time, the gap between their employers' growing profits and their own earnings led these patriotic miners to withdraw their labor-power, earning them charges of pro-Germanism. Adding to these tensions, none of the material questions facing them—the hazards of mining, inflation, the need for a washhouse—had been resolved. But President Farrington, backed up by the White House, had urged them to drop these "commonplaces." As southwestern Illinois coal miners struggled to navigate this web of conflicting feelings and loyalties, they gained and then lost a new co-worker by the name of Robert Paul Prager.

"White-Hot Mass Instinct"
The Lynching of Robert Paul Prager

In the early hours of April 5, 1918, a Collinsville mob hanged Robert Paul Prager. In the preceding weeks, rumors had surfaced that Prager planned, on German government orders, to blow up the Donk Brothers No. 2 mine in Maryville. The patriotic lynching capped a long ordeal in which miners paraded Prager down Collinsville streets, forcing him to kiss the American flag, sing patriotic songs, and affirm his loyalty to the war effort. Since Prager was one of the few to be lynched for explicitly patriotic reasons, his case drew considerable attention from contemporary observers, from Collinsville to Washington to London to Berlin. For several weeks that spring, the fate of one southwestern Illinois coal miner became part of national and even international politics. For working people in the region, Prager's death offered a grim reminder of just how divisive the "Great War" had become.

After traversing the Midwest for several years, residing briefly in St. Louis and working in a coal mine in Gillespie, Robert Paul Prager arrived in Collinsville in the fall of 1917. In the first few months in town, Prager attracted little attention and settled into his job working for baker Lorenzo Bruno and his wife. If he was an "outsider" to Collinsville in that he had just arrived, he was typical in many ways of young immigrant workers trying to make a way for themselves in the world. Considering the erratic employment that the coal mines normally offered, Prager's past as a "drifter" would not have been unusual.

In light of this, the suggestion that Prager came under suspicion because he was a "stranger" is itself somewhat suspect. His Collinsville neighbor Louis Fellhauer later explained that the two men had been friends for a year, indicating that they had been acquainted before Prager arrived in town. Prager did not live alone: he roomed at 208A Vandalia Street with a fellow miner, Valiso Vohella.[1] Another Collinsville resident who was fifteen when Prager arrived in town recalls him as a "very nice man," suggesting that he was known and accepted by others in the neighborhood of downtown Collinsville.[2]

It would also be said that Prager was stubborn and argumentative and that this had drawn attention to him. Of all the aspersions cast on Prager, this may be the only one that had some basis in fact. After Prager's death, when the wife of baker Lorenzo Bruno commented on Prager's character, she painted a generally complimentary portrait. In her view, Prager was "the best workman we ever had in the many years we are in business. He could do the finest bakery work, or any other work he was asked to do. And he was a fast worker, although he was somewhat of a physical cripple. He was very intelligent." There was one exception, however. According to Mrs. Bruno, "the only fault he had was a certain peculiarity in his makeup which, at times, made him quarrelsome with other people who did not agree with his ideas on ways of doing things. . . . But," she added, "as a rule he would soon get over his excitement and, when seeing that he was wrong, he would not hesitate to apologize for his queer actions."[3] The fact that Mrs. Bruno balanced her negative assessment of his stubbornness with an otherwise positive picture gives her observation the ring of truth. Still, possibly as a result of Prager's hot temper, Lorenzo Bruno fired Prager in early 1918.[4]

Once again he began to look for work, and once again he turned to coal mining. According to Mose Johnson, who asked him why he had sought work at the Maryville mine, Prager mentioned the hefty wages that miners were earning. Indeed, the unusually steady pace of work in the mines did mean higher than normal wages. Though Prager did not claim to have worked as a miner or loader, he did state that he had four years' experience as a timberman. On the strength of this, Donk Brothers Coal and Coke hired Prager as a night shift laborer, sometime in early March.

In the following month, Robert Prager became the object of suspicion by his coworkers. Prager was hardly the first German American to attract such suspicions, yet it is worth considering why attention focused on him. In the repressive atmosphere of early 1918, an obvious German accent could attract undue attention. While the region had a large number of German Americans, new immigration was dwindling by the years preceding the war. Miners whose first language was German were considerably fewer by this time than they had been two decades earlier. Though Collinsville and Maryville were filled with German Americans in positions of authority—Mayors John Siegel and Fred Neubauer, for instance—the propaganda of war put a spotlight on those who seemed obviously more "German" than "American." For instance, Albert Meyer, a Collinsville-born German American who grew up there during the war, recalls of a relative that "[h]e could talk good American and everything. The people who couldn't talk good American, they kind of stayed low. You know, they didn't get out and mix too much. Didn't want to have any trouble."[5]

The significance of the German language is also suggested by the recollections of William Jokerst, whose grandmother Mary Haupt Jokerst worked with Prager during his brief stint at the Bruno bakery. "Because Paul was from the same area [as she was] . . . they often spoke there at the bakery in German." Just as German Americans who bragged about the kaiser's successes were warned by family members to keep quiet, even those who persisted in speaking the language could find themselves in trouble. Since Mary Haupt Jokerst was "fond of her fatherland and she spoke German till she died, whether anybody liked it or didn't like it, and there was a lot of people that did not like that," her grandson explained, "she was warned several times that she should speak English."[6]

It was, however, not mainly Prager's German accent that seemed to invite attack in the waning weeks of March but his allegedly seditious political views. While a number of scholars have accepted contemporary allegations that Prager was a Socialist, the evidence is unclear on this point. Frederick Luebke writes that Prager was "given to Socialist doctrines," while Donald R. Hickey refers to him as "an active Socialist."[7] A Maryville miner testified later that Prager told him that the union leadership was persecuting him because he opposed the war and was a Socialist and for saying the country had made "a damn bad mistake" in entering the war.[8] The *Herald* wrote that "unconfirmed reports say violence began when Prager declared himself a socialist."[9]

On the other hand, a number of Prager's Odd Fellow brothers claimed that he was loyal to the war, disliked the kaiser, and applauded a patriotic speech at a St. Louis Odd Fellows rally.[10] After attending the rally, according to one Odd Fellow, Prager visited the St. Louis lodge and "in commenting on [Illinois grand master] Blood's speech told his friends there he would like to help hang the kaiser." The Hormonie Lodge was also at pains to deny charges, made public after his death, that Prager had failed to stand for the national anthem in the fall of 1917 at a public event in Niobara, Nebraska. Charles Specht, the lodge's treasurer, publicly responded to this charge by arguing that Prager could not possibly have been there at that time; he also pointed out that Prager had tried to enlist in the navy in St. Louis.[11]

The strongest testimony in support of Prager's patriotism came from John Pohl and his wife, who lived in St. Louis and worked in a bakery in Maryville. According to Pohl, "Robert Paul Prager was a crank on patriotism and was loyal at all times." How did Pohl know this? It seems that Prager had decided to display a large American flag in front of his rooming house on Vandalia Street. When Pohl objected—on what grounds is unclear—Prager not only argued with his fellow baker but also reported him to "Federal authorities." As a result, Pohl served thirty-two days in jail. Though he now had every reason to tarnish Prager's reputation, in the aftermath of the lynching, he "believed that it was his duty to tell the investigators what he knew of Prager's loyalty." Pohl's wife concurred, saying that "I was sick yesterday when I read of the untimely end of Prager. Although he caused my husband and myself much trouble I do not believe that it would be fair to this great nation of ours if I failed to tell of Prager's loyalty."[12]

Given the repressive atmosphere that developed by the spring of 1918, it is conceivable that a person in Prager's position, even if he did oppose the war, might well feel the need to offer reassuring signs of his patriotism. Display of the American flag, in particular, was seen to have a certain protective power. Joe Brabec of White City, who married a German-born woman, recalled that his German-born father-in-law was under suspicion during this period. "You know my father-in-law was a German," he said. "And a bunch of them youngsters one time decided to come tar and feather him, you know." Fearing the worst, "my mother-in-law, she call up a policeman or somebody." When the young patriots refused to leave, she said, "Come on and see," and invited them upstairs to his room. "He had American flags and everything. So he was a full-blooded American. Not German, no."[13]

On the other hand, in the minds of some workers, American patriotism, support for the war, and Socialism did not necessarily conflict. In the case of the Italian American pro-war Socialists from Benld, and for many other Socialists who rejected the St. Louis anti-war platform, the war became the ultimate Socialist crusade. That Prager may have shared these sentiments is suggested by Charles Otto, a fellow Collinsville boarder who commented that "although Prager was a radical socialist, he had said he was 'all for the United States' when this country entered the war."[14] Furthermore, Prager's reputed hatred for the kaiser would also not necessarily negate his Socialism.

In explaining why Prager met some resistance from UMWA Local 1802 in Maryville, Donald Hickey speculates that "his efforts to join the miners' union were unsuccessful, probably because he was an active socialist (it seems likely that his German birth was not the reason for his rejection since there were many German Americans in the Collinsville area who were union members)."[15] Though discussion of Prager's alleged Socialism must remain speculative, one can challenge Hickey's notion that miners who were active Socialists were unable to join Local 1802. Not only did a significant portion of Maryville miners vote Socialist in local elections but John Kettle, who ran on the local Socialist ticket and received one-third of the town's votes in the 1916 mayoral contest, also served as secretary-treasurer of the local.[16]

Of course, in the volatile politics of war, it may be that it had become difficult for Socialists to function openly in the union. This suggests that the role of Local 1802 president Joe Fornero should be given some attention. In the days leading up to Prager's death, Prager himself pointed to Fornero as the main force working against him. What little we know about Fornero is the following: Born in Italy in 1878, he arrived in the United States with his parents in 1897. By World War I, he had become a machine-runner at the Maryville mine and was married to the daughter of the former Maryville chief of police. He would die an early death in late 1918, of double pneumonia.[17] Though we have no direct evidence of his political views, a number of sources indicate that he and Mose Johnson were closely associated, suggesting that he may have been a Farrington supporter. It may well be that the dominant faction of the union, led by Fornero, helped seal Prager's fate. But simply to point to Prager's alleged Socialism explains little.

Clearly, what crystallized feeling against Robert Prager was the allegation that he planned to blow up the Maryville mine. The only "evidence" that led some miners to this conclusion surfaced in a reported conversation between Prager and John Lobenad, the mine examiner at the Maryville mine. After Prager's death, Lobenad submitted a statement, through Mose Johnson, to the coroner's jury. According to the *Herald*, it claimed that, presumably sometime in late March, "Prager had approached him [Lobenad] with the statement that he was studying to make himself a mine manager, and asking him various questions about the manager's work. Among other things, he asked to know what were the state laws and the organization laws regarding mine managers, something about the air controls in mines and about explosions and gases. The thing which excited the most suspicio[n] of Lobenad and the other miners was Prager's questioning regarding which way an explosion does the most damage to a mine."[18] This inquiry, if it indeed happened, became "proof" that Prager was a German agent. Around the same time, rumors also surfaced that a hoard of blasting powder had disappeared from the Maryville mine; however, no one ever came forward with evidence of this.

One can only speculate on John Lobenad's motives in this episode. It may be that Lobenad himself was under some suspicion of "slackerism," in that he had received an exemption from the draft on "industrial" grounds after having done a period of basic army training at Camp Taylor. In an interview with the *Herald*, Lobenad made a revealing comparison between his brief army experience and the work of coal mining. "There's a lot of difference between army life and digging coal," he told editor J. O. Monroe. "When that little captain tells you to do something, you do it," he said. "You don't stop to argue the case. And you don't call in the pit committee. And if you tried to strike you'd be put in the guardhouse on bread and water so quick you wouldn't know how it happened." His comment suggested that Maryville coal miners provided regular challenges to his authority. It also implied that miners somehow had it easy, which they may have resented, and that his subsequent release from the army, thanks to Donk's request, may not have sat well with them. In a similar case later that summer, Octavius Lumaghi, the coal operator's son who worked as an engineer and surveyor at No. 2, received a reclassification for his "industrial" status, incurring negative "street gossip."[19] In casting suspicion upon Prager, Lobenad may have been impelled, in part, by the need to draw attention away from himself.

Though at least some miners became suspicious of Prager, he did manage to win the confidence of three coworkers—John Tonso, Paul Schreiber, and Joseph Robino—who agreed to sign his union membership application and witness his statement that he was an experienced mine laborer.[20] In addition, when John Pohl attested to Prager's loyalty during the lynching trial, he also said that "many of the miners he knew thought Prager was innocent of the disloyalty charges."[21] Since Pohl worked in the tiny hamlet of Maryville, it is reasonable to think he would have been acquainted with at least some, if not many, of Prager's coworkers. Finally, if Prager did indeed make some attempt to talk politics with his fellow miners, as some sources suggest, that would imply a certain confidence on his part in the class consciousness of the Maryville miners. From what we know of the past actions of the Donk No. 2 miners, in relation to strike activity and the Socialist Party, that confidence would have been justified.

But whatever solidarity may have existed did not prevent other miners from singling out Prager for patriotic abuse in the early days of April. On Wednesday, April 3, as they left the washhouse at the Maryville mine, a group of miners accosted Prager. They not only forced him to kiss the flag, as they had done to coworker Theodore Schuster, but also marched him through Maryville, accused him of spying, and ordered him to leave town.[22] At this point, rather than buckle to local superpatriots, Prager decided to fight back and posted his "Proclamation to Members of Local Union No. 1802" around Maryville, a copy of which was found in his pants pocket when his body was cut down from the lynching tree.[23]

The very fact that Robert Prager decided to make such an appeal suggests a degree of self-confidence and boldness that is at odds with a picture of him as a mere victim. Prager made a dozen copies of the appeal and posted it around Maryville. To be sure, he took quite a risk in doing this. But it also must be accounted a courageous move, considering that his attackers had warned him to leave town. Not only was it an individual act of courage, but it reflects to some degree on the integrity of the UMWA. Though the proclamation failed to save his life, Prager did have reason to think that these union coal miners could be appealed to on the basis of class solidarity. He knew that the union had formal democratic procedures for handling all kinds of alleged transgressions by members. Thus, in addressing the members of Local 1802, Prager spoke to them as a fellow unionist and worker.

Though Prager insisted that he was a loyal American, his appeal did not focus on the spy charges surrounding him. Rather, he appealed to the miners to help him get his job back. This was his main beef with Fornero—that he had conspired to deprive Prager of his livelihood. He charged Fornero both with falsely accusing him of spying and with "the action taken by him to take away my daily bread." It seems that in the previous days, Fornero had taken some official action to prevent Prager from returning to the No. 2 mine.

In appealing to the miners, Prager now had a political problem: how could he make such charges against Fornero, a popular elected union official, and hope to win the support of those same miners who had elected Fornero? Perhaps alluding to this predicament, Frederick Luebke described Prager's approach as follows: "His emotions swept reason aside as he attacked Fornero as the chief author of his distress."[24] But in the hotly contested politics of the UMWA, charges against officials were part of the normal political culture. Miners in District 12 were used to a stream of "circulars" from besieged officials, failed candidates, and outraged workers. In and of itself, an attack on Fornero was not necessarily beyond the pale.

Second, and more important, the wording of his appeal, though it evokes Prager's strong emotions, conveys the approach of an experienced and disciplined unionist, not a wild, "unreasonable" accuser. The action of Fornero in branding him a spy and denying him employment, Prager argued, "is not the action or will of your people as a workingman's union. I have respect for your officials if on legal duty and will obey their commands to a letter. I have been a union man at all times and never once a scab, and for this reason, I appeal to you." Then Prager referred to the normal democratic channels of decision-making that the UMWA had developed to deal with charges by one member against another. "An honest working man as myself," he wrote, "I am entitled to a fair hearing of your committee. I ask in the name of humanity to examine me to find out what is the reason I am kept out of work."

Prager not only offered to submit to the collective discipline of the union but also assured the miners that he had followed correct union procedures in applying for membership. "I have kept the union informed from the very beginning of my employment at the Maryville mine. I have made and signed up two applications, the first with Mr. W. Wilhelm and the second with Mr. Ben Mettle. I have also had applications signed by three of your good standing members who have worked with me at various mines." This last statement suggests that Prager may have indeed worked in a mine in Gillespie before he came to Collinsville. Prager also explained that "I do not claim to be a practical miner"—that is, a miner or loader working at the face—"but do claim to have worked four years in the mines as a laborer, most of the time as a timberman."

Of course, Prager did take on the charge of disloyalty. "In regards to my loyalty," he wrote, "I will state that I am heart and soul for the good old U.S.A. . . . I am of German birth of which accident I cannot help," he continued, "and also declared my intention of U.S. citizenship, my second papers are due to be issued soon if I am granted." Despite this, he wrote, "I am branded as a liar in public by your President, Jim Farnaro [sic], by him I was branded a German spy which he cannot prove."

Prager also addressed the events of the previous day. Whereas Fornero and Mose Johnson later testified that they tried to place Prager in custody for his own safety, Prager presented a different view: Fornero "tried to have me arrested at Edwardsville, Maryville and Collinsville, and did not succeed in any of these places. . . . Mr. Farnaro," he wrote, "tried hard to have an angry mob deal with me. I was informed by him to leave my home at once and never come back to Maryville again if I knew what was good for my health."[25]

Among the various characterizations of Robert Prager by historians is Frederick Luebke's comment that the miner was "limited in intelligence." Not meant as a precise descriptive term, this allegation is one piece of Luebke's larger portrait of Prager as a hapless, naive, tragic victim. But even on its own terms, in light of Prager's written appeal to the miners, Luebke's appraisal falls short. The only "limitations" in Prager's writing are those of a worker who taught himself English. As for the authenticity of the document, the *Collinsville Herald* had no trouble believing that the miner wrote it and perhaps typed it himself. "The English shows distinct German twists," editor Monroe remarked, "which leads to the inference that he may have done it himself, or at least phrased it."[26] This would accord with Mrs. Bruno's characterization of Prager as "very intelligent."

What was the impact of Prager's appeal to the miners? Here again scholars can only speculate. Christopher Heilig claims that Prager's "attacks on the popular Farnaro [sic] only made them [the Maryville miners] madder. The note which Prager thought would help him just seems to have sealed his fate."[27] Certainly, a contingent of Maryville miners were incensed at Prager. Luebke suggests that as many as seventy-five "nurtured their animosities in their favorite Collinsville saloon" after reading Prager's appeal.[28] But nearly 600 mine workers were employed at Donk No. 2 in Maryville.[29] Even if Luebke's figure is correct, and it seems high in light of later testimony, the gang of miners stewing in anger at Prager that evening made up less than 15 percent of the Donk No. 2 workforce.

Given the history of struggle at the Maryville mine and the content of Prager's appeal for solidarity, it is likely that miners reacted in a variety of ways to Prager's words. Just as the reaction in Staunton's Local 755 to Severino Oberdan's appeal brought out a violent split in the union, Prager's appeal may have stirred similar feelings, even if miners did not openly vent them at the time or leave a written record of such sentiments. Heilig merely assumes, and does not attempt to prove, that the Maryville miners reacted in a uniformly negative way.

There is no doubt, however, that at around 9:30 that evening, a group of Maryville miners appeared on Prager's doorstep and ordered him to leave town. When Prager indicated that he would comply, the crowd began to break up. But for some reason, they made a fateful decision to call Prager out into the street. "All right, brothers, I'll go if you don't hurt me," Prager answered. "We won't hurt you," one of the miners reassured Prager. In retrospect, this comment takes on a bitterly ironic cast. But only in hindsight can one recognize here the beginning of a lynching. Neither Prager nor his harassers knew how the evening would end. After all, by this date, forced flag-kissings and patriotic singing had become fairly common in the coal towns of the region. Patriotic beatings were less common. The possibility of being covered with tar and feathers was certainly a painful and degrading prospect for Prager. Yet, rarely did any of these activities have a lethal outcome. Thus, the anonymous miner who reassured Prager may well have meant what he said.

Soon, a growing crowd paraded their patriotic spectacle down Main Street. It was at this point that Collinsville mayor John H. Siegel entered the scene. "As I left [a Liberty Loan meeting at the] opera house on the night of April 4," he testified, "a crowd of men was marching down the street; the central figure of the group being draped in a large American flag." As a measure of the level of official tolerance for such "harmless" patriotic activity, Siegel's next statement is revealing: "The crowd was orderly and there was no disturbance, so I crossed over to my [medical] office opposite the opera house."[30]

As this patriotic parade neared city hall, with the mayor safely ensconced in his office, miner John Hallworth, who had failed earlier to get Prager into police custody, approached police officer Fred Frost, who was patrolling the area. When Frost asked who Prager was, Hallworth explained "that the man was supposed to be a pro-German. Hallworth said he told Frost to take the man and lock him up." When some members of the crowd resisted Frost's attempt to seize Prager, Hallworth intervened, saying, "Let the officers have him boys." Frost then took Prager inside city hall and placed him in a jail cell.[31]

But like many a lynching victim who spent time in the "protection" of the authorities, Prager's stay in the city jail was quite brief. As the crowd, now grown to several hundred, milled around city hall, the character who would dominate the rest of the night's proceedings walked up Main Street toward the middle of town. This was Joseph Riegel, the former serviceman, Lumaghi No. 2 miner, wildcat striker, and now cobbler who would become the main defendant in the trial of Prager's accused lynchers.

By his own account, given in a detailed confession to the coroner's jury in the week after Prager's murder, Riegel recalled how he came upon the scene that night.[32] "I was standing in Schiller's Saloon, about ten o'clock in the evening," he said, "when the bartender got orders to close up." This order, made ostensibly to reduce the chance of mob violence that night, was relayed by a police officer who stopped by the saloon. Rather than accomplish this purpose, however, it seemed to swell the ranks of the mob.

"I finished drinking my glass of beer and went out," Riegel continued. "As soon as we got out, someone said that a bunch had caught a German spy and had taken him to the city hall." Walking up the street toward city hall, Riegel met up with a small crowd "talking about going to the city jail and getting this man. I stood with them and went over to the hall. . . . About that time I started," he added, "someone brought a flag and the crowd fell in behind it."[33] The flag bearer was Wesley Beaver, a Collinsville saloon porter, who would become one of the lynching defendants. Thus, as Prager sat in the city jail and an anxious crowd remained outside, Riegel, Beaver, and others approached with their own little procession.

Meanwhile, Mayor Siegel, notified that the police were holding Prager, left the comfort of his office, arrived at city hall, and tried to contact the county sheriff by phone. "Things were taking such a turn as to become menacing," he explained, "and I talked to the crowd in front of the City Hall for about five minutes."[34] Apparently, he urged people to go home and assured them that the spy charges against Prager would be handled by federal authorities.[35] Siegel then entered the building and went to see Prager. Given his actions at this point, the mayor seems to have shared the popular suspicion of Prager as a spy. "Prager answered several questions I put to him," Siegel recalled, "and showed me his permit [as an 'alien enemy'] to enter the barred zones." Siegel went back outside, presumably assured the crowd that he had the situation under control, and people began to leave. But as the crowd dispersed, Joseph Riegel's contingent arrived and led people back to the steps of city hall.

Among the faces in this increasingly restive crowd was miner Richard Dukes, who became a defendant in the lynching trial. Brother of James Dukes, whose death in France had grieved Collinsville one month earlier, Richard was scheduled to begin his own army training later that month. At the trial, Dukes testified that the "crowd acted as if it were mad." While they waited for word of Prager, Dukes recalled, he spoke briefly to Mayor Siegel, saying "that if the crowd got to Prager he wouldn't last fifteen minutes." Dukes "based this on the fact that the crowd looked so angry."

In contrast to Dukes's trial testimony, he admitted earlier before the coroner's jury that he might have made a more incriminating statement to Siegel, "something to the effect that *if he was permitted to go into the cell with Prager,* Prager wouldn't last fifteen minutes."[36] Since the coroner's jury proceedings were secret and could not be entered into evidence, Dukes was able to deny having previously made such an admission. Regardless of what he said, his testimony suggests the intense feelings of the crowd at city hall. Given the grief caused by his brother's fate and his impending induction, it would not be surprising for him to focus his anxiety and anger at a purported German spy.

With a large crowd again congregated before city hall, Riegel recalled, "Mayor Siegel was talking to the boys, telling them that they could not have the man. Just about that time someone came around the building and said he had been taken away." This rumor, quickly scotched, was the brainwork of two of the Collinsville police force who staged a fake getaway, without Prager in the car, hoping to convince the crowd to leave. After effectively speeding away in a police car, however, Officer Fred Frost returned shortly, thus ending the deception.

Before Frost returned, however, with the mayor insisting that Prager was indeed gone, some members of the crowd called his bluff and demanded they be allowed to search the city jail. At this juncture, Joseph Riegel assumed the leadership role that would prove fatal to Robert Prager. Stepping forward to speak to the mayor, he brandished his army discharge papers as irrefutable evidence of loyalty and asked if these credentials entitled him to lead the search. As Siegel testified, "Riegel told me he was an American soldier and they were going to get the man. I had learned Prager was taken away and made an investigation. I found he had been taken from the cell and was under the impression the police had spirited him away. I then gave my permission for the men to go into the City Hall." Prager had indeed been moved from his original cell—but only to another space in the same room. As Donald Hickey remarked of the mayor's testimony on this point, Siegel's alleged belief that Prager was really gone "seems improbable. It is unlikely that the police lied to the mayor or were mistaken concerning Prager's whereabouts. It seems more likely that both the police and the mayor knew that Prager was hiding in the basement and hoped he would not be found by the mob."[37] This then was the "protective custody" that Mose Johnson and James Fornero had offered Prager just days before.

Led by Riegel and the flag-bearing Wesley Beaver, a small crowd poured into city hall to find Robert Prager. After discovering an empty jail cell, the two ringleaders continued the search. After nearly giving up, they finally found the diminutive Prager hiding behind a store of sewer tile. "Beaver and I pulled him out and marched him upstairs," Riegel recounted. "When we got upstairs, we started him down to Main street, I holding his left arm and somebody else holding his right arm."

At the head of the procession, holding the flag aloft, were Beaver and James DeMatties, a nineteen-year-old miner who would also join the ranks of the lynching defendants. As the marchers turned left onto the St. Louis Road, toward the outskirts of Collinsville, Riegel said, "[W]e were making Prager kiss the flag and sing, though about all the singing he did was to repeat over and over the Star Spangled Banner and Three Cheers for the Red, White and Blue." Then, in an indication of the fury that lay behind these festive exercises, "somebody in the crowd hit [Prager] and knocked him down," Riegel said. Whether or not Prager knew that this was his death march, that he was literally singing for his life, still he had no choice but to get up and continue, as darkness enveloped the grim parade.

Once Prager became a prisoner of this procession, the Collinsville police were of no help to him. As Riegel and others dragged Prager out of city hall, one officer walked away to answer the phone. As for Officer Frost, he testified that he ran onto "Main street to follow, but went east by mistake and by the time he found the other officers and got a machine [automobile] the crowd was out of sight." Later, apparently, the four officers located the marching crowd and trailed a safe distance behind.

Once the marchers crossed beyond Collinsville city limits, the police returned to town, legally excused of duty.[38]

If their actions seem comical, akin to the antics of the Keystone Kops, it must be said that they clearly contributed to Prager's demise. Later they were charged with neglect of duty, though the charges were dropped once the lynching defendants were acquitted. But it is hardly surprising that the police, who answered to the mayor, did not take stronger measures to protect Prager. After all, Mayor Siegel himself had taken the lead in trying to form a vigilance committee the previous December. The city authorities, through the local Council of Defense, were intimately involved in hunting down alleged disloyalists. In effect, they had sanctioned the forced flag-kissing that had become commonplace by April. When the mayor first came upon Prager and thought merely that "the crowd was orderly and there was no disturbance," he implied his acceptance of patriotic vigilante action as legitimate. When the "white-hot" atmosphere that had developed by early April began to melt away the distinction between officially sanctioned flag-kissings and murder, the mayor and his "law enforcement" team were politically impotent to do anything about it.

After Prager's tormentors turned south on the St. Louis Road out of town, they passed by the Hardscrabble Saloon and a standing streetcar, full of passengers headed back into the middle of Collinsville. One of the passengers inside, Maude Gilmore, saw her father, Calvin Gilmore, in the crowd, recognizing his face that was illuminated by the lights of the stationary car. The younger Gilmore was returning from Belleville, where she and some other young women from nearby Caseyville had gone to visit a sick friend. Like a growing number of young Collinsville working-class women, Gilmore was a factory worker, employed at the National Carbon Works in Signal Hill.[39] Another passenger on the car recalled her "calling out of the window to her father in the crowd and telling her father to get on the car."[40] He refused to stop and continued along with his patriotic counterparts, down the St. Louis Road. Within weeks, Calvin Gilmore would be one of the eleven charged with lynching Robert Prager.

Others, however, who had come as far as the Hardscrabble now decided to call it a night. Miner William Brockmeier, for instance, had followed as far as this point. In the tumultuous events of the 1917 strike wave, he had played a crucial role in mobilizing solidarity among miners at Lumaghi No. 3 for the striking smelter workers. In publicly threatening to launch a sympathy strike of miners, Brockmeier may well have been suspected of disloyalty and pro-Germanism. What thoughts crossed his mind that night as he confronted the specter of another German American miner accused of even greater infamies? As he testified, and as was confirmed by a witness on the streetcar, Brockmeier got on the streetcar at the Hardscrabble and went home. Like Calvin Gilmore, however, he too would join the ranks of the lynching defendants.

After the departure of some miners thinned the ranks of the crowd somewhat, they continued on into the night. Leaving the Collinsville police at the city limits, Prager's captors continued about a quarter-mile along the St. Louis Road until they reached the crest of a hill. Here Prager's patriotic punishment was to take place. Though some individuals may have had murderous intentions from the beginning, the common plan seems to have been to administer a coat of tar and feathers. Consequently, a young auto mechanic named Harry Linneman who had followed Prager's tormentors in an automobile received orders to visit a nearby farm and fetch some tar and feathers. Linneman, along with seven young companions, rode to the farm, located near Monk's Mound, but could not find any tar; they then returned to the scene. The assembled crowd was illuminated by the bright headlights of druggist Louis Gerding's car. As they gathered around a large hackberry tree at the top of the bluff, someone found a towing rope in the trunk of Linneman's car. At this moment, whatever various individuals had intended, the remaining crowd became a lynch mob.

From this point forward, the action at the hackberry tree took on the classic trappings of a ritualized execution. Someone tied a noose and ran it up over a large tree branch. A voice called out that everyone present should touch the rope, symbolizing their collective responsibility for this solemn act. The rope was placed around Prager's neck. Mob members made one last attempt to extract a confession from Prager, peppering him with questions about his alleged bomb plot, asking why he had stolen powder from the Maryville mine. Riegel, the main interrogator, recalled that "[t]hen a lot of fellows in the crowd told me to ask him if he had any partners. I didn't know just what they meant, but I asked him and he said 'three.' Then the crowd wanted to know who they were. He shook his head. Then they wanted to know if he meant relatives and he shook his head." By this time, Prager was growing weary from his ordeal. "He didn't seem to want to talk anymore," Riegel said.[41]

With the noose tightened around Robert Prager's neck, Riegel pulled down on the towing rope but barely budged the miner's body. "Come on fellows, we're all in on this," he yelled; "let's not have any slackers here."[42] A number of others then joined Riegel and yanked Prager into the night air. But they were not finished. "His hands were not tied when we pulled him up," Riegel explained, "and he caught hold of the rope. He didn't say anything, but there was a funny noise in his throat. We let him down." Feet back on the ground, Prager asked to write something to his mother and father.

Led by twenty-two-year-old Charles Cranmer over to Louis Gerding's car, Prager dictated his parents' Dresden address, which Cranmer took down. Then Prager composed his brief farewell note. "He wrote very slowly," Riegel noted, "but it wasn't much when it was all written—just a little goodby to his parents." "Liebe Eltern," Prager wrote, "Ich muss heute den 4-4-18 sterben. Bitte betet fur mich, meine lieben Eltern. Das ist mein letze Brief oder Lebenzeugen von mir. Euer lieber Sohn und Bruder, Robt. Paul." Even as they granted Prager this tiny measure of dignity, they refused to drop their suspicious stance for a moment. As Riegel recounted, "We partly translated the note as we stood there—I can read a little German—to see that he wasn't putting anything over on us." "Dear parents," began the object of their scrutiny, "I must this fourth day of April, 1918, die. Please pray for me, my dear parents. This is my last letter and testament. Your dear son and brother, Robert Paul Prager."[43] Prager handed the pencil back to Cranmer and gave Riegel the note. He told Riegel "that he wished we would see that it got to his parents, and somebody asked him how it could be done. He answered[,] through Washington."

Then Prager made his final request. Granted permission to pray, he knelt down and offered a final prayer in German. According to a witness, "he asked forgiveness for his sins and asserted his innocence of disloyalty."[44] Prager then walked calmly back to the tree and the hanging rope. It was once again fastened around his neck, and somebody bound his hands with a handkerchief.

For the last time, the crowd pelted Prager with accusing questions. Once again, Prager remained silent. "Well, if he won't tell," someone finally said, "string him up." Maintaining his patriotic loyalty to the bitter end, Prager offered his dying wish to the mob. "All right, boys," he said, "go ahead and kill me, but wrap me in the flag when you bury me."[45] Now, pulling down hard on the rope, a handful of people ended Robert Paul Prager's life.

Who lynched Prager? Drawing mainly on the testimony given at trial, twenty-nine individuals can be placed at the lynching tree at the time Prager's murder took place. What proportion these comprise of the entire mob is unclear. Eyewitnesses at the trial offered estimates of the total size of the mob ranging from 30 to 100. The two individuals who gave these estimates were both eyewitnesses and rival Collinsville newspaper editors. It is reasonable to assume that both J. O. Monroe of the *Herald,* who gave the higher number, and A. W. Schimpff of the *Collinsville Advertiser,* who offered the estimate of 30–40, had a motivation to inflate the size of the crowd so as to diminish the significance of their own participation. Because of this, the lower figure is probably more accurate. If so, then the twenty-nine may be a majority of those who remained at the tree during Prager's fatal hour.[46]

One witness claimed that the group consisted "primarily of young men of draft age."[47] For fifteen mob members whose age can be either identified or roughly guessed, the average age was nineteen. These include five of the defendants: Joe Riegel, twenty-eight; Charles Cranmer, twenty-two; James DeMatties, nineteen; Cecil Larremore, seventeen; Frank Flannery, nineteen. (Six other defendants were most likely not at the lynching scene.) As in the cases of Livingston, Glen Carbon, and White City, youth played a conspicuous role in doling out patriotic justice on the streets. The fact that they were the ones who faced the possibility of trench warfare in Europe certainly accounts, to some degree, for this pattern. In addition, the contradictory dynamic suggested in the case of Joe Riegel would have been felt by young workers most of all. The main initiators of the mine drivers' strikes in the fall of 1917 were mainly young men. Flannery, DeMatties, and Larremore may well have belonged to this group.

On the other hand, half of the known individuals present at the hackberry tree were not particularly young. In addition to those whose age is unknown, there were a number of older and more established figures present. These included editors Monroe and Schimpff, electrician and alderman Notley Shoulders, mine engineer John Reese, and druggist Louis Gerding. In addition, during the trial, J. M. Bandy, who defended the accused lynchers, implied that other unnamed older men were present at the tree. In his closing statement, Bandy said that "[t]his hanging was done by old heads. The miners were afraid Prager would blow up the mine, and they put him out of the way."[48]

What about the gender composition of the lynch mob? It was certainly not unusual for women to take part in lynchings when they were carried out by the entire community. In the 1911 lynching of a black steelworker in Coatesville, Pennsylvania, for instance, nearly half of a crowd of 5,000 spectators were women. Nor was it unthinkable for a woman to stand trial for lynching, as a Wisconsin woman did in 1890 for the alleged retribution killing of her husband.[49] Moreover, in related types of "crowd action," women have historically played a prominent role.[50] As the next chapter indicates, women are known to have taken part in the violence attending the miners' rank-and-file rebellion in southwestern Illinois during 1919. Still, there is no available evidence that women took part in Prager's lynching.

As for the ethnic makeup of the mob, it is possible to draw an admittedly very rough portrait. Some thirteen of the twenty-nine can be identified as of "old immigrant" background, leaving aside Germany. Another thirteen appear to have been German Americans. The remaining three had names that suggested, respectively, Italian, Polish, and Greek ancestry. The disproportionately small number of such "new" immigrants on the scene is hardly surprising. Though these working people had a wide variety of political views and work experiences, they were more likely to share with Prager a lack of citizenship status and to have undergone their own experiences of victimization and scapegoating.

In addition, the presence of German Americans in the mob is important. These included prominent individuals such as editor Schimpff, garage owner Earl Bitzer, and Albert Kneedler, whose father had been mayor of Collinsville. They also included miner Joe Riegel, barber Bernhard Mueller, and horseshoer Paul Heim. The first case exemplifies those who were at least close to the local ruling establishment. It is likely that the second list comprised first-generation Americans, whose parents had been born in Germany. Riegel's passing comment that he knew some German suggests this possibility. It is likely that the war put particular pressure on this group of young people—who inhabited two worlds—to demonstrate their loyalty. In any event, the prominent presence of German Americans at the tree that night defies a simple characterization of the lynching as "anti-German."

What about the social and occupational background of the lynchers? Of the sixteen for whom occupation could be determined, there were three miners, two newspaper editors, and one each of the following: auto mechanic, stockyards worker, cobbler, barber, saloonkeeper, electrician, mine engineer, druggist, horseshoer, garage owner, and soldier (Kneedler). Naturally, little can be concluded from such a slim profile of a mob that may possibly have numbered 100. Yet a few features stand out. One is the sheer variety. For all the descriptions of "miners" having lynched Prager, they make up less than 20 percent of this list. Of course, it is likely that a certain number of the unnamed mob members, perhaps a majority, were miners. Given that they were executing Prager for allegedly plotting to blow up the Maryville mine, the group who helped Riegel pull down on the rope may have been mainly miners. And it is also possible that the three "new immigrants" were such. Still, the participation of many other workers, as well as more professional types, suggests that the lynching was truly a community affair.

Another way of looking at the participation of miners is to examine who was not at the lynching tree. Of the eleven defendants who went to trial in May, seven were coal miners. Yet, the trial testimony showed that four of these—John Hallworth, William Brockmeier, Richard Dukes, and Enid Elmore—were not at the scene of the lynching. They all went home early, before the harassment of Prager turned lethal. It may be that, more than observers realized, miners had listened to John Walker when he pointed out the dangers that mob violence posed to their own movement.

Aside from these general speculations on the composition of the lynch mob, what light can be shed on the motivations of the acknowledged leader of the mob, Joseph Riegel? "As I walked home [from the scene of the lynching]," recalled Riegel, "I began to wonder a little why we had done it. The liquor in me I suppose was dying down and I was getting sober." Thinking about the dead Prager, Riegel reflected "that I had never seen him before and I didn't know any harm he had done.... But it didn't worry me any," he added. "I thought it was kind of foolish, that was all." After a night of restless sleep, Riegel "thought about it a good deal more, and thought again how foolish it was. I didn't talk to anybody about it, but when I found out I had to tell about it, I made up my mind I would tell everything I knew." Having heard Riegel speak these words before the coroner's jury a week after the lynching, *Herald* editor J. O. Monroe remarked that "[l]istening to him, one was led to believe that if he had been asked to climb the tree he would have done so without question and would have adjusted the noose with the same automatic response. Had he been hypnotized he could not have responded more readily to immediate suggestion."[51] Indeed, Riegel did give the impression of someone who was obeying an outside force.

Why did Riegel act this way? In August, the German American army veteran and coal miner had endured taunts of pro-Germanism in order to support fellow miners in a fight with their common employer. He tried to be a loyal American and yet was frustrated in the attempt by his own unavoidable "subversive" action. Perhaps it makes perfect dialectical sense that this same rebel, precisely because of that rebelliousness, felt a compulsion to demonstrate his working-class Americanism to the hilt in April. For Riegel, the Prager lynching may have unconsciously provided the perfect opportunity to affirm his loyalty to the nation, once and for all. Perhaps his intense need for such affirmation drove him through the events of that night. If such an unconscious dynamic were at work, it might help explain his sense of being driven by an inexplicable force.

Beyond Riegel's motivations and the immediate context of the lynching, it is worth noting that in choosing to hang Robert Prager from a tree, Collinsville lynchers were drawing on a longstanding tradition of vigilantism in American history. Lynching was used not only against African Americans as a racist means of maintaining white supremacy but also against Americans of European descent at least as far back as the American Revolution.[52] Especially in the smaller towns of the West and Midwest, men and women were lynched for horse-stealing, thievery, murder, and immorality, among other reasons.[53] "Regulator" movements had operated in Illinois during the early and mid-nineteenth century. In fact, from 1882 to 1903, eleven whites were lynched and ten blacks.[54] During the World War I period, Illinois led the nation in murderous attacks on blacks from East St. Louis to Chicago. It was a riot against blacks in Springfield, Illinois, in 1908 that led to the founding of the National Association for the Advancement of Colored People (NAACP).[55]

Lynching has traditionally been viewed as a rather exotic phenomenon, particularly because of the highly ritualized form it can take. The role of ceremony and ritual in the case of Prager was certainly evident. The relatively large number of people involved, the highly organized and controlled nature of the execution, and the sense among the lynchers that they were acting as a surrogate for the law in upholding the safety of the community all fit the model of what W. Fitzhugh Brundage has typologized as the "mass mob." As opposed to the "private posse," which typically hunted down the accused criminal like a dog, or the "terrorist mob," which did not necessarily kill the victim, the mass mob came closest to performing the rituals of a public execution.[56]

While a focus on the ritual aspects of lynching is useful for making sense of a seemingly inexplicable and irrational practice, it can also obscure the essential brutality involved. As one scholar has commented, "[T]o say that a riot is a ritual is almost to smooth over its violence or to deflect attention from the sheer power struggles involved in this killing in the streets."[57] Similarly, after all was said and done on that night on the Collinsville bluffs, a group of people killed another human being.

To the degree that lynchings and associated violence have generally acted to maintain the political, economic, and social status quo, it is essential to view the killing of Prager not merely as a ritualized event with deep roots in history but instead as an inevitable result of the mobilization for war. Scholars of lynching are beginning to recognize that one needs to look at lynchings in their specific historical contexts rather than seek a single comprehensive explanation for lynching as a phenomenon.[58] The rising tide of vigilantism culminating with the Prager lynching is one such pattern that cannot be explained without a thorough understanding of the particular pressures brought on by war. Given the unrelenting patriotic campaigns carried out by public authorities from the White House to the mayor of Collinsville, it is a wonder that more lynchings did not result.

When Prager's lynchers tugged down hard on that one-inch towing rope in the early morning of April 5, they not only reached back into history but also catapulted Collinsville, Illinois, into the national and international political arenas. News of the lynching quickly spread over the wires. In Washington, Prager's death was immediately discussed by the Wilson cabinet. The Collinsville events became part of the ongoing debate over the proposed Sedition Act. They spurred a range of popular responses nationwide, expressed in a flurry of letters to top government officials and in public statements of protest. Finally, the lynching hit headlines in Berlin and received the prompt attention of the German government.

How did the Wilson administration respond to news of Prager's patriotic murder? This is itself a matter of some debate. Some thirty years after Prager's death, CPI chief George Creel reminisced about the outbreak of mob violence during the war. Creel argued that the Republican-dominated "superpatriots" in private organizations "were chiefly responsible for the development of a mob spirit" in America, which continued, he wrote, until the Prager lynching. Then, according to Creel, "I went to President Wilson at once, and his public denunciation of the mob spirit sobered the people as a whole, if not the superpatriots."[59] Of course, the government's campaign to develop a "white-hot mass instinct," led by President Wilson and by Creel himself, had contributed to the atmosphere favorable to patriotic lynching. Furthermore, the reaction of the White House was not encouraging.

The president made little immediate effort that spring to stem the rise in vigilante violence. On April 5, Wilson did meet with his cabinet to discuss the Prager lynching. After the meeting, however, Attorney General Thomas Gregory informed the press that the federal government would leave the matter to the Illinois authorities. Then Gregory gave what became the most common explanation of the lynching: "While the lynching of Prager is to be deplored, it cannot be condemned. The Department of Justice has repeatedly called upon Congress for the necessary laws to prevent just such a thing as happened in the Illinois town."[60] That is, if there were stricter laws on the books to prevent free speech, then mobs would not have to resort to violence.

The following day, Wilson spoke in Baltimore at the opening of the third Liberty Loan. The president made no reference to the lynching, even in oblique terms. Faced with the German battle offensive, he emphasized the need for "Force, Force to the utmost, Force without stint or limit, the righteous and triumphant Force, which will make Right the law of the world."[61] It would be over three months before Wilson spoke out explicitly against lynching.

In the weeks and months following Prager's death, a number of private citizens and local notables expressed their opinion on the Prager lynching in letters to the editor and to Wilson administration officials. Some of the letters reflected Attorney General Gregory's public statement that Congress was partly to blame for not having passed a Sedition Act. As one man wrote to the New York Times, he condemned the lynching but also contended that it was "the direct result of our namby-pamby policy of dealing with spies and traitors."[62] A Missouri circuit court judge wrote to Gregory that "unless persons who are guilty of acts of disloyalty, are promptly convicted and executed, the hope there will be no repetitions elsewhere of the Collinsville lynching, will not be realized."[63] Similarly, the chairman of the Council of Defense of Caldwell, Texas, wrote his congressmen calling for "a law inflicting proper punishment on disloyal citizens and aliens, and in severe cases, give them the death penalty." Only this would "avoid a repetition of acts of violence such as occurred at Collinsville. . . . You must punish them lawfully," he warned, "or the people will work on them individually."[64]

While these individuals blamed legal laxity for the violence, others pointed to hysterical war propaganda. Helmer Feroe of Des Moines, Iowa, sent two clippings to the attorney general. The first contained news of the Prager lynching; the second reported on a speech at the Des Moines Chamber of Commerce given by Henry Waters, associated with the *Kansas City Star*. "Every farmer in Iowa ought to plant an acre of hemp," Waters was quoted as saying. "That acre of hemp should be carefully harvested this fall and woven into enough ropes to hang every pro-German in the country." In Feroe's opinion, the Prager lynching was "the logical result of such distempered and criminally tainted assertions."[65] In a similar vein, a German American attorney from New York blamed the Prager lynching on "mad agitators" who called for extreme measures against Germans. "They are breeding riots and lynching and undermining law, order and justice," he wrote.[66]

Whereas the attorney general held the lack of sedition law responsible for mob violence, George Creel pointed the finger at "German sympathizers." Two days after the Prager lynching, Creel's "eighth message from the United States Government to the American people" appeared in magazines across the country. Rather than caution Americans against violence, it alleged that even violence against "pro-Germans" was cooked up by none other than "pro-Germans" themselves. This was a desperate attempt to absolve the government of any responsibility for the mob spirit that had developed. For its sheer audacity, Creel's piece is worth quoting at length:

> The German sympathizers in America have been taking advantage of every class quarrel and religious dissension and racial problem and political quarrel, in order to divide and disunite us. They are encouraging the campaign against price-fixing and persuading the farmer that he has a grievance in his $2.20 wheat. They have thousands of propagandists among the negroes, exciting them with stories of impossible atrocities committed against the colored people in the South. They are equally busy with attempts to incite the whites to negro lynchings, even while they are assuring the negro that under the Kaiser the colored race will have social equality with the whites. . . .

German agents are at work inciting the I.W.W., organizing leagues of conscientious objectors, and preaching violence in the West, while other German agents are leading mobs to tar and feather the victims of this German propaganda of social unrest.[67]

Applied to the Prager case, this argument would lead to the absurd conclusion that Joseph Riegel was secretly working for the German government when he egged on the mob in front of city hall. Needless to say, Creel's message to "unite and win" most likely had the effect of deepening the blind hatred for anyone suspected of disloyalty.

Though Prager proved to be the last victim of patriotic murder in southwestern Illinois, the wake of his lynching saw an upsurge of violence against German Americans and opponents of the war. In Conant, local "patriots" tarred a seventy-five-year-old Lutheran preacher of German descent for alleged disloyalty in a sermon.[68] Since many German Lutheran churches still conducted services in German, these became special objects of attack. Three weeks after the Prager lynching, Governor Frank Lowden referred to those who had interfered "with religious services conducted in German, by threats of violence under the guise of patriotism," and he vowed to "suppress mob rule whatever the form."[69] The day after Prager was lynched, a railroad worker in Mounds was "severely beaten" by some 300 coworkers for refusing to blow a whistle opening the third Liberty Loan campaign.[70] The same day in Steeleville, Edmund Speckman, a young farmer accused of "pro-Germanism," avoided tar and feathering only with the help of fifteen friends with shotguns and rifles who barricaded themselves inside his home.[71]

Along with this rise in the incidence of violence came an increasingly repressive stance by some area government officials. Across the river in St. Louis, for instance, Missouri governor Frederick Gardner, speaking at a Liberty Loan rally, threatened to place Missouri under martial law if he got word of any organized "pro-German" movement in the state. "A pro-German is no better than a spy," Gardner maintained. For him, these "traitorous wretches" included not only individuals who allegedly blew up coal mines and factories but "those who are against us." The worst examples of this type, added the governor, were Lenin and Trotsky of Russia. If Gardner had to impose martial law, "pro-Germans . . . would face a firing squad and thus suffer the fate which traitors so richly deserve."[72]

Similarly, a paid advertisement appeared in the *Collinsville Herald* several weeks later aimed at "slackers." These included men who would not serve in the army and also a man or woman who "does not take all the Liberty Bonds that he or she can possibly buy." These *"wretched creatures of feeble brain and feeble spine,"* the ad told readers, " . . . are not fit to live in this community, or *anywhere else in America.* They are not fit to *live at all."*[73] If there were ever a public call to patriotic lynching, this was it.

When George Creel wrote about the "superpatriots" and their responsibility for mob violence, he might have been thinking of this type of material, which was most likely not issued by the government. On the other hand, the ad appears with an official "Right Hand of Patriotism" seal used in government material, and it calls on citizens to buy Liberty Bonds, as did official representatives of the government. Similarly, Governor Gardner spoke at an official Liberty Bond rally. In neither case is there evidence that any federal government official criticized publicly what was being said.

April 1918 also saw a renewed campaign to eliminate the German language. The National Security League led the charge by asserting that "there is no longer any such thing as a German-American."[74] Governor Lowden lent credence to this in an address to the National Education Association, when he stated that "[y]ou do not get the true American spirit if you are educated in a foreign tongue. The English tongue is the language of liberty, of self-government and of orderly progress under the law."[75] Public schools eliminated German instruction in St. Louis, East St. Louis, and Edwardsville.[76] In Collinsville, the Holy Cross Lutheran School considered dropping German. Reverend H. A. Klein of Holy Cross supported the move, saying that "[i]t is in line with the thorough Americanization of our public and semi-public institutions."[77] In the face of rising violence, more and more German Americans publicly took part in the campaign against their own cultural heritage.

Many newspapers did denounce the Prager lynching. But even in denouncing it, they gave much ground to the lynchers. Following Gregory, most editors called for a stronger sedition law and seemed mainly concerned with the negative impact the lynching would have on America's "democratic" image. Among others, the *Chicago Herald, Chicago Tribune, St. Louis Post-Dispatch,* and *Cleveland Press* all called for stronger sedition laws. The *Tribune* argued, for example, that in order "to avoid" mob violence, Americans "must insist upon the repression of inflammatory sedition."[78] The *Collinsville Herald* warned that "there will be more of these lynchings unless Congress hurries to amend the laws dealing with this sort of thing."[79] "If there is one lesson above all others in the Collinsville affair," said the *St. Louis Republic*, "it is that Congress should act promptly in passing the espionage bill now before it. Unless we take steps to punish sedition legally, it will be done illegally."[80]

Numerous commentators also referred to the lynching as a "stain" on America. The *St. Louis Globe-Democrat*, for instance, charged the lynchers with "bringing shame on America, belying our proud profession of being a land of law and justice."[81] Illinois governor Frank Lowden also focused on how the Germans could use the Prager lynching for propaganda. "Even if Prager was guilty," he said, "the place in all the world where the act of the mob would bring the greatest satisfaction is the imperial court in Berlin."[82] It was as though the worst part of the lynching was not that an innocent man had died but that his lynchers had embarrassed the country.

The U.S. Senate took immediate notice of the Prager lynching. On April 5, Senator William Borah urged speedy passage of the Sedition Act, for "already the news comes over the wire that patriotic citizens are taking the law into their own hands." "If we do not do our duty," he warned his fellow senators, "the impulses of loyal men and women will seek justice in rougher ways."[83] Other senators, however, called for "rougher" measures. Henry Cabot Lodge of Massachusetts claimed that alleged spies "have been treated altogether too delicately." Echoing the proposals of Missouri's governor, he preferred to "try them by a court-martial and shoot them." Moreover, Lodge launched an attack on everything German. "Anyone who cherishes the idea that we can separate the German people from the Kaiser is cherishing the merest delusion," he said.[84]

On the Monday following the lynching, Senator Lawrence Sherman of Illinois raised Prager's case again. Sherman did favor sedition legislation, but he rejected the argument that it could stop mob violence. Only strict law enforcement could prevent the violence. He condemned the Collinsville lynchers as "a drunken mob masquerading in the guise of patriotism" and blamed "this ghastly tragedy" on the "inefficiency of municipal government." Sherman singled out Mayor Siegel as "a spineless mayor who is mainly concerned about his reelection." "Why did he not protect the victim?" he asked. At the same time Sherman lambasted

the lynchers, he made sure to demonstrate his own "loyalty" by saying
that "I have no apologies to make for Mr. Prager; he made a mistake: he
owed this country a better return for the protection it had given him."[85]
As Donald Hickey notes, Sherman's choice of words was "unconsciously
ironic."[86] In addition, they illustrate the severe limits within which civil
liberties "moderates" like Sherman operated. Each defense of free speech
was coupled with an attack on it.

The Socialist Party responded to the lynching with a public protest.
With national headquarters and eleven branches in Chicago, twenty-two
around the state, and at-large members in some thirty-nine towns, totaling some 8,000 members in 1918, the Socialists were keenly interested
in defending democratic rights in Illinois. Three days after the Prager
lynching, the Chicago locals of the party held an outside meeting at which
the attack was discussed. The circumstances of the meeting itself illustrate the repressive atmosphere created by the government. After reluc-
tantly granting a meeting permit, the city warned the Socialist Party leaders not to say anything disloyal. Police surrounded the gathering, listening
for any remark that they could use to close down the meeting. According to press reports, executive secretary of the party Adolph Germer "dep-
recated the mob violence that has been shown recently in Southern Illinois, and said that a man could not be held responsible for the place of
his birth."[87]

In a letter sent to President Wilson the following day, perhaps decided
on after the meeting, Germer appealed to Wilson to take a stand against
such mob violence. His letter provides a revealing look at Germer's political thinking at this time. In contrast with his public stand against the
war on the basis of class solidarity, Germer sang a sharply different political tune. "Mobs," wrote Germer, "arouse a bitter National hatred and
divide our own Country into conflicting and embittered groups." There
was ample evidence for this statement, and yet it also implied, oddly
enough for a Socialist, that the "Country" was not already divided into
conflicting classes. Germer also charged that Prager's lynchers "have no
confidence in the integrity of American institutions." This suggested that
perhaps there was some actual "crime" committed by Prager, which the
"normal" channels of justice might have prevented. On the other hand,
Germer wrote that rather than acting out of "devotion to the country,"
the miners killed Prager out of "savage prejudice," presumably against his
German birth. Finally, Germer echoed Governor Lowden's words in

claiming that "[b]rutal mob violence gives the greatest possible comfort to the enemy."[88] Once again, Germer's reference to "the enemy," though perhaps purposefully vague, could easily be understood to mean Germany. As a whole, Germer's letter indicates the hesitancy of a leading Socialist during this most repressive phase of the war.

The best-known Socialist, Eugene Debs, also condemned the lynching of Prager but did so without flinching from his militancy. Giving his famous speech in Canton, Ohio, in June 1918 that landed him in the Atlanta federal penitentiary, Debs offered a much more critical view of American "democracy" than did Germer. "They tell us that we live in a great free republic; that our institutions are democratic; that we are a free and self-governing people," Debs mocked. "This is too much, even for a joke." Instead, Debs proclaimed, "our hearts are with the Bolsheviki of Russia.... They have laid the foundation of the first real democracy that ever drew the breath of life in this world."[89] In denouncing the Prager lynching, Debs began by referring to the deadly effects of the vicious campaign against the IWW. "It is only necessary to label a man 'I.W.W.,'" Debs warned, "to have him lynched as they did Praeger [sic], an absolutely innocent man. He was a Socialist and bore a German name, and that was his crime. A rumor was started that he was disloyal and he was promptly seized and lynched by the cowardly mob of so-called 'patriots.' ... War makes possible such crimes and outrages," added Debs. "And war comes in spite of the people."[90]

Whatever defiance Debs and his supporters might offer the superpatriots, the "crimes and outrages" of vigilantism clearly had a dampening effect on Socialist activity. During a Socialist Party conference in the summer of 1918, the Illinois secretary of the Socialist Party reported that propaganda work had suffered due to "almost endless intimidation" all over the state. In southwestern Illinois, a "reign of mob violence ... finally wound up in a hanging bee in Collinsville." The lynching resulted in "scaring the daylights out of quite a large number of people." Since then, there has been "no particular activity in those two or three counties.... I think we probably will have more or less of that experience, not only here but all over the country," he concluded.[91]

If the Wilson administration might ignore the pleas of Adolph Germer, they could not afford to neglect the reaction of Berlin. Fears that the German government might use the Prager lynching for propaganda materialized within weeks. The first indication of a German response appeared when the Swiss legation forwarded a message to the State Department on April 11, allegedly from Berlin, that the German government would pay Prager's funeral expenses.[92] It later developed that the letter originated with Prager's family in Dresden.

Nonetheless, Acting Secretary of State Frank Polk inquired on the legal status of the case to the Justice Department. He learned from John Lord O'Brien, chief of the War Emergency Branch of Justice, that the lynching resulted from "popular impatience with the administration of law relating to alien enemies and hostile activities." O'Brien also informed him that the "situation was in the process of correction," as Congress would pass "additional legislation which has been requested by this Department."[93] The State Department then sent off a letter to Berlin, assuring the Germans that the government deplored the lynching and was taking steps to remedy the situation but that the lynching was legally a matter for the state of Illinois.

Before long, the German press featured stories on the Prager lynching. In early May, the *Vossiche Zeitung* reported that Prager had been accused of spying by his neighbor because Prager talked in German to an unknown woman from St. Louis. In condemning the attack, the *Zeitung* charged that the "American press is largely guilty owing to its love of sensation."[94] The *New York Times* answered by calling the Germans hypocritical for accusing Americans of brutality. "Compared with 10,000 atrocities committed by Germans in Belgium and France," they wrote, "the killing of Prager could almost be dismissed as an exhibition of bad manners, a manifestation of poor taste."[95] The *Times* chose not to respond to the German attack on the American press. But its characterization of the lynching as merely a faux pas almost seemed to bear out the German charge.

Back in Collinsville, the Prager lynching had more than symbolic effects; it seems to have hardened the lines of division among miners. Writing to his brother in the aftermath of the lynching, Jim Walker of Donk No. 1 in Collinsville noted the effect of Prager's death on the miners' cooperative store, a pet project of the union's Socialist wing. "Mose Johnson and the whole Farrington crowd is not only staying away from the store but they are getting others to quit it," Walker wrote. "I think some of them quit because we dident gloat over the murder of that inisent man down here."[96] Walker's implication that some miners did gloat over Prager's murder suggests the depth of divisions among some working people in Collinsville. The apparent glee with which some miners greeted the murder, moreover, casts doubt on the statement of one local historian that "[s]urely, no one took any satisfaction from a Collinsville crime that disgraced our community all over the country."[97]

Walker's statement also indicates that there may have been some political basis for differing reactions to the lynching. This supports the idea, raised earlier, that there may well have been a variety of opinions in the Maryville UMWA local. Indeed, the Fornero leadership was eager to make an example of miners who had associated with an accused German spy. At least three miners suffered penalties for signing Prager's petition for membership to the union, which allegedly contained false information about Prager's work history. For this "crime," Local 1802 slapped John Tonso, Paul Schreiber, and Joseph Robino each with a fifty-dollar fine, well over a week's pay. In the volatile atmosphere that followed the lynching, pressure mounted on workers to demonstrate their loyalty.

In the week following the lynching, Mose Johnson played a role similar to the one he had played during the fall 1917 wildcat strikes. Without presenting any hard evidence, he repeatedly asserted that Prager had been working for the German government. On the day following Prager's death, Johnson, like Attorney General Gregory, "deplored" the lynching but deplored even more "the fact that it had not been possible to have Prager arrested and grilled in the expectation of getting valuable information from him."[98] A week later, Johnson offered his "evidence" that Prager had asked John Lobenad about explosives.

If his union did not come to his posthumous defense, Prager's fraternal brothers in the St. Louis Hormonie Lodge of the Odd Fellows did take a stand on his behalf. In an April 9 resolution denouncing the Prager lynching, they began by noting that one must "pledge loyalty" to the United States before joining the order. They reported that Prager, "during his short career as an Odd Fellow has proven himself worthy and entitled to our fellowship and our association." Finally, their resolution said, "we most profoundly deplore and most emphatically denounce this barbarous act and call upon all those in authority to employ all legal means at their command to bring the guilty parties to the bar of Justice." Copies of the resolution went to the press, the governor of Illinois, the Madison County coroner, and President Wilson.[99] In addition, the grand lodges of both Illinois and Missouri supported the prosecution of the lynchers and affirmed Prager's loyalty.[100] In contrast to the tempered denunciations by the attorney general and other authority figures, the Odd Fellows resolution gave no ground to claims that Prager was a spy.

In Collinsville as well, members of Madison Lodge #43 of the Odd Fellows also honored their fraternal commitment to Prager, though much more quietly. Only days after the lynching, lodge records show, the lodge arranged to pay for the transport of Prager's body to St. Louis for burial. While Prager had not formally joined the Collinsville lodge, he was still an Odd Fellow, and lodge minutes refer to him as "Brother Prager." Given the intensity of feeling surrounding Prager at this point, it seems significant that lodge members were willing to take on this responsibility, even if they did not issue a public protest.

The lack of public comment from the Collinsville lodge is hardly surprising, given the atmosphere in town at this juncture. But several other factors are worth considering. First, the Odd Fellows observed, at least in theory, a rule that forbade discussion of political or controversial topics in lodge meetings, although the St. Louis Hormonie Lodge clearly had not let this prevent them from taking up the issue of the lynching. Second, and probably more important, there inevitably had been lodge members at the lynching or connected to it in other ways. At the very least, Collinsville Odd Fellow Notley Shoulders, though not a defendant, was present at Prager's demise. And one of the elderly members of the lodge, Wesley Beaver Sr., who regularly drew sick benefits, was the father of a man who did become a central defendant in the trial of the lynchers.[101]

On April 10, five days after his murder, Prager was buried in St. Louis. Some 500 people attended the memorial service at the William Schumacher funeral home, held under the auspices of the Hormonie Lodge. According to Prager's dying wishes, a "large American flag was spread over the casket," and flowers, sent by "unknown persons," covered the flag. With the room "filled to overflowing," those in attendance heard Reverend W. S. Simon, of the Jesus Evangelical Church, speak, and "there was scarcely a dry eye in the room."[102] After the short service, Prager's fraternal brothers took his body to St. Matthew's Cemetery and there interred him. His headstone, weathered today by age, bears a faded photo of the man and reads "ROBERT P. PRAGER, Born Feb. 28, 1888 at Dresden, Germany, Died Apr. 5, 1918 at Collinsville, Ill., THE VICTIM OF A MOB."[103] While Prager's service and funeral were not explicitly protest gatherings, many attendees may have found the occasions a welcome opportunity to grieve not only Prager as an individual but also the loss of democratic rights that the "white-hot mass instinct" had caused.

In Collinsville, only two days after Prager's body was laid in the ground, the *Collinsville Herald* stirred yet more animosity toward the alleged spy by publishing the following sensationalistic headline: "Prager Took Young Girls to Men; Sought Correspondence with Women Under Plea of Marriage." After scouring Prager's Vandalia Street apartment for any material he could find, editor J. O. Monroe claimed to have found a series of letters. They allegedly showed that Prager sought help from a "matrimonial agency" in finding a female companion and that Prager supplied young girls to male friends in St. Louis. One letter from a St. Louis brewery worker named Hertling to Prager supposedly referred cryptically to the girls as "chickens." At one point, Monroe claimed, Hertling complained that Prager "brings him . . . '——— chickens' and says the men at the brewery laugh at him that a man ——— should have anything to do [with] children." He then asked that "[t]he next time Prager brings him any chickens from Collinsville, he bring him 'a nice fat old hen.'" Based on this alleged evidence, Monroe concluded, "Taking the fact that Prager went out with young girls and took them to friends in connection with the fact that he wrote also letters to women he had never seen, it would look as if he might have been immoral possibly to the extent of doing a regular business in young womanhood."[104] Following this potential lead, a St. Louis newspaper reported, "The woman angle to the case is being investigated, both by the county authorities and by the police in St. Louis."[105]

By adding a moral element to the indictment of Prager, Monroe and others may well have helped to ease the troubled consciences of those who wondered if the lynch mob had killed an innocent man. Disloyalty was bad enough, but this offense was unforgivable. It offered a reason for the entire community to detest Robert Prager. Not only did jumpy miners afraid of being entombed underground have a reason to stop Prager; anyone with a young daughter now had a big stake in the outcome of the case. Prager now became a kind of sacrificial lamb. With his lynching, the community had been morally cleansed. Indeed, the weight that the immorality charge carried in the months following April 5 is suggested by the way that the *Collinsville Advertiser* responded later to the news that the indicted lynchers had all been acquitted: "The verdict was in line with the desire of almost everyone who had followed the case. Prager was an ex-convict, a white slaver in morals and a decidedly foolish man."[106] Accusations of sabotage and Socialism were conspicuously absent.

To the extent that popular feeling against Prager—at least after his death—drew its strength from the charge that he was a "white slaver," how did Collinsville residents understand that term? Historian Nancy MacLean, in her analysis of another well-known World War I–era lynching—that of Leo Frank—has taken an approach that is suggestive for Prager's story. In reinterpreting the Frank lynching, which took place in 1915, MacLean persuasively argues for a connection between the increasing incidence of young women earning wages, mounting popular anxieties about the potentially freer exercise of young women's sexuality and life choices, and, finally, the way that these fears were focused on Mary Phagan, the young factory worker whom factory owner Frank was accused of raping and murdering.[107] Especially since previous accounts of the Prager lynching have uniformly ignored its hidden gender dimension, some scholarly speculation is warranted here on how such dynamics may have operated in southwestern Illinois.

A white slaver was defined by one authority of the time as "any man or woman who traffics in the sexual life of any woman or girl for financial reward or gain."[108] As opposed to ordinary prostitution, which might be voluntary, white slavery was by its nature coercive. Especially between 1909 and 1915, Americans were blanketed by lurid white-slave tracts and films that depicted young working women as innocent, newly arrived in the big city, and in danger of abduction or seduction by evil "procurers," who typically were portrayed as conniving foreigners.

The picture painted by some of a vast, highly organized white-slavery network was exaggerated. Rather than address the complex reality of the problem, the intensity of the campaign against white slavery, including the enactment into law of the White Slave Traffic Act (Mann Act) of 1910, tended to turn it into a convenient scapegoat for deeper social problems. At the same time, white slavery was not entirely a myth. From 1910 to 1915, there were over 1,000 convictions for this crime. While there was not a formal, hidden white-slavery "ring," there was an informal network that included some 10 percent of all prostitutes, according to one estimate.[109] The southwestern Illinois region seems to have been no exception to this phenomenon. In 1918, for example, newspapers reported that seventeen-year-old Myrtle Gardner had brought federal suit under the Mann Act against one Steve Unk and several associates. According to the lawsuit,

Unk had kept Gardner a "white slave prisoner" at his St. Louis hotel for more than two years, where "she was compelled to receive the attentions of men brought to her."[110] Whether or not this suit had merit, the people of the southwestern Illinois coalfields certainly had reason to think that white slavery had invaded their region.

Still, popular concern over prostitution, as one scholar notes, "had at least as much to do with the anxieties produced by the transformation of American society occurring in the progressive era as with the actual existence of red-light districts." As young women flocked to urban centers and increasingly entered the paid workforce, that is, they began to exercise an unprecedented degree of social and sexual independence that was profoundly unsettling for many Americans. The prostitute—aggressive, sexually independent, money-earning, bold—served as a convenient symbol of these changes; the anti-prostitution campaign thus was aimed not so much at a sex-for-hire industry but at the "new woman" of the early twentieth century.[111]

And the southwestern Illinois coalfields certainly had its share of "new women." Maude Gilmore, who called to her father from a streetcar near the Hardscrabble Saloon, would certainly seem to qualify. In the company of her working-class peers, she traveled from home, on public transportation, and arrived home well after dark. Her financial self-sufficiency and freedom of mobility, moreover, seem to have been matched with a degree of self-assurance. In a kind of role reversal, as if catching him playing hooky, she confronted her father and practically ordered him to return home. Lola Higgs, Mary Killian, Lillian Walker, "Miss Baehler," and "Miss Higgins"—the telephone operators who had gone on strike in Collinsville the previous fall—would also qualify as "new women." Indeed, telephone operators in the second decade of the twentieth century were viewed as the quintessential "new women." In their attire and social lives, it was suggested, many of them seemed to fit the immoral "flapper" image, which conveyed a new and threatening degree of female freedom. In going on strike and refusing to back down in the face of stonewalling by Bell telephone, especially in the context of government pressure to stay on the job, Mary Killian and her fellow operators challenged the prescribed female roles of the time.

Women also challenged tradition by taking a more visible role in public and political life. Collinsville women were part of the national network of women's clubs, which had blossomed in the 1890s. In 1914, some

150 women attended a district meeting of the Federation of Women's Clubs in Collinsville.[112] Boosted by the 1912 victory of the women's suffrage movement in Illinois, women's temperance activists also began to mobilize in southwestern Illinois to shut the saloons down tight. That year, Margaret Turner, a young activist, and other local women organized a Collinsville chapter of the Women's Christian Temperance Union, gathered hundreds of signatures in order to place an anti-saloon resolution on the ballot, and campaigned vigorously for their cause.[113] Although Collinsville remained a "wet" town, the women had boldly entered local politics.

Considered in the context of changing gender roles and relations, the "white slaver" accusation against Robert Paul Prager was a powerful weapon in the hands of newspaper editors, police authorities, and politicians who wished to minimize opposition to the superpatriotic wave of April 1918. If we recall that anti-Socialist religious crusaders like David Goldstein had made an explicit connection between Socialism, sexuality, and "moral degradation," the possible association in the popular mind between white slavery, "foreigners," immorality, and Socialism would certainly have made a potent mix. Prager seemed to qualify on all four counts.

Given these marks against him, it was clear from the outset that conviction of Prager's lynchers would be nearly impossible to obtain. Indeed, the expectation of community approval is a key ingredient in almost every lynching.[114] Though everyone knew who had led the mob, the coroner sought arrest warrants, only to be told by four justices of the peace that "they didn't care to get mixed up in the affair."[115] After further warnings from Attorney General Edward Brundage and after Joseph Riegel made a full confession naming four other men, the coroner obtained warrants, and the men were arrested. Eventually, eleven men were indicted for murder. Eight were miners—Joseph Riegel, Richard Dukes, William Brockmeier, Enid Elmore, John Hallworth, Frank Flannery, James DeMatties, and Cecil Larremore. Wesley Beaver was a saloon porter, Calvin Gilmore a plumber's helper, and Charles Cranmer a stockyards worker.[116]

There seems to have been at least one person in Collinsville who was determined that Joseph Riegel pay for his crime. This was Emma Riegel, his estranged wife, who cared for their two-year-old child and lived with her mother near the Madison County town of Troy. Because of some serious trouble in their relationship, according to a *Herald* article, "The young wife is intensely embittered against Riegel. . . . Hearing Wednesday afternoon that he was in jail, she came here to see him. Not finding him in jail she went to the shoe shop to find him and gloat over his undoing." "I hope [he] hangs," Emma Riegel told some customers. "If he doesn't, I'll hang him myself."[117]

Despite Emma Riegel's wish to send her husband to the gallows, she was clearly the exception. It was only after examining 750 potential jurymen that twelve were finally selected.[118] Not one was from Collinsville or the surrounding towns.[119] The trial, which ran from May 13 until May 30, shared a number of ritual elements with the lynching itself. The defendants wore red, white, and blue ribbons. At a key point in the trial, the wafting strains of the national anthem were audible in the courtroom. Some members of the Great Lakes Naval Training Band, visiting in Edwardsville, performed outside, assured that they would not disturb the proceedings.[120] To his credit, Judge Louis Bernreuter ruled that evidence of Prager's disloyalty was inadmissible because Prager was not on trial. On the other hand, the judge undermined that ruling completely in his instructions to the jury. "It isn't necessary for the defense to prove Prager a spy," he stated. *"If it can be shown that the defendants thought him one, that would be sufficient to mitigate the crime and lessen their punishment."*[121] The defense took full advantage of this opening, arguing that since the lynchers believed Prager a spy, they acted in legitimate self-defense.

The jury acquitted the defendants after deliberating for forty-five minutes. Riegel and his associates had indeed gotten away with murder. But the question of who actually bore the guilt for Prager's death was more complicated than that. Leaving aside for a moment the larger political and social forces as "culprits," the courtroom testimony suggests that, as mentioned above, a number of the defendants were not at the lynching tree. John Hallworth, Wesley Beaver, William Brockmeier, Richard Dukes, Calvin Gilmore, and Enid Elmore all testified that they did not follow the crowd that far. No one contradicted their testimony, and there is no reason to believe they were lying.

For those who were placed at the tree, the defense strategy was not to deny this fact but to ask why these men had been singled out. The same was true of witnesses who admitted to being present in the crowd at city hall. For instance, when former mayor R. Guy Kneedler testified about the scene there, defense attorney J. M. Bandy inquired, "Oh, you were one of the crowd, then." "Yes, I was one of the crowd," answered Kneedler. Similarly, when Bernhard Mueller admitted to being at the tree, Bandy made a motion that Mueller be charged along with his clients. "Your theory is, then, that anyone who saw the occurrence is guilty?" asked Judge Bernreuter. "Yes," answered Bandy. He was overruled, but he had made his point. In his summation, Bandy continued the argument, asking why Mueller, Louis Gerding, editor J. O. Monroe, saloonkeeper William Horstman, and even Mayor Siegel were not indicted.

While someone did commit the crime, and while some of Bandy's clients were among them, the attorney had a point. The very process of selecting those to prosecute was a highly political process. Outside of Riegel, who confessed and gave authorities some names, why did, say, someone like William Brockmeier appear on the defendant list? No one testified that he took part in the actual lynching. It is possible that his selection might have something to do with his role as leader of the Lumaghi No. 3 miners. During the period of the autumn strikes, for instance, miners there discussed a number of grievances and resolved to take action on a number of fronts. One of these was a decision to demand that mineowner Louis Lumaghi remove John Siegel as company doctor. Whatever tensions between Siegel and the miners this demand expressed might well have played a part in the politics of the lynching indictments. At the very least, it is worth considering the possibility that such dynamics were at work. The simple, quick, and predictable not guilty verdict in the lynching trial may well have masked a more complex underlying reality.

The acquittal of Prager's accused lynchers once again cast Collinsville onto the world stage. A week after Prager's lynchers walked out of the Madison County court, the German Foreign Office sent a note to the State Department. Berlin expected "prompt and telling atonement to be made for the shocking deed" and specifically called for the federal government "unconditionally to answer, whatever may be the cleaving line of the jurisdiction of Federal and State courts in this case, for such an atonement." The Foreign Office demanded "safeguarding of German-Americans against any repetition of the outrage." If the American government failed to give such protection, the Germans warned that "it would be constrained to resort to retaliatory measures."[122]

Several days later, members of the German Reichstag heard a discussion of the Prager lynching between delegate Ernst Mueller from Meiningen and Dr. Walter Simons, privy councillor from the ministry of foreign affairs. After relating the story of the lynching, Mueller charged Collinsville authorities with complicity in Prager's death. The federal government, he charged, "merely started a kind of mock investigation, as in other cases of the lynching of labor leaders who had opposed President Wilson," presumably referring to the Frank Little case. Mueller than asked Simons what the Imperial government would do in response.

Simons informed the Reichstag that the "Swiss legation in Washington has quickly and emphatically intervened in Germany's interest . . . and has demanded an explanation and a guarantee against similar riots from the American government." The letter had been sent several days earlier. Adopting a more militant tone than had the official letter, Simons held the U.S. government "responsible for the indignant incident" since it had "for years . . . tolerated . . . a bloody defamation campaign of the Entente among the American populace." No matter that federal law was "insufficient to penalize the culprits," he said. International law required the federal government to "secure the rights, freedom and lives of the Germans in America against barbarous persecutions."[123]

When news of the Reichstag discussion of Prager appeared in the *New York Times* several days later, both the State Department and the Swiss legation denied that they had received any protest note from the German government on the lynching. A *Times* editorial even ridiculed the privy councillor for "talking nonsense" by pretending that the Foreign Office had sent such a letter.[124] It is worth noting that this denial came months after the State Department had already sent an explanatory note to Berlin. It cannot be proved but seems likely that the State Department sought to suppress the fact that it was corresponding with the German government on the subject of the Prager lynching. No doubt, the prospect of lynching in a nation claiming to fight a war to make the world safe for democracy was beginning to embarrass the Wilson administration.

Voices in and out of government continued to pressure Wilson to make a definitive public statement on mob violence. When Adolph Germer wrote to President Wilson urging him to make a statement on lynching, he followed on the heels of African American leaders who had been raising the issue with Wilson for at least the preceding year, which witnessed 259 black victims of mob violence. The U.S. entry into the war coincided with an upsurge in both violence against black people and their resistance to it. In addition to waging countless anonymous acts of self-defense, the NAACP launched a visible political campaign against lynching during 1917. Highlighting this campaign was a silent protest parade in July down Fifth Avenue in New York. Banners in the march read "Mr.

President, Why Not Make AMERICA Safe for Democracy?"[125] Since the murderous attack on the black residents of East St. Louis, black leaders had
been pressing President Wilson to make a public statement denouncing
lynching, but Wilson had refused to meet with an NAACP delegation
following the violence. Under tremendous pressure in August 1917, he
finally issued what they considered a very weak statement.

In the wake of the Prager affair, black leaders saw a new opportunity
to press Wilson for a strong condemnation of lynching. The day after
Attorney General Gregory made his "deplore but not condemn" statement, prominent black educator Leslie Pinckney Hill wrote him with this
object in mind. After congratulating Gregory for discussing the Prager
lynching with the president, Hill asked him to consider the "heartache
and mind distress of twelve millions of Negroes who still see their fel-
low-men lynched with a brutality which the Germans themselves cannot outdo . . . without so much as a word of denunciation from our Government and with not a single man in authority like yourself to present
our cause to the Chief Executive."

According to Hill, thousands of black men and women were wondering how it was "possible for the Federal Government to have more sympathy for Germans who have blown up our mills, bombarded our ships,
attempted the destruction of our bridges . . . than it has for millions of
loyal Negroes who are offering their lives every day for the defense of that
very nation, whose executive officers do not lift a finger or say a word in
their defense." Can you imagine how difficult it was, Hill wrote, "to teach
colored boys and girls loyalty and patriotism? . . . Will you help us?" he
asked.[126] After reading this letter, Attorney General Gregory received a
note from his secretary asking how to respond. Gregory's answer revealed
the racism operating at the highest levels of the Wilson administration:
"I do not think it necessary to reply to the letter, which is based upon
misinformation."[127]

Despite this dismissive attitude, the Prager affair and the larger issue
of lynching refused to go away and continued to draw international attention. Algie Simons, for instance, a pro-war American Socialist in London during the war, writing to a British newspaper, the London Justice,
referred to the "one lynching case, of which so much is made by paci-
fists in this country."[128] Just as the New York Times attempted to diminish the severity of Prager's murder, so did Simons try to shift attention
from Prager's death to the Germans. Responding to an article by a labor

unionist critical of the Prager lynching, Simons asked, "Why has nothing ever been said in your columns concerning the outrages of German agents upon American lives and property? . . . I have never seen any protests when hundreds of lives were taken by explosions, fires, and wrecking of bridges and plants, in time of peace, by those against whom popular rage is now directed." It is likely that the international publicity the Prager lynching received helped prompt Wilson into action.

On July 26, Wilson finally issued a written statement on lynching. The president repeated the by-now familiar arguments: lynching gave comfort to Germany, the country that had "made lynchers of her armies"; lynchers brought discredit upon "Democracy"; and, in addition to being an embarrassment to America, lynching was unnecessary. "No man who loves America . . . can justify mob action while the courts of justice are open and the governments of the States and the Nation are ready and able to do their duty."[129]

Though Wilson seemed to condemn lynching as such, the logic he used undermined the force of his condemnation. By assuming that lynching victims were guilty, he gave potential lynchers an advance justification for their action. In trying to condemn the Prager lynching and all others, Wilson accepted a basic premise held by the lynchers themselves: if the government failed to "do its duty," then lynching was legitimate. The implication was that victims of lynchings had truly done something deserving of punishment—sedition or spying in Prager's case, rape in the case of black men. The problem, in other words, was only one of effective punishment. And of course, Wilson's statement was entirely silent on the specific question of African Americans. Even though Wilson's lynching statement appeared on page 1 of the *Official Bulletin,* which every newspaper in America received daily from the CPI, it made very little impact. The *New York Times* carried it on page 7. Wilson received praise from more accommodationist black leaders, like Booker T. Washington's successor at Tuskeegee, Robert Russa Moton, who commended him for a "wise, strong, frank, patriotic statement."[130] On the other hand, the NAACP noted that in Georgia, Wilson's statement had the effect merely of keeping lynchings out of the newspapers.[131]

Both on the battlefields of Europe and on home fronts worldwide, World War I incited in large numbers of working people a mindless hatred of each other. The war launched millions of young men, who had never seen each other and had never harmed each other, into mortal combat. The successful prosecution of the war required that these human beings not reflect on that fact, as Joseph Riegel belatedly did, through a drunken haze, on the morning of April 5. Conversely, the possibility that working people on opposite sides of the trenches might view each other as fellow human beings, exemplified by British and German troops in the famous "Christmas truce" of 1914, was impermissible to the high command. To the degree that soldiers were willing to continue to slaughter each other, a certain kind of political and moral hypnosis was necessary. In this sense, on the night of April 4–5, Joseph Riegel and his associates had literally brought the war home to Collinsville.

In doing so, they provided powerful evidence against the idea that a working-class version of patriotism could somehow serve as a vehicle for advancing the interests of working people. Once the United States entered the war, UMWA leaders from John White to Frank Farrington to John Walker to Mose Johnson had argued that coal miners could use the great patriotic crusade to bolster the legitimacy of the union in the eyes of the public. Union leaders not only adopted the political language of the Wilson administration in boosting the war; Farrington and others were also willing to use the repressive machinery of the state to keep miners on the job. But by invoking the patriotic genie in their behalf, the UMWA leadership unwittingly unleashed a monster.

In his account of Woonsocket textile workers during the 1940s, Gary Gerstle notes a similar dynamic at work. Members of the Independent Textile Union (ITU) who had used patriotic rhetoric, ostensibly for their own progressive, even radical purposes, found that in the aftermath of World War II, it came to be used against them in a conservative way. As he puts it, "[T]he language of Americanism had slipped out of the ITU's control."[132] The story of Prager's murder, however, suggests that working people were never free to harness patriotism for their class purposes. American patriotism was not just a set of words, a freely floating signifier available for the use of any social class. Rather, it was materially rooted in the reality of class rule, no matter how cloaked it normally appeared.

While the UMWA bore a degree of responsibility for making vigilantism likely, it was the Wilson administration that provided the fertile ground in which superpatriotic violence flourished. Several authors, including David Kennedy and Frederick Luebke, have made this abundantly clear in general surveys of the period. Wilson, however, still seems to have escaped the kind of critical scrutiny he so richly deserves. For instance, Joseph McCartin briefly treats the topic of wartime vigilantism, focusing on the deportations of striking copper miners from Bisbee, Arizona. In explaining the president's unwillingness to take a strong stand against a flagrant violation of democratic rights, McCartin writes that "the administration lacked the resources and the political consensus that might have allowed it to control vigilantism."[133] But even if, as McCartin maintains, there were Wilson administration figures, including Secretary of Labor William B. Wilson, who were unhappy with the deportations, the Wilson White House itself helped lay the foundation for vigilante attacks. As Yvette Huginnie writes, "In its war against the IWW, the Wilson administration had ignited anti-radical flames; Bisbee copper companies merely spread them."[134] In regard to southwestern Illinois, as well, Wilson's own war-related propaganda and repressive measures inevitably led to bloodshed on the home front.

But if southwestern Illinois coal miners paid an unexpected and heavy political price for their patriotism, if the war inevitably accentuated their disunity, it also cost their class adversaries dearly. By mobilizing miners to fight for "democracy" and imposing one sacrifice after another, the Wilson administration laid the basis for a profound working-class upsurge that swept the nation in 1919. After presenting the specter of murderous patriotism to the nation in April 1918, the miners of Collinsville and the entire region once again exhibited a fierce current of class solidarity in the aftermath of the war. The rulers of America had indeed unwittingly provided "the proletariat with weapons for fighting the bourgeoisie."

"The Great Class War"
Postwar Rebellions in the Coalfields

I n early 1919, a prominent American business newsletter surveyed the postwar political and economic scene for its wealthy subscribers. "A period of trouble and depression is ahead," began the report from the Babson Statistical Corporation. "We can prepare for the reaction and prevent it from being disastrous but to stop it is impossible." The war had already brought enormous upheaval in its wake, the report continued. "The industrial classes in many parts of the world are at the point of revolution. Insiders well know that the uprising of the masses in Germany was a vital factor in ending the war." Though businessmen had learned much about the "terrible conditions" in Russia, they were less acquainted with the mass unrest in England, Ireland, Italy, France, Portugal, Spain, and even Japan, where the "rice riots . . . show the temper of the people, who are beginning to revolt against the imperialistic designs of their leaders." Summing up this discontent, the newsletter remarked, "The war of nations in Europe is over, but the great class war apparently has just begun."[1]

To place the patriotic violence of 1918 in proper perspective, it is not enough to chronicle the events that preceded it; one also must move beyond the armistice and consider how the southwestern Illinois miners experienced the following year, which proved to be a milestone in the history of working-class politics. Without an account of 1919, the story of the Prager lynching would become a film stopped midreel. For in that volatile year of mass strikes and political radicalization, the working people of Collinsville and its vicinity did not come to a political standstill. To the contrary, the miners of the region played a significant role in leading the *Nation* to label the events of 1919 "the unprecedented revolt of the rank and file."[2]

After sketching out the conditions facing miners and their families after the armistice, this chapter charts the political trajectory of the southwestern Illinois miners by examining their participation in four closely intertwined developments of that year: a nationally organized political strike in support of freedom for Tom Mooney in July 1919, the movement for independent labor political action, a statewide rank-and-file rebellion against the Farrington leadership of District 12, and a nationwide strike starting November 1. Taken together, the events of 1919 in the southwestern Illinois coalfields suggest that despite the deep human and political costs exacted by the war on working people, the government and coal operators also had a price to pay.

In early 1920, Secretary-Treasurer Walter Nesbit of the Illinois UMWA recalled how coal miners experienced the end of the war. In mid-1918, "[i]ndustry was going full blast. Production reached its height. Advances in wages and steady employment increased earnings. Time rolled on." Then on November 11 "came the glad news that hostilities had ceased and the armistice was signed." Following these happy tidings, however, "came a lull in business and a stagnation of industry, but worst of all the Influenza Epidemic, leaving in its path sickness, death and unlimited suffering." As a result, "[e]arnings were reduced." Moreover, "[t]he already high cost of living continued to soar, poor work continued and discontent was rife; the promises labor had received had not yet materialized; the crisis was here."[3]

As Nesbit suggested, late 1918 was a bittersweet time for coal mining families in southwestern Illinois. To be sure, news of the armistice brought great celebration. In Collinsville, by 5 A.M. on the day of the historic signing, there "were hundreds on the downtown streets, gathered mainly about the *Herald* office, cheering, shouting, blowing bugles and beating drums and tin pans. After daylight they organized impromptu parades and marched up and down the streets, partly to display their enthusiasm and partly to keep warm. Then most of them went home for breakfast."[4]

But the great relief that the armistice brought to working people in November 1918 was mitigated by a number of factors. First, since news from the front took time to travel back home, the next month brought continued casualty reports into the region. In late November, for instance, word arrived in Livingston that Private Jonas Wajcuila, a member of

UMWA Local 2656, had been killed in action a month earlier. And the family of Corporal R. East, a Worden miner, learned that their son had been missing in action for over five weeks.[5] Collinsville received notice on November 29 that Bernard Rissi had been killed in action. Brother of Frank Rissi, who worked at Donk No. 2 mine in Maryville, Bernard had worked at the St. Louis Smelting and Refining lead smelter before entering the service.[6]

Then there was the flu. As Alfred Crosby has noted, though the 1918 Spanish influenza epidemic has appeared as a minor footnote in the written histories of this period, "It was a demographic catastrophe, comparable in its destruction of human life in this century only with World War II." Worldwide, over 21 million died from the virus. Over a half million perished in the United States. Most commonly, they died from pneumonia, which developed rapidly in influenza victims, often within days of infection.[7]

The most deadly phase of the 1918–19 epidemic hit the St. Louis area in the period surrounding the armistice. In the last four months of 1918 combined, the death rate from influenza and pneumonia in St. Louis rose by more than 250 percent.[8] Across the border in the Illinois coal towns, the epidemic may not have spread as quickly, but it took its toll. In Pawnee, Illinois, fifteen-year-old Joseph Buckles drove a mule at the Peabody mine. Of that fatal autumn, he recalled that "there was an awful lot of people that died. They had the town quarantined. You'd come uptown in the daytime and buy your groceries. Then [at] night it was closed down. We used to go uptown—they didn't even have street lights on. Fred Crowder run a restaurant over next to Clete's on the corner and we used to go up there and hang out at night. We'd get in there and play cards by candlelight. It was just some place to go and loaf until that was over with."[9]

The death records of the Illinois UMWA reflect the epidemic. Entries for late 1918 and early 1919 are littered with cases of influenza and pneumonia.[10] Crosby notes that the incidence of influenza was underreported since those listed as dying from pleurisy or bronchitis were not included in the epidemic death count. Such a person might have been R. C. Delaney, a miner at Donk No. 1 in Collinsville, who had been elected alderman on the Socialist ticket. Showing no signs of ill health, Delaney got sick in mid-December and died "very suddenly." His official cause of death was "bronchitis."[11] Another victim was none other than Joe Fornero of the Maryville mine, who succumbed October 15.[12]

Of course, the union records are silent about the toll of influenza on women and children in coal mining families. Once one parent or child became infected, the others were almost sure to follow. Whereas most flu viruses tended to strike hardest at the very old and very young, the 1918 strain, for unexplained reasons, was most lethal to children under five and young adults. Thus, young mothers and small children were the perfect candidates for the disease. The flu was certainly a family affair in the region. Despite the relative unpopularity of AFL president Samuel Gompers among southwestern Illinois miners, it is likely that more than one of them shared Gompers's grief: he lost his daughter Sadie to the epidemic while on a trip abroad in early 1919.[13]

What produced the crisis of 1919 alluded to by Walter Nesbit, however, was not of purely natural origin. The biological assault on mining families came on top of the unnatural disasters of inflation and unemployment. As one top UMWA official noted, "Never before have these problems presented themselves in such an aggravated and in such a live and forcible way."[14] The Washington Agreement wage hike of October 1917 put only a temporary dent in the high cost of living. In the five-year period from December 1914 to June 1919, according to the federal Bureau of Labor Statistics, the cost of necessities for coal mining families rose an average of 79 percent. In the same period, taking into account three pay raises, miners' tonnage rates had gone up only 37 percent.[15]

What made inflation particularly pressing after November 11 was the disappearance of steady work. For Illinois mines as a whole, the average number of days worked dropped by one-third—from 238 in 1918 to 160 in 1919. The low 1919 average represented a return to the prewar depression days of 1914–15. In a real sense, the wartime boom proved to be a fleeting interruption in Illinois miners' long-term bleak employment prospects. Aside from Indiana, which was slightly worse, the 1919 Illinois figure was the lowest absolute number nationwide and showed the biggest percentage drop from 1918.[16]

Even in Maryville, where the Donk No. 2 miners were used to steady work, the postwar slowdown took its toll. Frank Rissi, for instance, worked as a machine runner at the Maryville mine. He and his wife, Ernestine, had six children. In a letter to President Wilson, Ernestine Rissi explained what mining families were facing. "Since the Armistice," she wrote, ". . . miners have not been able to earn a living wage, and there are a number of Boys and girls 14 and 15 years of age working at different occupations because their fathers can not earn enough to feed his family." Her own husband brought home the equivalent of only three dollars per day, due to the intermittent work at the Maryville mine. "We have 6 children under age," she explained, "and they do not know what Milk, Butter and Eggs taste like, as we can not afford to buy them on $3.00 per day, and I admit my children are underfed."[17]

The combined effects of influenza, inflation, and unemployment suggest the misery spreading across the region in early 1919. These conditions alone, however, did not produce the rebellions of that year. What galvanized this inchoate social discontent into political action were the unfulfilled expectations raised by the war. For nearly two years, the working people of the southwestern Illinois coalfields had sacrificed for the alleged war for democracy. They willingly gave their lives, their sweat, their last dollars. In doing so, they had been assured by all that their loyalty would carry a reward once peace arrived. As UMWA International secretary William Green put it, "The working people throughout the world are aroused. The ideals of which they once dreamed are now becoming political realities. They are no longer content with being regarded as cogs in the industrial machine or mere producing units used for the purpose of increasing the profits of employers."[18]

Employers, moreover, were aware of this explosive dynamic. The Babson report warned them that we are "destined to have great labor troubles unless employers immediately adopt different methods." The "trouble" would start in textiles, copper, or possibly steel. "The coal and electrical industries will also be affected." Moreover, "[t]hose who try to dam the flood will be washed away." This tidal wave of change was largely due to expectations raised by the war, the newsletter explained. "Our government has said so much about democracy that the masses are now determined to have it, and to have it apply to industry as well as to politics."[19]

As 1919 opened, these expectations fused with the postwar conditions facing miners and their families to produce a multifaceted "great class war" in southwestern Illinois. First, there was the movement to free Tom Mooney—the militant Socialist and union leader convicted of exploding a bomb that had killed ten—which culminated in the July 4 strike. Over the previous two years, mounting pressure from labor had helped prevent the execution of Mooney and fellow unionist Warren Billings. In early 1917, sentiment built for a strike to free the two men. Though the plan was opposed by top AFL officials, workers continued to organize protest meetings and aggressively publicized Mooney's side of the story. Southwestern Illinois miners played their part in this campaign, providing both financial and moral support. Among others, Lumaghi No. 3 miners in Collinsville fired off a protest to California governor William Stephens in May.[20] UMWA locals in Maryville, Collinsville, Edgemont, Belleville, Virden, Lenzburg, Carlinville, New Athens, Worden, Freeburg, and Livingston donated money to the defense effort.[21]

Just as the Prager lynching became a diplomatic embarrassment to the Wilson administration, the miscarriage of justice in Mooney's case also became a foreign policy matter. President Wilson learned of the Mooney case from David Francis, U.S. ambassador to Russia, after workers in Petrograd demonstrated in front of the U.S. embassy, chanting Mooney's name. Upon hearing from President Wilson on the potential negative international repercussions of the planned execution, Governor Stephens postponed the execution in May 1917, six days before Mooney and Billings were scheduled to hang. In the meantime, evidence surfaced showing conclusively that key prosecution witnesses had been paid to perjure themselves on the stand.[22] Soon, the Wilson administration launched its own investigation. And as more public officials joined the chorus of critical voices, Governor Stephens finally commuted the sentence of Mooney and Billings to life imprisonment on Thanksgiving Day of 1918.

Rather than quiet the Mooney defense forces, however, the commutation emboldened them to push further. In mid-January, hundreds of representatives of labor organizations from around the country met in Chicago at the American Labor Congress on the Mooney Case. Convened by the International Workers Defense League (IWDL), a coalition of San Francisco–area unions, the congress had the backing of the influential leadership of the Chicago Federation of Labor (CFL), headed by John Fitzpatrick, who would play a central role in the steelworkers' strike later that year. Of the delegates, some 200 represented locals of the UMWA, many of them from Illinois. The congress, though it focused on the Mooney case, proved to be a rallying point for the more militant forces in the labor movement. Delegates discussed a wide range of political topics. One resolution they adopted explained that "the Mooney case symbolizes all the oppression and bitterness of the struggle of the toiling masses of humanity to rise up and shake off the shackles that kept in bondage the workers of the world." Though the congress refused to seat Socialist Party activists unless they represented a union local, they did invite Eugene Debs to address the meeting. Wiring his regrets, as he was in federal custody, Debs noted: "Free speech prevails in Russia but is dead in the United States since the world has been made safe for democracy."[23]

Some of the more moderate UMWA delegates, such as John Walker, sought to restrict the attention of the congress narrowly to the matter of Mooney and Billings.[24] But the younger, more radical delegates put their stamp on the meeting. For example, the congress adopted unanimously a resolution calling on the Wilson administration to withdraw U.S. troops from Russia. Closer to home, a group of southwestern Illinois miners' leaders, including Jim Walker of Collinsville (now Subdistrict 7 president) and William Airey of Belleville, proposed a resolution that called for the government to take over the "mines, mills and factories, railroads, meat industries, and all other large industries." George Stouffer, a miner from St. David, Illinois, and a returning war veteran, attended the congress in full field artillery uniform. He proposed a plan to organize a Soldier and Workman's Council—or Soviet—"to protect the interests of returned men in his community and in Illinois and the nation." This was one of a number of proposals that workers in uniform made to counter the anti-labor American Legion formed that year.

On the subject of Mooney and Billings, congress delegates agreed on a series of actions to advance their fight. They demanded freedom, or a new trial, and full restoration of citizenship rights for the two men; they called for a campaign to pressure the Wilson administration and for new laws in California relating to trials and evidence to prevent a repeat of the frame-up; they launched a new round of publicity on the case; and most controversially, delegates agreed to organize a vote in the labor movement on a general strike to take place July 4–8 to free Mooney and Billings.[25]

Taken as a whole, the Mooney congress reflected the political ferment bubbling to the surface in the wake of the armistice. It heralded the heightened aspirations of working people, noted by the Babson statistical experts. The political significance of the congress is indicated by a letter sent by John B. Lennon of Bloomington, Illinois, to Hugh Kerwin in the Labor Department. A longtime leader of the Journeyman Tailors' Union and national AFL treasurer from 1888 to 1917, Lennon wrote as a kind of unofficial adviser to Kerwin to "communicate to you my impressions as to the present attitude of the working classes toward After the War questions. . . . The action taken in Chicago yesterday calling for a general strike if a new trial is not given to Mr. Mooney . . . and the demands that are growing out [of] the movement by the Labor Party, I fear is going to stir the pulses of the wage workers of the United States to a degree never before known," Lennon wrote. "The things that ought not to be done seem to be uppermost and the reasonable methods that should be followed are ignored. . . . These are rumblings," Lennon warned, "and they are not meager by any means[,] that portend distrubances [sic] equal to any in Europe."[26]

Though the Mooney strike idea did indeed "stir the pulses" of many miners in the region, the strike was not popular with UMWA officials. After John Walker received a letter from his brother Jim about the strike proposal, he recalled, "I wrote him that I believed Mooney was innocent and ought to be free, but I was positive there would be no general strike, and if a few men in that district came out they would crucify themselves and not help Mooney."[27] A Peoria district official noted that "I helped to raise many dollars for the Tom Mooney Defense Fund," but he advised against the strike, which would be of "no consequence." Moreover, it would violate the UMWA contract with operators. The "contract should be held inviolate," he said.[28] Arguing along these lines, on April 8, 1919, the UMWA International Executive Board issued a circular to miners nationwide forbidding them to participate in the proposed Mooney strike.[29] At least one group of miners from the region, Local 99 of Belleville, protested this decision at the time.[30]

Well aware that the Mooney strike would run into opposition from the top layer of union leadership, the IWDL appealed directly to the rank and file of the labor movement. In a letter sent to unionists in March, the Defense League deliberately used patriotic language, hoping to head off charges of subversion that the strike plan incurred. The league drew upon the rhetoric of the American Revolution as well as upon the words of Wilsonian war propaganda. To begin with, the strike date of July 4 was chosen for its symbolic power. Moreover, Mooney's defenders affirmed the right to strike in terms of freedom and slavery. In their circular entitled "The Right to Strike for Liberty," the IWDL began, "We boast and proudly proclaim ourselves freemen. The fundamental difference between freedom and slavery is that the freeman's work is voluntary, while that of a slave is compulsory. The right to quit work, to strike for the betterment of living conditions, not alone of individuals, but of whole peoples is therefore the inherent right of a freeman." Moreover, the "right to strike to preserve liberty and democracy," as the Mooney campaign proposed to do, "is a more valuable right than the right to strike for bread." Then, going over the heads of the official union leaders, the appeal added, "[N]o institution has control over this right except the people themselves who must suffer in the loss of these great principles." Unless workers struck to free Mooney, the appeal warned, "precedents will have been established that will make America safe for plutocracy, but very unsafe for democracy."[31] As John Laslett comments, the Illinois miners' support for Mooney went beyond "a concern for civil liberties. . . . It also symbolized their disillusionment with the outcome of the First World War; their discontent at the increasingly bureaucratic nature of the UMW . . . and the determination . . . to take the running of the organization into their own hands."[32] The rhetoric of Mooney's Defense League echoes all of these themes.

But the red, white, and blue language of the Mooney circular failed to convince top UMWA leaders to support the planned walkout. UMWA officials not only were opposed to the strike but also refused to help organize a vote on it, as the Defense League requested. In light of this stand, the mere act of voting on whether to strike became an act of defiance. The balloting took place nationwide on May 20. In many locals where Farrington loyalists held sway, no vote took place. Not surprisingly, the miners of Subdistrict 7, which encompassed mainly St. Clair and some of Madison County, voted in large numbers. At least twenty-nine out of thirty-six locals organized a vote. Of 4,789 miners who took part in the balloting, 81 percent voted to strike. In Collinsville, no vote was recorded for Locals 264 (Consolidated No. 17), 848 (Donk No. 1), or 826 (Lumaghi No. 3). On the other hand, miners at Lumaghi No. 2 voted 160–28 for the strike.[33]

The largest single vote tally took place at a mine technically in Subdistrict 6 but right in the area—the Maryville miners voted 429–67 to strike for Tom Mooney.[34] A year before, in the face of accusations against Robert Paul Prager, at least some of the Maryville miners had simply assumed his guilt in the absence of a real bombing or solid evidence of a plan. Now, after a real bomb had killed and the convicted plotters had come within days of execution, a majority defended the presumption of innocence, even at the risk of condemnation from their union officials. The willingness of the Maryville miners to strike for Tom Mooney suggests that, under a leadership that appealed to their instincts for class solidarity, they were highly capable of being mobilized on that basis.

Even before the vote, strike supporters in the region organized a Southern Illinois Mooney Defense League, headed by miner Dan Thomas, a Socialist and the UMWA subdistrict president. The league's secretary was Bert Gray of the Maryville mine.[35] In a "Proclamation" sent out on the eve of the strike, the league urged other workers to join the miners in walking off their jobs on July 4–8. Like the national appeal, this document made generous use of the language of liberty. At the same time, it had a sharper class character. Of Mooney and Billings, for instance, the league declared that their "only crime has been the heinous one, of loyalty to the WORKING CLASS, thereby arousing the hatred and malice of the capitalist class and its henchmen."[36]

On July 4–8, thousands of miners in southwestern Illinois joined other workers nationwide in the Mooney protest strike. July 4 fell on a Friday. Since this was normally a holiday, and miners were used to taking off July 5 if it fell on a Saturday, the only real days of the strike were Monday and Tuesday. Given that St. Clair County formed the heart of the strike and that mines there had been working so little, it also seems that many miners would not have gone to work in any event. In this sense, the Mooney strike was hardly a dramatic shutdown of industry. Considering the controversy attending the voting, the walkout itself was something of an anticlimax. But the miners succeeded in drawing attention to Mooney's plight.

Later in the year, in an address to the delegates of the UMWA International Convention, Rena Mooney, Tom's wife and a tireless activist for his cause, brought his message of gratitude to the miners. "When I left Tom in California a few days ago," she told them, "he said there was nobody he felt nearer to than the mine workers, and he wanted me to thank you personally for everything you had done, both through your contributions and the strikes you have participated in."[37] If Mooney and his supporters were gratified by the miners' support, however, the employers of St. Clair County were not so pleased. Though the miners considered the strike to be outside the realm of the contract, the mine owners at St. Louis and O'Fallon Coal Company and Southern Coal and Coke disagreed. When miners there opened their paychecks on July 15 and July 30, they received a rude awakening. Seven months after the armistice, miners had three days' worth of fines deducted from their pay, under the provisions of the wartime strike penalty clause.

Before turning to the August-September rank-and-file rebellion sparked by these strike fines, it will help to first place the Mooney agitation in a broader political context by examining a development closely connected to that movement in the spring of 1919—the miners and the birth of the Illinois Labor Party (ILP). From the Labor-Greenback campaigns of the 1870s to the labor-populist alliance of the 1890s, Illinois miners had shown an active interest in independent labor political action. In the opening decade of the new century, the CFL had renewed calls for a labor party, though they went unanswered. The increasing use by employers of the court injunction against strikes played a key role in stimulating interest among workers in a third-party effort. By 1918, under the impact of the Bolshevik revolution, the massive upsurge of American labor, and the widely admired example of the British Labour Party, the CFL, under the leadership of John Fitzpatrick, gained a wider hearing than ever before for a working-class political alternative. Following the armistice, Fitzpatrick and his associates organized the Cook County Labor Party, which ran the CFL president for mayor of Chicago in the spring of 1919. CFL forces also teamed up with leaders of the Illinois Federation of Labor, including John Walker, to campaign for a state labor party, a proposal endorsed at the IFL convention in December 1918.[38]

The political program of the Cook County party was expressed in "Labor's Fourteen Points," which were adopted by the CFL in November 1918. Named in imitation of President Wilson's plan for his new world order, the "Chicago program," as it became known, offered a working-class version of Wilson's rhetorical crusade for democracy. Demands included the right of labor to organize; an eight-hour day and minimum wage; public works projects to end unemployment; a profiteering tax; equal pay for men and women doing similar work; nationalization of basic natural resources; restoration of free speech and freedom for political prisoners; labor representation in all branches of government, including the Paris Peace conference; and finally a League of Workers, to supplement the League of Nations.[39]

Coal miners offered strong support for the CFL's political project. Leading up to the 1918 convention, the IFL conducted a statewide referendum of all affiliated locals on whether a state party should be formed. Taking the UMWA locals in the region for which a vote is recorded, some 80 percent voted to endorse the new party. In Collinsville, the combined vote among the four locals was a lopsided 1008–6. Though no vote is recorded for the Maryville local, other evidence suggests strong support there. Miners endorsed the party unanimously in a number of other towns as well, including Gillespie, Benld, O'Fallon, Edwardsville, and Virden. And in others, such as Glen Carbon, Livingston, Mt. Olive, Carlinville, and Belleville, a substantial majority supported it.

In some locals, the Labor Party was soundly defeated. Rather than reflecting conservatism, however, this may well have reflected the continuing loyalty of some miners to the Socialist Party, which took a hostile stance toward the Labor Party effort. Thus, in Mascoutah, a stronghold of German American Socialists, one miners' local voted 95–0 for the Labor Party, while the other voted 0–84 against it. In Belleville as well, one local opposed the new party 0–348. Even the vote in locals such as in Glen Carbon and Mt. Olive, which approved the party by an impressive margin but by a lower-than-average one, in the range of 75 percent, may have reflected the ongoing presence of the Socialist Party.[40]

In early 1919, local and county branches of the planned state labor party began to crop up in the region. Maryville miners established a local party in February. Dominick Oberto, the former pro-war Socialist, became secretary-treasurer and was nominated to run for village clerk in the April municipal elections. In Collinsville, the UMWA locals banded together to form a party branch in early March. The executive board included Bert Gray of Donk No. 2 and leaders of Consolidated No. 17. Among those nominated to run in the spring elections were Harry Ewing of Donk No. 1, who had run on the Socialist ticket several years before. The presence of the former Socialists suggests that despite the tensions between the Socialist Party and ILP, on the local level, the lines between Socialist and Labor miners were quite fluid.

At a meeting to boost the Collinsville party, longtime UMWA leader T. J. Reynolds explained why miners were turning their backs on the Democrats and Republicans. "We have gone to these people on our knees and have failed to get anything," he said. "We have got to the place where we must organize politically as well as industrially." In the event of a strike, Reynolds observed, miners would gain by having men from their own ranks in office. Noting that the Labor Party movement had already drawn fire from the established parties, Reynolds rose to its defense. "They say it is a class institution," he said, "Let it be so. Heaven knows we have had enough of class institutions and class rule in the past—only it was the other class interest."[41]

As the comments of Reynolds suggest, the miners' interest in the Labor Party came out of the bitter experience they had with both Democrats and

Republicans wielding state power in the interest of their employers. This experience no doubt included the intervention of the Wilson administration in the mine and smelter strikes the previous fall. The use of a federal injunction by SLSR and the role played by Edward C. Knotts in prosecuting the strikers raised questions for working people regarding whom the government truly represented. In this sense, the Labor Party drew its strength from mass struggles and the conclusions miners were beginning to draw from them.

Not surprisingly, the Labor Party did well at the polls in the mining towns of southwestern Illinois. The full Labor slate was swept into office in Glen Carbon and Livingston. In Maryville, as well, voters elected a Labor president of the village board, Nelson Kinder; chose Dominick Oberto for clerk; and selected three Labor trustees. In Williamson, home to the giant No. 2 mine, three aldermen won election.[42] And in Collinsville, James Darmody, a miner and official of UMWA Local 264 at Consolidated No. 17, defeated John H. Siegel and became a Labor mayor.[43]

At the same time that the Labor Party emerged from the struggle of the rank and file, it also reflected the determination of the more conservative labor leaders to keep the postwar working-class upsurge within safe political boundaries. For instance, in their official call for a founding convention of the ILP, issued in early April, John Walker and Victor Olander explained that the party would help save the country from revolution. If better conditions for working people could be secured under the leadership of the Labor Party, they wrote, "the breeding places of so-called Bolshevism will have been destroyed. It will be impossible for it to exist in our country." Similarly, on the eve of the April voting, the CFL's *New Majority* campaigned for the Labor Party candidates by appealing to businessmen. In an editorial entitled "Help Prevent Revolution," the paper hoped that "[e]very business man, big or little, who loves his country and desires to aid in saving the U.S.A. from disorders will vote the Labor Party ticket on April 1."[44]

It is likely that this logic resonated with some miners in southwestern Illinois. Consider, for instance, the resolution on nationalizing the mines, cited earlier, which Jim Walker and Belleville area miners introduced at the January Mooney congress. To motivate the proposal, the preamble stated the following: "We feel that if some drastic change isn't made in the near future that our country is going to drift into a state of unemployment which will result in hunger and misery which will breed anarchy and revolution. To prevent the above," the resolution supported nationalizing the coal mines and other industries.[45]

The politically moderate nature of the ILP was reflected in its program. All units of the party incorporated "Labor's Fourteen Points" into their program. But particularly in the local and county bodies in the region, the Labor Party ran on a platform that stressed good government, fiscal efficiency, fair taxation, and the provision of better services.[46] Membership in the party was not restricted to unionists but was open to all who endorsed the platform and paid their dues. In many ways, the party's approach was indistinguishable from previous "reform" campaigns under the name of the "Citizen Party," "Progressive Party," or "Independent Party." Moreover, there was a high degree of continuity between the established local and subdistrict UMWA leaders and the leadership of the local labor parties in coal mining towns.

In Collinsville, Darmody was nominated to run for the mayor's spot precisely because he was considered to be conservative and "respectable." He had previously served as alderman on an "improvement" platform and also served as city treasurer. "Darmody is a property owner," the *Herald* added, and "the head of a family . . . of some prominence in the community."[47] Newly elected Mayor Darmody explained that the watchword of his administration would be "economy." In order to save money, he planned to eliminate the positions of city attorney and city physician and reduce the number of monthly city council meetings from four to two. Polishing up the local law enforcement apparatus, Darmody appointed a new chief of police and some new patrolmen. As for the trio of police officers who had done nothing to save Robert Prager, they were retained by the new mayor.[48]

But despite the mild reformism of the new Labor Party, the deep working-class impulse that led to the establishment of the ILP was reflected in the range of political issues that were taken up at the founding convention, held just after the spring elections. Miners were prominent among the delegates, with thirty-nine from the southwestern Illinois region alone.[49] Among the resolutions passed by the delegates were those calling for independence for India and Ireland, freedom for Tom Mooney, an end to the Allied blockade of Europe, an end to secret diplomacy, no universal military training in the United States, and the ouster of U.S. Postmaster General Albert Burleson. Delegates also made a point of voicing their support for the miners' demands for the six-hour day, the thirty-hour week, and the nationalization of mines.

Finally, the delegates approved a resolution in support of Soviet Russia. Though few miners were ready to adopt the Communist program, or were even familiar with it, many felt a solidarity with the young workers' republic. The ease with which this resolution sailed through the convention suggests the political space for such views during the brief opening of 1919. The authorship of the resolution was credited to Frank Hefferly, a prominent moderate Socialist miner who attended the convention with credentials from the Maryville local. "Whereas, the Russian people overthrew imperialism and a government of industrial and political autocracy and have proclaimed Russia to be a democratic soviet republic," the resolution began, and given that "the American and allied troops are waging war on the Russian soviet government and the Russian people," the ILP delegates made three demands: that American troops stop hostilities with Russia and withdraw as soon as possible, that the United States influence other Allied countries to withdraw, and that the Wilson administration immediately recognize the Soviet government and restore "friendly diplomatic and commercial relations."[50] Thus, while the *New Majority* railed against Bolshevism at home, the ILP delegates, led by a miner who worked alongside former coworkers of Robert Prager, heartily endorsed it in Russia.

The contradictory character of the Labor Party, as well as the fears it raised among employers, is further suggested by the case of John Lennon of Bloomington. As cited earlier, Lennon wrote to the Labor Department in the wake of the Mooney congress, warning officials about the dangerously high expectations that the congress and the Labor Party movement were creating among working people. The very next day, the conservative, "respectable" Lennon was nominated by the newly organized Bloomington Labor Party to run for mayor. Over the next few months, the local Merchants and Manufacturers Association campaigned against Lennon, calling him a Bolshevist and an anarchist. The Illinois Coal Operators Association joined in the campaign against the Labor Party, running an article against Lennon in its newspaper and circulating it widely.[51]

The fact that Lennon got swept up in the Labor Party campaign and "became" a radical, even as he privately warned against the Labor Party, reflects well the internal contradictions of the movement. Even while the CFL touted the antirevolutionary credentials of the ILP, the Bloomington employers saw more clearly that within the conservative shell of John Lennon, there was indeed a radical kernel that reflected the "great class war" warned about by the Babson Statistical Corporation. The very fact that working people dared to organize independently threatened the established parties and the powerful employers they served. The participation of the miners in the Labor Party movement was just one indication of the great "flood" of change unleashed by the war.

In John Lennon's case, the "Bolshevist" label was mainly a rhetorical barb meant to undercut the appeal of the fairly nonradical Labor Party. It is worth noting, however, that while most miners who were persuaded to abandon the Democrats and Republicans in 1919 gravitated to the Labor Party and others remained loyal to the Socialists, a small number of miners in the region did join the fledgling Communist movement. These miners went beyond sympathizing with the plight of the young Soviet Republic. They believed that the best way for working people to support the Russian revolution was to organize a revolution in the United States.

In Collinsville and Maryville, a handful of Croatian-born miners joined the South Slavic branch of the Communist Party in 1919. Three of the five were U.S. citizens. One had lived in the country for fourteen years, another for nine. They were recruited by Milos Vojonovich, a Croatian-born meatpacker and the secretary of the St. Louis South Slavic branch. Among the many items of literature that Vojonovich sold to area members, perhaps including these miners, were "The Manifesto of the Communist International," "The Class Struggle in America," and "The Communist Manifesto."[52]

Vojonovich and his comrades are known to posterity thanks to the vigilance of a federal agent sent to investigate Bolshevism in St. Louis and southern Illinois in late 1920. The evidence in his report, which also concerns miners farther south in Franklin County, is highly fragmentary and colored by the views of a government agent, but it suggests that pockets of Communist support, especially among newer immigrant miners, were not a rarity in the Illinois coalfields after the war. The presence of Communist coal miners in the Collinsville area after the war, even if only a handful, suggests that the attacks on the rebels of 1919 as "Bolshevists" were not mere rhetoric. The rise of the first workers' republic from the ruins of World War I deeply inspired a number of working people in southwestern Illinois to emulate the example of the Russian workers and peasants.

At least one observer in Collinsville noted this development. In late June 1919, one week before the planned Mooney strike, *Collinsville Herald* editor J. O. Monroe commented that "we see a good deal of Bolshevik literature floating around, directly and indirectly criticizing the form and organization of our American government." Of those who looked to Russia as an example, Monroe warned, "we don't believe they have any conception whatever of the danger that lies in committing control of the whole economic and industrial fabric to the Soviet heads through the abolishment of all private ownership in property and personal rights. That notion is not only revolutionary but to us it is revolting." Monroe's solution to this apparent spread of Bolshevism? "It might not be a bad idea for the Council of Defense to reorganize."[53] Thus, to paraphrase the Babson Statistical Corporation, the great war for democracy was over in Collinsville, but the great class war had only begun.

Into the broader context of independent labor politics came the July 1919 Mooney protest strike in the southwestern Illinois coalfields. If the Mooney strike represented the "rumblings" of discontent over "after-the-war" problems, the strike fines proved to be the shock that brought the earthquake of rebellion out into the open. Monroe's proposal to reinvigorate a wartime agency pointed to a question that became central in the controversy over the Mooney strike fines in late July: was the war actually over? When the miners at St. Louis and O'Fallon No. 2 found that the company had fined them, according to the provisions of the wartime penalty clause, they were outraged. They could not believe they were being penalized on the basis of what one miner called "the miserable technicality that the war is not over."[54] The provisions of the Washington Agreement were to expire either at the end of the war or in April 1920, whichever came first. By fining the miners under the penalty provision, St. Louis and O'Fallon was technically correct, since the peace treaty had yet to be signed.

But eight months after the armistice, miners had ample reason to consider the agreement invalid. In February, the Wilson administration had lifted wartime price controls on the coal operators. Moreover, miners pointed out that the U.S. Fuel Administration, one of the three parties to the agreement, no longer existed. In June, director Harry Garfield closed down the Fuel Administration offices and went back to private life.[55] Despite their anger, the miners stayed on the job in late July, hoping that local union officials would get the fines refunded. But when they refused to call a meeting on the issue, a group of the St. Louis and O'Fallon miners called their own meeting near the mine and quickly decided to refuse work until the company lifted the Mooney fines.

What began as a strike to protest the Mooney fines among miners at St. Louis and O'Fallon's two mines in the waning days of July soon grew into a major rebellion in the entire region, involving tens of thousands of miners. In early August, a mass meeting in Belleville voted to expand the strike throughout the region until the fines were dropped. Moreover, miners issued a call for a special district wage convention to reopen the wartime contract immediately, push for a wage increase from operators, and scotch the hated penalty clause. When the Farrington leadership refused to call such a convention, invoking the technicalities of the district constitution, the rebels formed their own State Policy Committee and called their own convention in Springfield, which met in mid-August and formulated a militant program. This included a demand that operators turn over ownership of the mines to the miners.

In response, Farrington gave local loyalists the authority to hire miners as special deputy sheriffs to put an end to the rebellion. In a series of blistering circulars mailed to miners statewide, the district president charged that the Socialist Labor Party (SLP) was behind the rebellion, that rebels aimed to split from the UMWA, and that rebel leaders were Bolsheviks and anarchists. Under threat of revoking their local union charters and facing union-sponsored armed strikebreakers working with local authorities and this barrage of red-baiting, many miners returned to work by the end of August. Others, however, stayed out and tried to spread the movement throughout the state. Hundreds of rebel miners, known as "crusaders," marched from town to town, enlisting the support of new contingents of miners. Women also played an active and visible role in maintaining the rebellion. In early September, Farrington, with authority from UMWA International acting president John L. Lewis, revoked the charters of twenty-four of the most tenacious locals. Farrington also openly invited area coal operators to discriminate against the most outspoken rebels, and in the aftermath of the rebellion, many miners lost their jobs, and men and women were jailed. Several weeks later, at the UMWA International Convention in Cleveland, the regular delegates voted not to seat delegates from the expelled locals. But their presence was very much felt in the decisions of the convention. Most important, the miners voted to declare the Washington Agreement null and void as of November 1 and authorized a national strike to begin on that date.

While the story of the rank-and-file rebellion has been told before, there are a number of unexplored aspects of these events in southwestern

Illinois that will help illuminate the broader theme of workers and World War I.[56] In particular, it is worth examining the experiences of Local 685 president Robert Bertolero, who was swept up in the events of the August rebellion; James Walker of Donk No. 1; and District 12 president Frank Farrington. While existing accounts of the revolt center on the mines around Belleville, the focus here is on the Collinsville vicinity. Just as the miners "set the nation wondering" the previous year by seeming to shift from militant class solidarity to militant patriotism, they once again made a dramatic shift. The members of Local 1802 in Maryville, who apparently would not countenance dissent in 1918, embraced it in 1919.

The course of events in Collinsville roughly paralleled that of Belleville, but with some significant differences. Answering quickly to the call of the St. Louis and O'Fallon miners, the Collinsville and Maryville miners joined the strike in early August. They sent delegates to the policy committee and the state rebel convention. After those at the convention declared their work completed, the Collinsville miners returned to work on Thursday, August 21. But the following day, Donk Brothers Coal and Coke fired a number of the strike leaders, including Charles McDaid and John Kreumeich, who worked at the new No. 4 mine, under construction, and Bert Gray of the Maryville mine. By Monday, as more former strikers were fired, nearly all the miners went back on strike. One week later, Farrington carried out his threat and revoked the charters of the four locals in Collinsville and one in Maryville. Rather than demoralize the strikers, however, this move just angered them further. Two days later, they set off on a crusade to convince miners farther north to rejoin the strike. Though the leading scholar of the rebellion described the mid-August rebel convention as the "crest" of the movement, the Collinsville rebellion was still going strong in early September. In fact, miners there did not return to work until September 21, after the UMWA International Convention had set the November 1 strike deadline. In all, they had stayed out for nearly seven weeks. Considering this fact together with the high number of locals expelled (only Peoria sported a higher number), Collinsville could rightly be considered the single most rebellious town in Illinois.[57]

What motivated the rebels? According to Frank Farrington, the "trouble" resulted from "a well organized and long planned scheme on the part of the Socialist Labor Party and the Industrial Workers of the World to wreck the United Mine Workers of America." By using "deception and by appeals to passion and prejudice," Farrington claimed, "they were able to delude hundreds of honest, loyal men to follow them in their work of destruction."[58] Farrington also claimed that some of the rebels were Bolsheviks. At the debate over the rebellion at the March 1920 Illinois miners' convention, he presented his evidence for the delegates to see. "Here is a picture of Jukov, first chairman of the Bolshevik Revolutionary Tribunal, here is one of Trotsky. Here is one of Lenin—all taken out of a union meeting hall in the Belleville district."[59]

Despite his transparent and classic attempt to blame the rebellion on outside agitators, there was a grain of truth in Farrington's charges. There was a degree of sympathy for the Russian revolution among the miners. And members of the SLP played key leadership roles at a number of points. These included Henry Schilling and Philip Veal of Belleville and David Reid of Collinsville, who headed the State Policy Committee. The ideas and peculiar language of the SLP were clearly reflected in the resolution passed by miners in Priester's Park on August 3 in Belleville. That document, introduced by Philip Veal, called on workers to hold an "industrial congress" that would demand that employers turn over all industry to the workers and urged miners to pull the control of their organization "out of the claws of the labor fakirs."[60]

Moreover, Farrington produced copies of SLP literature showing that the party hoped to capitalize on the dissatisfaction in the ranks to win miners away from the UMWA. After the local charters were revoked, for instance, state SLP leaders reported that "[t]he sentiment among the miners here of completely pulling away from the U.M.W.A. and joining the W.I.I.U. [Workers International Industrial Union] is running high. That seems to be the next logical move on their part and it behooves all of us to explain what the W.I.I.U. is and how it differs from the I.W.W. from now on."[61] The SLP had high hopes for pulling Illinois coal miners out of the hands of Farrington and his allies, whom they called the compliant "poodles" of the mine owners.

But both the SLP and Farrington exaggerated the extent to which miners had rebelled against the UMWA. For the bulk of miners, the rebellion is best seen as an attempt of the rank and file to make more effective, democratic use of their cherished union. Rather than trying to break from the union, the rebels were attempting to push their leaders into action. During the summer, in anticipation of the September International Convention, numerous locals in the region passed resolutions reflecting the militant demands they wanted the convention to adopt. From locals in Belleville and New Athens in St. Clair County; Virden, Girard, and Carlinville in Macoupin County; and Maryville and Collins-ville in Madison County, miners consistently urged that the UMWA adopt the following demands: a six-hour day, a five-day week, double time for overtime pay, a substantial wage increase (50–60 percent), and nationalization of the mines. During the rebellion, the Freeburg local did pass a resolution arguing that, due to corruption in District 12, all dis-trict officials should be barred from the next wage negotiations. Still, they did not call for abandoning the UMWA.[62]

The Maryville miners' resolution had appeared in print on April 5, 1919, exactly one year after some members of Local 1802 had helped lynch Robert Prager. Prefacing their demands, the miners noted the severe shortage of work and pointed out how loyal coal miners had been dur-ing the war. Miners "proved their loyalty to the government, first in pro-ducing all the coal necessary, and second by the purchase of Liberty Bonds and donations to all war funds." Given the hardship caused by un-employment and the high cost of living, the Maryville miners were now ready to be rewarded for their patriotism. It was this kind of sentiment among miners in the spring that proved so explosive in August.

Given this sentiment, how did the rebels go about organizing the strike? A crucial tactic was the "crusade." The scene of miners marching from one town to another to spread the strike hearkened back to the great struggle of 1897. As in the earlier case, the marchers of 1919 were dubbed "Coxey's Army," referring to the famous 1894 march of unemployed workers from Massillon, Ohio, to Washington, D.C., led by quixotic busi-nessman and reformer Jacob Coxey. In both 1897 and 1919, it was the independent action of the crusaders that provided the power behind the strikes. More than any of the resolutions passed by the State Policy Com-mittee in 1919, the disciplined action of thousands of rank-and-file min-ers taking to the streets and roads of the coal regions was the aspect of the rebellion most threatening to the Farrington leadership. In his cir-cular of September 8, for example, Farrington described the marchers in alarming terms: "Hundreds of self-constituted committees went madly over the district trying to incite all of you to join in the rebellion."[63] Not surprisingly, it was the crusaders were who most subject to the attacks of special deputies hired by the Farrington forces.

In Collinsville, the marchers did not set off until September 4, when many miners elsewhere had already returned to work. Early that afternoon, the 170 crusaders assembled near city hall, joined by hundreds of other miners and women from coal mining families. The crusaders were headed by a forty-man contingent of miners who had served in the war. They marched in full army uniform and included a drummer and flag bearer. At the sendoff rally, policy committee chairman David Reid addressed his remarks particularly to the veterans among the miners. "The war in which you lately fought, I cannot say, was particularly in the interests of working people," Reid began. "But this war you are entering concerns no one else. . . . In the late war you learned the necessity for discipline," Reid continued. "I will depend on you to enforce discipline among your fellow marchers in this war for the workers. Do nothing that will conflict with the laws of the country." Finally, Reid portrayed the rebellion in-terms of the war against autocracy. "It is just as necessary that you clean out the kaiser and the bunch of despots in our state organization as it was to clean out the German kaiser and his despots," he said. Clarifying his point, he added that "[y]ou are seeking to purify, not to disrupt, the organization."

The picture presented here offers a fascinating contrast to the scene at city hall on the fatal night of April 4, 1918. Both gatherings featured patriotic displays and the use of Wilsonian war rhetoric. But on this afternoon in 1919, instead of embodying George Creel's "white-hot mass instinct" for devotion to the war against German autocracy, the miners pursued a much different agenda. By mobilizing around demands to transfer mines to the miners, end the hated penalty clause, and force a militant program on the upcoming UMWA convention, the miners set themselves on a collision course with their employers and the administration in Washington.

Before the crusaders departed, Robert Bertolero of Local 685 also addressed the crowd. During the war, Bertolero had been one of Collinsville's most enthusiastic war boosters and had served on the local Council of Defense. But in his speech, Bertolero took the occasion to denounce the penalty clause. It was wrong "because it works only one way," the *Collinsville Herald* reported. "When the men fail to work they are fined, he said, but when the mine blows for work and then does not work the company excuses the inconvenience to the men on the ground by saying there were no [railroad] cars. He said the penalty clause was necessary and right in war times but not now." Bertolero also explained that he did not fully sympathize with the strike at the outset, "but he felt bound to act with the men who had elected him local president or resign."[64]

This last comment points to an important dynamic among local union leaders during the rank-and-file rebellion. Bertolero was one of many local officers who were unwittingly swept by union members into the strikes of August and September. At the International Convention in mid-September, Bertolero explained how he got involved. "When [the St. Louis and O'Fallon] strikers came to my mine and asked for support, I said, 'so far as having the fine refunded, there is a proper way to get it back without striking.' I was local president, and some of the boys [at Lumaghi No. 2] said I was getting cold feet. I said I was not getting cold feet and asked if they were willing to go home, and if they were, I was willing to go, too. As local president I was not supposed to start any trouble, but when a majority of the men who elected me were going home I thought I had a *right* to follow them."[65]

Bertolero's experience was repeated by many other union officials who found that no amount of speech-making would make the miners return to work. Even Socialist miners with a certain reputation for militancy, such as Subdistrict 7 leaders Dan Thomas and Jim Walker, ran into a brick wall when they tried to reason with the strikers. "I could see the mood of the men," Thomas recalled. "They had no patience with an officer, the agreement, the constitution or anything else." Similarly, Walker explained that "[w]e tried to get the men to remain at work." But "[i]n these mass meetings the men did not seem to pay much attention to what we said. They didn't seem to care whether they went to work or not." Still, even as he made the effort, Walker defended the actions of the rank and file, just as Bertolero did. "Probably the men did violate the [UMWA] constitution," he said. "But . . . since the war closed men all over the world have been blowing up. It is not the so-called rebels in the Belleville District that are responsible for the rebellion that is tearing up things all over the world . . . it was the profiteers and high cost of living that caused them."[66]

Not only did Robert Bertolero follow his flock out of the mines, but the former superpatriot unintentionally played a role in widening the rebellion on the eve of the August Springfield convention. When he arrived in that city as a delegate of Local 685, he was beaten up on the street by a number of Farrington loyalists. They had been tipped off to his impending arrival by a telegram from Mose Johnson to Farrington. The rebels later got hold of the telegram, and the incident galvanized many

Springfield miners to join the rebellion.[67] Thus, pressure to strike from Local 685 members combined with the violence of the Farrington establishment to turn Bertolero from a celebrated loyal American into an alleged Bolshevik.

After hearing from Bertolero, Reid, and others on September 4, the Collinsville crusaders formed ranks and stepped off on their march. Whereas the 1897 marchers were provisioned from a horse-drawn carriage, the miners of 1919 were accompanied by an automobile truck carrying fifty dollars' worth of food, donated by local merchants. They headed north to Maryville, where some 250 miners joined in the march, then continued on to Glen Carbon and Edwardsville. They passed into northern Madison County, where meetings were held in Worden, Livingston, and Williamson. Finally, they reached Staunton, where most miners remained at work. Though the Staunton miners refused to join the strike, they let the crusaders pass through peacefully, and at least one of the working miners generously donated a pig to the hungry crusaders.[68] At the dawn of the automobile age, the miners still lived the semirural life of twenty years earlier; this proved crucial in surviving the strike.

As in the 1897 strike, coal mining women played an essential role in convincing miners to stay away from the mines. In mid-September, for instance, a crowd of Collinsville strikers assembled early in the morning at the Pennsylvania Railroad depot, where working miners made a brief train ride on a spur to Consolidated No. 17. According to the *Herald,* "The men near the depot were joined by a dozen Russian women who live in that vicinity and who put themselves at the head of the insurgent party." When a handful of miners tried to pass by the crowd to the train, "they were accosted only by the women, who stretched out their arms and jabbered in their broken tongue." The men on strike "stood behind and at times offered arguments against the workers going on." In a few cases, the women threw rocks at the strikebreakers and hit two of them on the arm.[69] The centrality of women in this activity is confirmed by the comment of a miner from this region who told fellow delegates at the UMWA International Convention in mid-September that "[t]en days ago I took my dinner bucket and went out to the mine and the women folks chased me back home."[70]

Coal mining women not only took the lead in such confrontations but also suffered the consequences, along with coal miners, of the state repression visited on strikers. For instance, coal operators of Marissa refused to rehire strike leaders, filing charges against strikers and their supporters in St. Clair County court. They secured indictments against fifty-six miners and thirteen miners' wives and daughters on the charges of intimidation, riot, and conspiracy. According to Rose North, who saw the women being taken away, one of them was nursing a six-month-old child. Some of the women spent up to eleven nights in jail before being released. Authorities offered to let off one woman with a twenty-five-dollar fine if she would plead guilty. But as William Lami, who headed up a defense committee for the jailed rebels, commented, "This she nobly declined to do."[71]

The mobilization of Collinsville women at the Pennsylvania depot spurred Mayor Darmody to issue an order to the police forbidding any further mass meetings. Shortly thereafter, six insurgent leaders were arrested on charges of "rout." At a later mass meeting, which Darmody attended, some miners began to talk of breaking from the UMWA; the Labor Party mayor then interrupted the discussion, declaring that he had given permission for a meeting only to discuss returning to work. In Maryville, too, village board president Nelson Kinder, who worked as a non-UMWA mechanic at the Donk No. 2 mine, lost the support of many working people when he answered the company's call to return to work during the strike. Thus, the militancy of both the men and the women strained the political limits of the Labor Party.[72]

As they challenged the authority of the state in carrying out their rebellion, coal miners made sure to show just how patriotic they were. Uniformed American Expeditionary Force veterans of the war led the Collinsville crusaders out of town. Even miners like David Reid who raised questions about the democratic aims of the war still used the rhetoric of democracy and autocracy to describe the rebellion's goals. It is clear that miners aimed to lend legitimacy to their actions by draping them in the mantle of the flag. It is less clear that this strategy succeeded. For instance, when a contingent of crusaders headed south into Perry County, led by uniformed war veterans, its members, including Glen Carbon Socialist Dan Slinger, were attacked at Pinckneyville by special deputies and then arrested by the county sheriff.[73] Their evident patriotic loyalty seemed to avail them little. Like the men and women thrown into the Marissa jail, the Belleville marchers in Perry County failed to convince either Frank Farrington or the coal operators that they were other than subversive.

At the September UMWA International Convention, the protective power of patriotism was briefly debated by miners in a way that sheds light on this incident. A resolution proposed that every miner who had done military service be presented by the UMWA with a bronze medal, reading "A gallant member, For heroic service performed in the great World War 1917–1918." After the text of the resolution was read, someone raised an objection from the floor but declined to elaborate. Then, James Gillespie of Stonington, Illinois, rose and clarified his fellow miner's objection: "I presume the delegate over here feels that if the miners' medal is put on one of his brothers and he is sent to one of those unorganized fields he would get his head cracked," Gillespie explained. "If an organizer went there with such a medal, would it save him? Not on your tintype!"[74] Miners were hardly of one opinion on this question. But the Pinckneyville incident suggests that even in UMWA strongholds like Illinois, miners learned that patriotic displays might be of little help in the heat of class battle.

Still, the idea that miners were not true patriots incensed them and spurred them on to further action. For instance, one of the initial leaders of the policy committee, starting with the second big mass meeting in Belleville, was Belleville miner and flag striker Luke Coffey. He explained how the tide had turned among his coworkers. At first, many of the St. Clair County miners were impressed when in late July, Frank Farrington notified John L. Lewis that the Washington Agreement no longer applied and that miners needed a new contract immediately. Farrington seemed to be sharing their militant stand. But when the miners "went on strike and got a copy of the *Belleville Democrat,* according to which he accused every man in that strike of being a Bolshevik, and I.W.W. and everything on the map outside of being a man, you can imagine the outcome," Coffey said. "The men got sore, not only at Lewis but at Farrington also, and the fight was on."

Coffey's case provides a kind of mirror image of Joe Riegel, who seemed to jump from radicalism to reaction. In the hot spring of 1918, Coffey went to extreme lengths to demonstrate the miners' patriotism. Then by the summer of 1919, accusations of unpatriotism sent him off in the direction of deeper class solidarity with his fellow miners. In early 1920, facing disciplinary action by the Farrington administration, Coffey vowed that "[i]f I am deprived of the right to dig coal under the United Mine Workers I will find a living in some other walk of life—I will not dig any scab coal. I never fed a child of mine a mouthful of scab bread in my life, and I'll be damned if I do it now!"[75]

How effective was the rebellion? After reconstructing the events of the strike in her study of rebel unionism, Sylvia Kopald assessed it as "a struggle that had been lost" by the insurgents. "Thus," she concluded, "a violent and almost spontaneous uprising created by a tense 'bread and butter' unrest, which had eventually metamorphosed into a struggle between union officials and union rank and file, had been successfully crushed by the union organization."[76] Certainly the Farrington leadership successfully harnessed the ample resources of the district against the strikers. As Kopald and others have noted, district secretary Walter Nesbit acknowledged in 1920 that the union spent some $27,000 in putting down the rebellion, though he refused to itemize it.

In fact, in a testament to the union democracy still prevailing at that late date, Nesbit was forced in 1922 to provide District 12 members a detailed itemization of this budget. His report proves that the District 12 executive board did hire hundreds of miners as official strikebreakers and special deputies, paying the handsome fee of $6.50 per day, more than twice what Frank Rissi had been making at the Maryville mine. In addition, testimony given before an investigating board suggested that some of the money paid for guns and a generous supply of alcohol, which both served as tools to convince miners to return to work. Moreover, it seems that, following the pattern of the Virden fight in 1898 and the Collinsville smelter strike of 1917, a good number of the strikebreakers were African American miners, thus deepening the divisions that had already developed along racial lines.[77]

But if Farrington did succeed in forcing miners back to work, what about the larger objective of the rebellion? In Collinsville, opinion among miners was divided on whether the strike had accomplished anything. In tallying up the cost of the struggle to miners, J. O. Monroe estimated that they had collectively sacrificed over a quarter million dollars in pay. Many of the miners Monroe talked to believed the strike had been in vain. But others, like rebel leader Tom White, argued that the struggle had been well worth it. After the International Convention voted to strike on November 1, White told the *Herald* "that he believed the [Illinois rebel] movement alone had brought International President Lewis to his recommendation for the abrogation of the war time contracts and agreement on November 1 instead of April 1, 1920 and . . . for the elimination of the automatic penalty clause." This change in position, "coupled with Lewis's threat to strike all the mines in the country," White thought, would "bring the men greater benefits than those they would have derived from continuing to work under the old contract."[78]

The rebellion, in White's view, acted as a lever that the ranks of miners used to force their leaders into action against the coal operators. Though the rebellion appeared to be an affair between factions of miners, White perceived that the rebels ultimately aimed their fire at their employers. Far from a unconditional loss for the rank and file, then, the rebellion was a fundamental factor ensuring that the UMWA officials agreed to launch the national strike in November. To the degree that the national strike was a powerful weapon in securing some gains for miners and their families, the rebellion can be counted a success.

The participation by southwestern Illinois coal miners in the national coal strike is the fourth and final chapter of the "great class war" of 1919. At the International Convention in Cleveland in September, the UMWA delegates authorized a strike beginning November 1. In the six weeks following that decision, union and operator representatives met in Buffalo for negotiations but got nowhere. Last-minute discussions convened at the White House by Secretary of Labor William B. Wilson also failed to produce results. By October 25, the stage was set for a showdown, and the operators were hoping for full government cooperation in breaking a nationwide miners' strike.[79]

It is difficult to exaggerate the level of political alarm that the planned miners' strike aroused that October. Just as Frank Farrington tried to tar the rebels of August and September as wild radicals, Thomas Brewster, the leading national spokesperson for the coal operators, publicly asserted that the strike had been ordered by Lenin and Trotsky, financed with Moscow gold.[80] Brewster may have been influenced by his own recent experience with the "Bolsheviks" of southwestern Illinois. He owned the Mt. Olive and Staunton Coal Company, which ran mines in Staunton and Williamson. The Collinsville crusaders had marched through Brewster's terrain only a month earlier.

Similarly, on October 31, the *New York Times* editorialized against the imminent walkout under the title "A Causeless Strike." Of the nation's miners, the *Times* wrote that "[i]t is hard to believe that they are not tinctured with that embittered revolutionary radicalism which is the greatest danger of labor associations and is striving so hard to break up the American Federation of Labor." Affecting concern for the "responsible" labor movement, the *Times* warned that "if class selfishness or the inoculation of violent ideas threatens disaster to the whole country, what but disruption and destruction can come to labor unions so conducted?"[81]

On the other hand, it would be a mistake to dismiss these dire pronouncements as mere paranoia. The nation had never seen anything like this before. For employers, the prospect of over a half million steelworkers and miners on strike was a new and terrifying prospect, especially in industries that were so interconnected. The degree of working-class unity required to even contemplate such struggles was unprecedented. Moreover, these were walkouts sanctioned by top union officials, not wildcat strikes. In a sense, mobilizing massive union power in this way was a radical challenge to the power of coal operators and steel magnates.

Though there were sharp limits to the solidarity within and between these strikes, there were close connections between the miners and steel strikers. At the request of William Z. Foster of the steel strikers, for instance, Frank Hefferly of the Maryville miners' local was assigned by John L. Lewis to help organize the steel strike in Pittsburgh and Youngstown. Writing on September 30 to Harry Ewing of the Donk No. 1 mine in Collinsville, Hefferly reported that "I addressed several overflow meetings at Homestead," which were attended by the hated "cossacks," special deputies armed and paid by the steel companies.[82] "Tonight we had a monster mass-meeting in the labor temple here—20,000 strikers. We could not speak to half of them at the time. Yet [Judge Elbert] Gary [of United States Steel] says there is no strike. The press is vicious and lying as usual. The men are sticking fine. There are about 450,000 out in the U.S., the biggest affair that ever was. I believe the men will win."[83] Hefferly's assignment in 1919 presaged the central role that UMWA officials would play in organizing steelworkers as part of the Congress of Industrial Organizations in the 1930s and 1940s.

In late October, facing the likelihood of 400,000 coal miners joining the steelworkers, President Wilson fired off a preemptive strike against the UMWA. On October 25, in a statement prepared by Joseph Tumulty and Walker D. Hines for the bedridden president and approved by him from his sick bed, Wilson stated that the miners' planned strike was "not only unjustifiable; it is unlawful." Miners threatened to curtail the production of coal when "the war itself is still a fact . . . when our troops are still being transported and when their means of transport is in urgent need of fuel," Wilson charged. Miners, in other words, would be violating the Lever Act, which forbade "conspiracies" to stop the production of food or fuel. "I cannot believe that any right of any American worker needs for its protection the taking of this extraordinary step," the president told the miners. "[A]nd I am convinced that when the time and money are considered it constitutes a fundamental attack, which is wrong both morally and legally, upon the rights of society and upon the welfare of our society."[84]

This proved to be only the opening salvo of the government offensive against the miners. On October 31, Attorney General A. Mitchell Palmer obtained a temporary restraining order from federal judge Albert Anderson in Indianapolis, with a full hearing on permanent injunction scheduled for November 8. But the statement from President Wilson, who had posed as the friend of labor and been received as such by millions of working people, caused an immediate political uproar among miners and their families. Among those who wrote to Wilson in the days following his statement was Mrs. J. A. Faulkner, "a Minar's wife" from Cutler, Illinois. Her letter eloquently evoked the feelings of betrayal felt by many working people in 1919 after having made so many sacrifices during the war. At the same time, she evinced a deep patriotism and an abiding religious faith. For the sheer poignancy of her words and the way they illuminate broader themes, her letter is worth quoting at some length:

> I want to explain facts which i know to be gospel truths When the war started we had Been on half time for two years or more an almost every family was in Dept more or less. and when your call came for men we Responded and when your call came for more coal we Responded, with all the strenght of our Beings then when your call came for conservation, we done with out Sugar flour and other things which you needed for the Soldiers, they was our soldiers as well as yours and we was proud of them, and glad that we could send so many to preserve our Beloved Constitution. then when the call came for aid to help the Red Cross and Y.M.C.A. and the Salvation army We Responded to our full ability then came the Liberty Bonds and War Savings Stamps.... Now the capital press say that the miners had an unprecedented chance to Save money while the war Lasted. Did we[?] ...
>
> ... after the armistice was Signed the Mines Shut Down to half time or less and the Nessarys of Life Sores higher and higher untill the time is at hand when we cant live at all. an what we are allowed to Earn hedged around with this War Emergency Contract as we are. We just haft to have Some Reliefe and that at once.... Why i know lots of familys that cant send their children to School Because they cant get them shoes and clothing and the same cause

is keeping adults as well as children away from church and Sunday School Why I myself havent had a Dress or a pair of Shoes Since the war started. . . .

Now the Miners Dont wante to Embaress the Nation, or Cause any suffering for they Realize that what will make one suffer will make all suffer. But if they give in now when there is pressing need for coal and waite untill Spring the operators will make big profits all this Long Winter while we half Starve and go Bear in a Land of plenty. . . .

i know full well that they are willing (the miners i mean) to make conssesions if they are aproached in a spirit of give and take But you wise man that you are seemed to Loos Sight of the human Side of this proceedings. . . .

your honor i have wrote this in an effort to show you that the miners are not extemest or anarkist. But out of the fullness of my heart which Begs for a Little More Equal Rights and Less Special Privelages for the Moneyed Enterest of our Beloved Nation. . . .

i will still continue to pray for your full Recovery to Normal health as i have in the past, for we need you Still. May god Bless and keep you amen.[85]

It would be hard to imagine a more moving illustration of the tug-of-war experienced by the working people of the Illinois coalfields in the aftermath of the armistice. In her letter, Mrs. Faulkner tries desperately to maintain her own sense of patriotic loyalty, obedience to authority, subordination in a female role, and political moderation. The miners don't want to "Embaress" the country. Wilson is a "wise man." In condemning the strike, he "seemed to Loos Sight" of things. Perhaps you are simply uninformed, she seemed to be saying. The miners are not extremists or "anarkists." They are loyal citizens.

But her letter also offers a devastating answer to the president's statement, one that cannot help but express a sharp sense of class injustice and militancy. The newspapers who condemned the miners, for instance, are the "capital press." The miners need relief, not after April 20 but "at once." The miners, she explains to Wilson, have to strike now, or else they will lose their leverage with the operators. That is, the "extraordinary step" that Wilson decried was indeed necessary. If miners waited, they would "go Bear in a Land of plenty," the central and continuing irony of capitalist life that mining families had faced for decades. Finally, even as Mrs. Faulkner spoke of the suffering of the "nation," she pointed to the "Moneyed Enterest" of that nation as the culprit.

Though general surveys suggest that the "public" tended to take President Wilson's side of the controversy, the miners won many supporters in southwestern Illinois. In Staunton, for instance, the editor of the *Star-Times* took quite a different position from his counterparts at the *New York Times.* "All that the miners are asking is that they may earn enough money to properly provide for their families and live as Americans ought to live," he wrote. "There is nothing unjust about such a demand and it should be granted without quibbling."[86] At the *Collinsville Herald,* J. O. Monroe shared the miners' impatience with the Washington Agreement. The "technicality of waiting four or fourteen months for the signing of the peace treaty doesn't fill any stomachs," he wrote. As far as their wage demands, Monroe wrote that "[p]ersonally and from every consideration of the welfare of Collinsville, we should like to see them get the sixty percent wage increase." On the other hand, Monroe thought less of the miners' demands for a shorter workweek. "As for the thirty hour week," he wrote, "we think that is nonsense. We don't believe the Good Lord intended a man to rest two days in seven." In any event, Monroe predicted the strike would be short. "[B]efore the middle of November, we venture . . . the matter will be settled somehow."[87]

On November 1, the miners struck. The mines of southwestern Illinois were shut down tight. In Collinsville, the *Herald* reported, miners responded "100 percent to the call for the strike."[88] During the first week of the walkout, all eyes were on Indianapolis to see how Judge Anderson would respond to Palmer's request for an injunction to make the strike illegal. In the meantime, the Wilson administration placed federal troops on alert in the West Virginia coalfields and sent out secret agents to Indianapolis, who conducted surveillance on UMWA headquarters and put a tap on Acting President John L. Lewis's phone.[89]

On November 8, Anderson handed the government the injunction and gave the UMWA three days to end the strike. The injunction barred a total of eighty-four international and district officials from doing anything to advance the strike, including distributing strike benefits. According to Melvyn Dubofsky and Warren Van Tine, "It was the most sweeping injunction issued against a major union since the Pullman Boycott of 1894."[90] As Illinois miners waited for the response of their leaders, they received word from Farrington to stand firm and stay away from the mines. At their meeting of November 10, for instance, the Collinsville miners at Consolidated No. 17 heard Farrington's communication that, according to the minutes, instructed "the Members to stay away from the Mines and do everything in your favor in a lawfull way to make the strike effective."[91]

Faced with the Anderson injunction, Lewis called an emergency meeting of the executive board. Apparently Alexander Howat, the militant leader of the Kansas miners, and Frank Farrington took the position that the UMWA should defy the injunction. But Lewis and his allies prevailed, and in the early hours of November 11, the board voted to obey Anderson's order. In a public statement, Lewis said, "We will comply with the mandate of the court. We do this under protest. *We are Americans. We cannot fight our government.*" Another top UMWA official said, "We expect the men to obey the withdrawal order. All of the power and influence of the union will be brought to bear immediately to get the men to return to work."[92]

As is well known, the ranks of miners did not obey the withdrawal order. In most places, including southwestern Illinois, the strike remained solid. According to Dubofsky and Van Tine, Lewis knew that the miners would ignore his order and would understand that he was simply going through the motions of canceling the strike. The decision to cancel, that is, was a clever political move that put the ball in the Wilson administration's court. They would have to make the next move. And three days later, in fact, Secretary of Labor Wilson offered a compromise solution to the wage dispute, proposing that miners and operators agree on a 31 percent wage hike. At the same time, President Wilson called Harry Garfield back to Washington and the U.S. Fuel Administration back into being. For his part, Garfield proposed a compromise of 14 percent, which was actually below the 20 percent offered by the coal operators.

To some extent, the benevolent interpretation of Lewis's actions was shared by miners in Collinsville. Initially, according to the *Herald,* the decision to cancel initially caused a "wave of bitterness." But when most local union presidents received copies of the press coverage of Lewis's order, they did not take them seriously. The order was not on UMWA stationery and did not include Lewis's signature. The majority of miners believed that the order "did not represent the real judgement of the officials on the merits of the strike situation." Contrary to the statement of top officials that the union would force the men back to work, most Collinsville miners believed that "the officials were aware that the men would not return to work and did not expect them to do so." Thus, the miners imagined that as John Lewis looked solemnly at reporters and ended the strike, he gave the miners an invisible wink, as if to say, "Just kidding." One Collinsville UMWA official even told the *Herald* "that he thought somebody had been joking with federal judge Anderson who approved the withdrawal order."[93]

On the other hand, at least some miners in the region were incensed at Lewis's public capitulation to the Anderson injunction. The day after Lewis declared his unwillingness to fight the government, the Benld miners held a special meeting to discuss his action. In a telegram to Lewis, sent that day, the members of Local 730 informed him that "your decision in calling off the strike order was condemned by a unanimous vote, and motion was adopted to stay out until a new contract is negotiated and ratified by a national convention. Also, a motion was adopted asking for resignation of J. L. Lewis and Secretary William Green." Adding insult to injury, the miners addressed the telegram to Lewis not to Indianapolis but in "care of William B. Wilson" at the Labor Department.[94]

The Benld miners not only fired off their telegram to Lewis but also made some effort to mobilize broader opposition to Lewis's decision. At a union meeting on November 24, for instance, members of Collinsville's Local 264 read and discussed the Benld resolution. Since these miners could not agree on their response, they tabled the question.[95] Still, the fact that the Lewis announcement initially caused a "wave of bitterness" in town suggests that more than a few Collinsville miners may have sympathized with the sentiments of their fellow unionists in Benld. Perhaps it is appropriate that Lewis's agreement to call off the troops came on the first anniversary of Armistice Day. But Collinsville miners apparently did not appreciate the coincidence. According to the *Herald,* "Miners found occasion to contrast the holiday idea with their disappointment at the day's developments in the mine strike situation, word being received early in the morning of the withdrawal of the strike order by President Lewis."[96]

Furthermore, miners at a mass meeting in Carterville, in southern Illinois, openly defied the injunction. In a printed statement "To the Public of Carterville and the U.S.A. in General," the Carterville miners ridiculed the miraculous reappearance of the U.S. Fuel Administration's Garfield. Since February, the coal operators had been profiteering off inflated coal prices, they charged. "And where was Dr. Garfield? . . . We suppose he was setting eggs for nine months and leaving the profiteering to his own kind." But "the moment the miners asked for their rights as wage workers Dr. Garfield comes to life again and says the contract of the miners is not out." In conclusion, they resolved that "the miners . . . are good law abiding citizens and willing to do anything for our government that is fair, but we are not willing to abide by the decision of Judge Anderson." And in open defiance of the law, the Carterville miners resolved that "every member of our union stay at home on and after Tuesday, November 11, 1919, until we have an agreement to work by." An almost identical resolution was made by miners in Peoria.[97]

In the three weeks following November 11, Illinois miners held firm. By early December, with the temperature plummeting, southwestern Illinois was feeling the effects of the walkout. "The fuel situation has become acute," announced Mayor Darmody of Collinsville. The lead smelter was shut down, the electric plant operated only half-time, and residents began to substitute wood, kerosene, and crude oil for coal. Facing this dire situation, Illinois employers appealed to the government for sterner action. Writing to the Justice Department on December 2, a manufacturer in Champaign proposed that "martial law be established in the mining districts and that every miner residing in such districts be compelled to mine coal or move out. . . . Any quibbling over technicalities while the people are starving and freezing," he warned, "are liable to be swept away in an attempt to over-throw the government by these radical union leaders."[98]

In early December, the government offered 100,000 federal troops to protect strikebreakers and declared martial law in the Wyoming coalfields. Bureau of Investigation and Immigration Service agents stepped up their harassment of strikers. Even though Lewis had publicly called off the strike, Judge Anderson cited all Indiana UMWA officials for contempt on December 3 and issued warrants for their arrest. In the wake of this action, the Belleville Manufacturers Association wired its approval to Attorney General Palmer. "[W]e heartily endorse your decision to enforce the law to protect the public[.] [I]n general we insist that the federal government use all the power at its command to compel immediate resumption of all coal mines pending adjudication."[99]

Coupled with this continuing repression, the Wilson administration proposed a new compromise offer. If miners returned to work with a 14 percent wage hike, there would be a federal coal commission appointed, and the president would guarantee that miners' other demands would receive fair attention. Once again, Lewis convened top union officials, and once again, after much discussion, they agreed to the government's proposal. In the course of the discussion, Lewis argued for ending the strike with the following words: "I will not fight my government, the greatest government on earth." On December 11, Lewis unveiled Wilson's offer to the nation's miners and requested that they go back to digging coal. He also announced that miners could vote on this proposal at a special International Convention in January 1920.[100]

In taking a stand in favor of ending the strike, John L. Lewis sparked much controversy then and since. As Dubofsky and Van Tine have noted, Lewis was criticized by UMWA radicals for "selling out the miners in 1919." As these authors summarize the critique of Lewis: "Had the miners remained on strike, the government would have forced the operators to concede to union demands, and the UMW and organized labor in America would have entered the 1920s a rising instead of declining power in society." In defense of Lewis, his biographers make the following points. First, Lewis knew that when Eugene Debs defied an injunction and went to prison in the 1894 Pullman strike, the strike collapsed. The lesson: no officers, no strike. Second, "[A]ll of the UMW radicals shared Lewis's perception of reality in December 1919: John Brophy, Frank Farrington, Alex Howat and Robert Harlin all signed the call for the strike's termination and not one voted against the December 10 decision." Third, even if the UMWA called on miners to stay out, they would have buckled under the impressive array of repressive tactics available to the government. "No one enjoys dwelling within sight of armed troops nor living under constant surveillance with mail intercepted and phones tapped nor fearing summary deportation nor enduring constant legal process," Dubofsky and Van Tine write. "That would have been the fate of coal miners had the strike continued." In sum, "Lewis did what he had to do in December 1919, what circumstances and the realities of power demanded. Had he been more radical and less conservative, more idealistic and less opportunistic, he probably would have acted similarly." Put simply, Lewis had no choice.[101]

Considering that Lewis justified his decision with a ringing statement of working-class patriotism, a major theme of this story, it is worth assessing Dubofsky and Van Tine's argument, with southwestern Illinois in mind, by posing four interrelated questions. First, is it true that miners' determination would have crumbled without their eighty-four district and international officers? Probably not. Miners in Collinsville had just been through a series of strikes that had been carried out with great organization, discipline, and effectiveness against the leadership of their officials. One notable feature of the rank-and-file rebellion was the way in which new, unknown leaders seemed to appear out of nowhere. In both the 1917 strikes and the 1919 rebellion, the decisive factor was not the union officials—it was the organized power of the rank and file. In the case of the national strike, the relatively big wage increase of 27 percent that coal diggers ultimately won in February 1920 can be attributed largely to the fact that miners did not listen to their officers when they ordered them back to work on November 11.

Second, what about the contention that all of the "radicals" shared Lewis's perception of reality? The fact that Frank Farrington backed up John Lewis proves little about UMWA radicals. To be sure, Farrington postured as something of a militant in 1919. As president of the Illinois district, he could not help doing so. Dubofsky and Van Tine do show that Farrington allied with more radical miners in power struggles against Lewis in the early 1920s. But they confuse his opportunistic maneuvering in the elite politics of the UMWA with principled radicalism. Certainly the Illinois rebels who had been ceaselessly red-baited by Farrington would have been surprised to hear him, of all UMWA leaders, called a radical. To include Frank Farrington as a barometer of radical opinion seems a questionable choice.

There is, however, a deeper problem with this portion of their argument. If there were no top officials offering a radical alternative to Lewis in December, there were thousands of Illinois miners who offered their own rank-and-file political alternative in November and December. As even fragmentary evidence from Illinois suggests, miners in Benld, Carterville, Peoria, and some in Collinsville openly took issue with the Lewis strategy. In effect, they said, "We can fight our government, even if it is the greatest government on earth." And they continued to mobilize their class solidarity, even while being labeled Bolsheviks, anarchists, and un-American.

Third, given the willingness to fight, could the miners have withstood the repression of the federal government? To be sure, there was a limit to how far the miners could push their struggle at this time, in the face of armed repression. Even with the most militant leadership, there was a balance of forces to be considered. But one must recall the odds already weathered by Illinois miners from 1917 to 1919. Nearly every one of the repressive tactics that the government held in store had already been used on the miners of the region. During the 1917 wildcat strikes, Farrington himself had worked with Justice Department agents. Local postmasters censored Socialist publications sent to miners. German American miners, such as Anton Korun, were deported to internment camps. Patriotic pugilists had doled out a crescendo of vigilantism culminating in the Prager lynching. And during the rank-and-file rebellion, many miners found themselves at the wrong end of the barrel of a gun. Others landed in jail. In fact, a number of St. Clair County miners were still in local jails when the November strike began. Given this experience during the war years, the argument that the miners would have simply withered in the face of further repression is not convincing.

Lewis's actions stemmed from a lack of confidence in the power of the rank and file. That Lewis made the choice he did is hardly surprising. He went on to create a decades-long dynasty of autocratic rule in the UMWA. In a sense, the "radical" argument summarized by Dubofsky and Van Tine, which holds Lewis responsible for the fate of the labor movement in the 1920s, is a straw man. There were clearly broader forces at work in the decline of the unions. But the "circumstances and the realities of power" of the time offered several alternatives to John Lewis. The Benld and Carterville miners and others ready to defy the Anderson injunction presented one option. Lewis chose another.

The events of November and December had serious political repercussions. The repeated legal attacks by Judge Anderson against the strike, at the request of the Wilson Justice Department, angered many miners. In early November, John Walker issued a statement saying that "[a]s for the action of Judge Anderson and his court, it is unspeakable. Judge Anderson in my opinion ought to be either in an insane asylum or in the penitentiary." In early December, at a miners' meeting in Springfield, John Walker and Frank Farrington blasted the Wilson administration's actions. "The government is applying methods of intimidation and oppression instead of justice to the settlement of the strike," Farrington said. When Local 264 in Collinsville received a message from IFL president Duncan McDonald on December 8 calling for Judge Anderson's impeachment, the Consolidated miners agreed to circulate a petition at the mine that they would forward to the U.S. Congress.

Government officials were well aware of the political cost of the stand taken by President Wilson. Keeping A. Mitchell Palmer informed of miners' reactions to government actions, U.S. District Attorney Edward C. Knotts wrote of the actions of Judge Anderson, "The injunction at Indianapolis has so far operated to chrystalize [sic] sentiment among the miners against returning to work. As a class they have been educated to hate injunctions as applied to industrial disputes, and this they regard as the most flagrant attempt at so-called 'Government by Injunction.'"[102] It is no surprise that in the aftermath of the strike, two new branches of the ILP were organized—in Livingston and Staunton.[103]

The actions of the Wilson administration also prompted miners to reevaluate their views on the war. At the Illinois miners' convention in 1920, for instance, Jim Walker explained how his views had changed. "The world war was to be fought for democracy," he recalled. "However since I have seen what has come out of it I have felt that statement was a lie. I think we are in a worse condition today than we were when the war was fought." For Walker, the Anderson injunction showed that the legal system was rigged. Of the laws that working people were obliged to follow, Walker said, "It is not so with the other side. They don't have to comply with those laws. They have money enough so that when they violate those laws they do not have to suffer."[104]

Another indication of the political impact of the government's strike-breaking in the region is suggested by an article written by a *Chicago Daily News* reporter who visited the Macoupin County coalfields during the national strike. In an article entitled "Why Illinois Miners Don't Trust the U.S.," the reporter wrote that "[t]he miners of Virden and Carlinville are as far from holding bolshevist notions as are the bankers in La Salle Street. They are sore, hot under their flannel collars and ready to throw a few monkey wrenches into the wheels of a machinery they conceive to be grinding the life out of them." Even if they are not Bolsheviks, he wrote, "[w]hat has happened in this little strip of Illinois is nevertheless important and—perhaps—dangerous. The miners around these parts have lost their respect for their government. They no longer consider it a virtuous or square institution." One miner he interviewed explained that "[t]he trouble with this government of ours is that it's got the feeling of respect for big business and private property and private interests too deep in its mind."[105]

Finally, the political fate of Frank Farrington in the aftermath of the strike deserves some attention. Despite his hostility to independent rank-and-file action, Farrington could not avoid being swept up in the militancy of the national strike. On December 3, Judge Anderson issued his contempt citations. On December 6, U.S. Marshal Dallman arrived at the doorstep of Farrington's Springfield home. Dallman arrested Farrington and brought him to the office of Edward Knotts. After Farrington spent a night in jail, Knotts released the District 12 president on $10,000 bail, with an order to appear in Peoria federal court.[106]

The next month, at the reconvened International Convention, Farrington was one district official who argued against the compromise settlement that Lewis had accepted. It is entirely possible that Farrington took the stand with an eye to challenging Lewis for the UMWA presidency. He was widely considered to be Lewis's most powerful rival. At the same time, it is quite possible he was still smarting from his December arrest and angry at the treatment the miners had gotten at the hands of the Wilson administration. In any event, his anti-Lewis stand, in combination with his previous arrest and denunciation of the Anderson injunction, soon drew the attention of Justice Department officials, who had just conducted the infamous Palmer raids on the nation's Communists. In late January, Farrington wrote to Palmer and complained that the government had labeled him a subversive. "I have been informed," Farrington wrote, "that the Department of Justice has me tabbed as being one of the very radical leaders in the Miners' Union. . . . [T]he information comes to me from what I regard as a very reliable source. . . . In fact," Farrington added, "my informant is a very good friend who had the pleasure of a long conversation with your Mr. Creighton." To dispel this rumor, Farrington enclosed a sheaf of circulars he had sent out to miners during and after the war. They illustrated his deep commitment to the war effort and his strenuous efforts to put down the August-September rebellion in Illinois. "They are self-explanatory," Farrington wrote, "and a perusal of the same may be helpful in enabling you to judge my personality."[107]

During the war, Frank Farrington had urged the miners to give "until it hurts." He had promised that if miners dropped "commonplaces" while the nation fought its heroic battle against autocracy, they would be richly rewarded after the war. More than anyone in the Illinois UMWA, Farrington had argued that patriotism pays. But more than a year after the armistice, Farrington found himself rather underappreciated by his former friends in Washington. Despite his most diligent efforts to stay in the good graces of "the nation," he ended up on the wrong side of the law. Just as Joe Riegel's rebelliousness played havoc with his desire to remain a loyal American, Frank Farrington's unavoidable involvement in the giant miners' strike made it impossible for him to maintain his sterling patriotic credentials. No matter how much he did to maintain the "honor" of the UMWA, once miners went into battle on a grand scale,

Farrington fared no better than the champions of "individual action" he had lambasted during the war. In the eyes of the government and employers, he was a rebel miner, pure and simple.

Though Palmer's Justice Department was wrong to classify Frank Farrington as a left-wing radical, government investigators unwittingly pointed to an essential truth: as much as they tried to deny it, the miners were inevitably pushed by the daily workings of capitalism to rebel time and time again. Even the new Donk No. 4 mine, north of Collinsville, which had yet to produce an ounce of coal, succeeded in producing more working-class rebels. As Marx wrote, "Modern bourgeois society . . . is like the sorcerer who is no longer able to control the powers of the nether world whom he has called up by his spells."[108] It was this inexorable dynamic that lay behind the "great class war" in the southwestern Illinois coalfields in 1919, from the emergence of the Labor Party to the Mooney strike to the August rebellion to the national strike. In the spring of 1918, the miners embodied George Creel's "white-hot mass instinct" with fatal results for Robert Prager and for working-class unity. One year later, they displayed their own white-hot class instinct, a kind of rejection in action of "working-class Americanism," which succeeded in mediating the worst effects of the open-shop movement that gained momentum in the aftermath of the war.

Even as they wielded the weapons that the government and employers had unwittingly provided them by mobilizing for the "war for democracy," the working people of the coalfields desperately held on to their self-identity as patriotic Americans. On July 4, they struck for "liberty" and the rights of "freemen." In August and September, veterans of the American Expeditionary Force marched in a new miners' crusade, bearing aloft the American flag. And in November and December, men and women in mining families requested a "Little More Equal Rights and Less Special Privelages for the Moneyed Enterest of our Beloved Nation," as they proceeded to defy the highest legal authority of that nation.

Despite the fears of a Champaign manufacturer that the miners' "radical union leaders" planned to "over-throw the government," no such possibility lay on the immediate political horizon in 1919. And yet, the gravitation of even a tiny number of southwestern Illinois coal miners to the Communist movement, in the context of real Socialist revolutions abroad, signaled something quite new. As the perceptive reporter from Chicago found in talking to Virden miners in November 1919, the experiences of the war years had eroded a basic trust among working people that the government in Washington was their government, that America was truly a republic of all the people. To be sure, the war cost miners dearly. The Prager lynching crystallized the fatal divisions among them on the home front. But the U.S. government also paid a political price for the war. The "white-hot mass instinct" would never again be so easy to ignite.

Epilogue

The dramatic and ironic political shifts that the working people of Collinsville experienced during the World War I era were shared by workers worldwide. In his epic *History of the Russian Revolution*, Leon Trotsky described a similar process involving lethal violence, alleged German spies, and political radicalism. During the "July days" of 1917, the Kerensky government jailed prominent Bolsheviks and hunted for Lenin, who became public enemy number one. Letters appeared in the newspapers, later shown to be forgeries, which allegedly proved Lenin was in the pay of the German General Staff. Trotsky writes that most Russian soldiers, if they had found Lenin, would certainly have killed him on the spot. Only months later, many of these same workers and peasants in uniform hailed the alleged German spy as their hero.[1] All proportions guarded, the same fundamental shift took place in the United States, as the patriotic passions of 1918 gave way to the rebellions of 1919. As David Montgomery writes, "American workers may have been out of step with their European counterparts, but they were marching to the same drummer."[2]

In the decade following the war, southwestern Illinois miners continued to march to that inexorable beat. By the crisis of the early 1930s, as the Lewis leadership of the UMWA cooperated more openly with coal operators to save "the industry," rebellion once again brewed in Illinois. Rank-and-file outrage at John L. Lewis's dictatorial methods and his unwillingness to confront the operators led to a succession of rebel movements, culminating in the formation of the Progressive Mine Workers of America, which led dozens of mining locals out of the UMWA. Collinsville and Maryville miners were once again in the forefront of this movement, as were Macoupin County miners from Mt. Olive. Key to the strength of the Progressive Mine Workers was the Women's Auxiliary, led by the former Agnes Burns, now Agnes Burns Wieck, who had addressed the Illinois miners in 1916 as a young Women's Trade Union League organizer.[3]

Lewis stirred controversy far beyond the ranks of the UMWA during World War II as he led, and in some cases followed, coal miners out of the pits in a series of four national strikes. Once again, the high cost of living, government regulation of industry, and mining hazards combined to produce widespread revolt. And just as coal miners had endured charges of pro-Germanism the first time around, this time Lewis and miners were accused of being undemocratic, treasonous, and, in some cases, even Nazis. Enduring two federal government seizures of the coal mines, threats to draft them, and the blatantly antilabor Smith-Connally Act, coal miners held firm and ended up winning gains, even though their patriotic reputation took some blows.[4]

During these decades, memories of the Prager lynching quietly haunted Collinsville. Much as newspapers had denounced Prager's hanging as a "stain" on America, the patriotic murder of April 5, 1918, seemed to many local residents as a curse on the town that they could never erase. In the words of one scholar who has studied the lynching, "It was a dark mark on the town."[5] In fact, the most often repeated comment that older residents make about the case concerns the supposedly unusual or violent ends met by those involved in the lynching. As Karl Monroe, the son of *Collinsville Herald* editor J. O. Monroe, put it in a 1989 interview, "Some of these guys that were tried came to disagreeable ends. . . . Dick Dukes ended up as the town drunk," Monroe explained. "And Wesley Beaver didn't do well." That was putting it mildly. Some seventy years after the fact, Monroe may have forgotten that less than one year after the trial, Beaver committed suicide by shooting himself in the head.[6] But as another scholar has pointed out, the only other individuals connected with the events of the lynching who died anything like "violent" deaths were Madison County coroner Lowe and Joe Fornero, both of whom were victims of the terrible 1918 flu epidemic. In contrast, coal miner and lynching defendant Cecil Larremore owned a popular café on Main Street for decades and later served as city parks supervisor, living forty-seven years beyond Prager's death.[7]

The widespread belief that those responsible for the lynching were "cursed," a rumor that some Collinsville residents still repeat today, seems to have little basis in fact. Cecil Larremore is certainly a glaring exception, and there are others.[8] The myth probably draws its power from the need, if only a subconscious one, for Collinsville to somehow come to terms with what happened on the St. Louis Road early on the morning of April 5. If Collinsville residents can believe that the lynching defendants were somehow punished, perhaps by a higher power, that might well make them rest easier.

In probing the story behind the Prager lynching, however, this study has suggested that in order to understand what happened in Collinsville, one needs to appreciate the uncomfortable truth that deep social conflict marked southwestern Illinois during the World War I period. In many ways, Collinsville mirrored a process that working people nationwide experienced during the war, as their divided loyalties were strained to the breaking point. Throughout the nation, working people were suspicious of the claim that America was fighting a war for democracy. And many refused to put their class battles on hold "over here" while the government exhorted them to fight the enemy "over there." Especially in heavily German American regions, as in southwestern Illinois, the consequent emotional, physical, and political need to demonstrate loyalty to the nation was intense. In a sense, the fatal punishment dealt to Robert Paul Prager and the less lethal medicine given to other "disloyalists" in the region were a perverse tribute to the impressively high level of labor solidarity that working people had developed over the previous decades. The fact that this tradition of class solidarity was severely weakened by war does not diminish its historical reality. From the standpoint of working-class history, then, Collinsville should be proud of its heritage of collective struggle for a better world, not ashamed of the fact that it was not one big happy, patriotic family.

Keeping in mind all the ways that working people consciously used patriotism to give their struggles legitimacy in the World War I era and the ways that extreme patriotism emerged, in part, as a kind of defense mechanism, still it would be a mistake to deny that most southwestern Illinois miners sincerely believed in the democratic promise of America. As Frederick Engels, not one given to overestimating the patriotism of working people, observed in 1892, "It is remarkable but wholly natural how firmly rooted bourgeois prejudices are even in the working class in such a young country, which has never known feudalism and has grown up on a bourgeois basis from the beginning. Out of his very opposition to the mother country—which still wears its feudal disguise—the American worker, too, imagines that the traditional bourgeois regime he inherited is something progressive and superior by nature and for all time, a *nec-plus ultra*."[9] Even as they rebelled against government authorities from the county sheriff to the president, the working people of southwestern Illinois continued to reaffirm their patriotism.

It is one thing, however, to recognize and account for this and another to uncritically embrace it. In recent decades, the trend among scholars of labor history has been to celebrate the appropriation by workers of Americanist "discourse." But the story of southwestern Illinois coal miners and World War I suggests the hazards of this enterprise. The working people of southwestern Illinois, like any other human beings, naturally wanted to have it both ways—to fight for their collective needs as workers and still remain patriotic Americans. My study has concluded that this was an impossible dream. As Andrew Neather writes in a recent collection on the study of patriotism, nationalism, even in its most "progressive" form, "implied that, at some level, workers were members of the same fictive national 'family' as their class opponents."[10] Working people paid, and continue to pay today, for the fundamental illusion that such a "family" meaningfully exists. But for historians, making this political judgment is not enough. What needs to be recaptured, reconstructed, reimagined even, is that process of workers struggling with this contradiction inside and among themselves. That is what my study, centered around the most dramatic illustration of working-class patriotism one can imagine, in the context of unceasing class struggle, has attempted to do.

In terms of the history of the working-class movement in the United States, the World War I era is often seen to mark the end of the possibility for large-scale political radicalization. In his study of the Socialist Party, for instance, James Weinstein looks back fondly on that era, seemingly never to be recaptured, when Eugene Debs could poll one million votes. For Weinstein, and for many sympathetic to Socialist ideals, "the legacy of 1919 was the alienation of American socialism."[11] But the narrative surrounding the Prager lynching suggests instead how the war marked both an end and a beginning. The old forms of evolutionary socialism and patriotic unionism proved unable to lead working people forward. But in the heat of the war crisis and its aftermath, working people, under the influence of a worldwide working-class upsurge, including the Bolshevik revolution in Russia, began to reach in political directions that were better suited to the new world that had emerged in the coalfields of southwestern Illinois in the half-century after the Civil War.

In the late 1990s, with the further mechanization of coal mining, Illinois produced fully two-thirds the amount of coal as in the peak year of 1918 with only one-eighth the number of mines. Nearly half of Illinois coal is strip-mined, retrieved from giant open pits by workers operating enormous steam shovels. As of 1999, Illinois coal was dug by a grand total of 4,000 men and women, less than one-twentieth the number during World War I. With the state's high sulfur coal increasingly losing out to competition in the West, Illinois coal miners might seem to be a vanishing breed. [12]

But the multifaceted war experienced by working people in southwestern Illinois has hardly vanished. In September 1998, a group of researchers and labor activists were preparing to commemorate the 100th anniversary of the Battle of Virden. They had hired professional actors—all unionized—to reenact key events, invited UMWA officials to speak, and planned a kind of living history tour for what they expected would be a modest crowd. What they did not expect was that area coal miners working for Freeman United Coal, a subsidiary of General Dynamics Corporation, would coincidentally create their own commemoration of the battle by going out on strike. On September 11, 1998, the workers at the No. 2 mine in Virden, together with miners in two other Illinois towns, walked out when Freeman refused to guarantee health benefits for retirees. A month later, on October 11, some 350 striking miners converged on Virden, joining some 600 others who had come to commemorate the Virden massacre. The strikers chanted union slogans, dressed in full camouflage, and walked in formation into the downtown square. [13]

The strike echoed history in several ways. Just as the 1898 contest was sparked by a coal company refusing to abide by a national contract, so had Freeman dropped out of Bituminous Coal Operators Association negotiations with the UMWA in 1997, demanding a more "competitive" deal with the union. Moreover, as in the early days, Freeman hired private armed security guards who policed the struck mines; this time they wielded not only guns but also video cameras. Virden miners also noted that a majority of the guards were black, a fact the company said was pure coincidence. Some strike activists saw this as another deliberate attempt, as in 1898, to spark violence and discredit the strike. "We're not biting that bait," said one organizer. "Our fight is with Freeman Coal." [14]

The Virden miners also confronted intervention in the strike by the federal government in the guise of the Federal Bureau of Investigation (FBI), which was responding to company complaints of violence directed toward strikebreakers. Eighty-six-year-old Georgia Yard, whose grandson David was a strike leader accused by the company of violence, reported that FBI agents had appeared on her doorstep asking to search a backyard shed for "evidence." She refused them permission to conduct the search, and they eventually left. When they returned with a warrant, they searched and found nothing. In response to this government harassment, the strikers circulated a leaflet bearing Georgia Yard's picture, a copy of the search warrant, and the incredulous question, "You want to search my house for what?!" In an interview, David Yard commented, "My grandmother is almost 87 years old and has survived three heart attacks. The F.B.I. are nothing more than strikebreakers. Their goal is to intimidate people like myself and our membership."[15]

Like Joe Riegel, Robert Prager, Mrs. Faulkner, and others, David Yard and his grandmother found themselves on the wrong side of the law, suspected by the very government that they had been taught was theirs but that they could not help but suspect belonged to someone else. The German kaiser is long dead and buried, forgotten by all but historians and a few late-night viewers of documentaries on the History Channel. But there are new public "enemies," from Osama bin Laden to Saddam Hussein to Kim Jong-il to Fidel Castro to the ever-present nameless terrorists that allegedly threaten America. And in the remaining coal mines of southwestern Illinois, as everywhere, new generations of working people living in a declining empire struggle with how much they can continue to sacrifice for the powers that be.

APPENDIX
NOTES
INDEX

APPENDIX
People Present at the Prager Lynching

Albert Altman	R. Guy Kneedler
Vic Biama	Cecil Larremore†–D
Earl Bitzer	Harry Linneman
Louis Blumberg	J. O. Monroe
Louis Compton*	Bernhard Mueller
Charles Cranmer–D	Clarence Nagel
George Coukoulis	Edward Nagel
Edward Delaney	John Reese
James DeMatties*–D	Joseph Riegel–D
Louis Gerding	Stanley Semkowski
Paul Heim	A. W. Schimpff
Frank Flannery*–D	Notley Shoulders
Louis Hazzard	Ernst Tucker
William Horstman	William Tucker
Albert Kneedler	

This appendix is a partial list of those individuals who were at the tree where Robert Paul Prager was lynched on St. Louis Road, April 5, 1918. It is based on uncontradicted testimony at the lynching trial, as reported in the local press at the time of the trial. As the discussion in chapter 5 indicates, these twenty-nine men may have been a large majority of the total present.

* Testified that he left the scene before Prager was hanged.

† His testimony conflicts with witness testimony.

–D Defendant in the lynching trial. The uncontradicted testimony of the other six defendants (Wesley Beaver, William Brockmeier, Richard Dukes, Enid Elmore, Calvin Gilmore, and John Hallworth) suggests they were not at the lynching scene.

NOTES

Introduction

1. Rosemary Feurer, ed., *Remember Virden, 1898* (St. Louis: St. Louis Bread and Roses and Illinois Labor History Society, 1998), 1.

2. H. C. Peterson and Gilbert C. Fite, *Opponents of War, 1917–1918* (Seattle: University of Washington Press, 1957).

3. For scholarly treatments of the Prager lynching, see Peterson and Fite, *Opponents of War*, 202–7; Donald R. Hickey, "The Prager Affair: A Study in Wartime Hysteria," *Journal of the Illinois State Historical Society* 62 (Summer 1969): 117–34; Frederick Luebke, *Bonds of Loyalty: German-Americans and World War I* (DeKalb: Northern Illinois University Press, 1974), 3–24; and Christopher Heilig, "A Community Torn Apart: The German-American Community of Madison and Saint Clair Counties, Illinois, June, 1914 to January, 1919" (master's thesis, Southern Illinois University Edwardsville, 1988), 81–99. The episode is also briefly mentioned in David Montgomery, *The Fall of the House of Labor: The Workplace, the State, and American Labor Activism, 1865–1925* (Cambridge: Cambridge University Press, 1987), 378, and David Kennedy, *Over Here: The First World War and American Society* (New York: Oxford University Press, 1980), 68. For primary documents related to the case, see Franziska Ott, "The Anti-German Hysteria: The Case of Robert Paul Prager, Selected Documents," in *German-Americans in the World Wars: The Anti-German Hysteria of World War One*, vol. 1, ed. Don Tolzmann (New Providence, N.J.: K. G. Saur, 1995), 237–365, and Raymond K. Cunningham Jr. and John Foschio, "Collinsville, Illinois—The Robert Paul Prager Lynching April 5, 1918," <http://www.staff.uiuc.edu/ ~rcunning/lynch.htm> (July 14, 1999). In addition, there is a U.S. government file on the case; see Robert Prager, Straight Numerical File 191395, Box 2760, Record Group 60, Department of Justice, National Archives, Washington, D.C.

4. Paul Boyer et al., *The Enduring Vision: A History of the American People*, vol. 2 (Lexington, Mass.: D.C. Heath and Co., 1996), 754.

5. John H. M. Laslett, "Swan Song or New Social Movement? Socialism and Illinois District 12, United Mine Workers of America, 1919–1926," in *Socialism in the Heartland: The Midwestern Experience, 1900–1925*, ed. Donald Critchlow (Notre Dame: University of Notre Dame Press, 1986), 167–214; John H. M. Laslett, *Colliers across the Sea: A*

Comparative Study of Class Formation in Scotland and the American Midwest, 1830–1924 (Urbana: University of Illinois Press, 2000).

6. David M. Emmons, *The Butte Irish: Class and Ethnicity in an American Mining Town, 1875–1925* (Urbana: University of Illinois Press, 1989).

7. David Corbin, *Life, Work, and Rebellion in the Coal Fields: The Southern West Virginia Miners, 1880–1922* (Urbana: University of Illinois Press, 1981), 180–81.

8. In a notable exception, the relationship between the lynching and class conflict has been explored recently in E. A. Schwartz, "The Lynching of Robert Prager, the United Mine Workers, and the Problems of Patriotism in 1918," *Journal of the Illinois State Historical Society* 95 (Winter 2002–03): 414–35.

9. Sean Wilentz, "Against Exceptionalism: Class Consciousness and the American Labor Movement, 1790–1920," *International Labor and Working Class History* 26 (Fall 1984): 5.

10. Corbin, *Life, Work, and Rebellion*, 241, 244.

11. Gary Gerstle, *Working-Class Americanism: The Politics of Labor in a Textile City, 1914–1960* (Cambridge: Cambridge University Press, 1989), 166, 181. For a somewhat different study that argues for a "progressive" patriotism, see Jonathan M. Hansen, *The Lost Promise of Patriotism: Debating American Identity, 1890–1920* (Chicago: University of Chicago Press, 2003). Examining the thought and activity of a key group of Progressive Era intellectuals—William James, John Dewey, Jane Addams, Eugene Debs, W. E. B. Du Bois, Randolph Bourne, Louis Brandeis, and Horace Kallen—Hansen argues that they "enlisted American patriotism in the daily, never-ending struggle for social and political justice" (x).

12. Joseph McCartin, *Labor's Great War: The Struggle for Industrial Democracy and the Origins of Modern American Labor Relations, 1912–1921* (Chapel Hill: University of North Carolina Press, 1997), 7.

13. For an effective critique of "labor republicanism" from a materialist standpoint, which is very suggestive for viewing twentieth-century working-class patriotism, see Bryan Palmer, *Descent into Discourse: The Reification of Language and the Writing of Social History* (Philadelphia: Temple University Press, 1987), 106–19. For another more critical look at labor republicanism, see Andrew Neather, "Labor Republicanism, Race, and Popular Patriotism in the Era of Empire, 1890–1914," in *Bonds of Affection: Americans Define Their Patriotism,* ed. John Bodnar (Princeton, N.J.: Princeton University Press, 1996), 82–101.

14. Brian Kelly, *Race, Class, and Power in the Alabama Coalfields, 1908–21* (Urbana: University of Illinois Press, 2001), 160.

15. Karl Marx and Frederick Engels, *The Communist Manifesto* (New York: Pathfinder Press, 1987), 25.

1. The Southwestern Illinois Coalfields

1. Charles Dickens, *American Notes* (New York: The Modern Library, 1996), 233–35.

2. DeLorme Mapping, *Illinois Atlas and Gazetteer* (Freeport, Maine: DeLorme Mapping, 1991), 59–60, 67–68, 75–77, 82; Illinois Central Railroad Company, *Annual Report*

of the Second Vice-President for the Year Ended June 30, 1900, 50, Section 3.4, Box 8, Illinois Central Railroad Collection, Newberry Library, Chicago; Stuyvesant Fish to J. C. Welling, Esq., and J. T. Harahan, Esq., March 21, 1906, in "Reports of Messrs. Parker and Moorshead on Coal Properties in Springfield Division and other points on line in Illinois," "Papers relating to Coal Lands in Illinois," Illinois Central Railroad Collection; W. H. Stennett, comp., *Yesterday and Today: A History of the Chicago and North Western Railway System* (Chicago: n.p., 1910), 188; Chicago and North Western Railway Company, *Fifty-third Annual Report of the Chicago and North Western Railway Company, Fiscal Year Ending June 30, 1912*, 19, Newberry Library; John F. Stover, *History of the Illinois Central Railroad* (New York: Macmillan, 1975), 210; Illinois Bureau of Labor Statistics, *Statistics of Coal in Illinois* (Springfield, 1887), 91–92, 104–6, 121–22; Department of Mines and Minerals, *Thirty-fifth Annual Coal Report of Illinois* (Springfield: Department of Mines and Minerals, 1916), 200–201, 224–25. On UMWA District 12 in the World War I era, see Laslett, "Swan Song or New Social Movement?"

3. For a richly illustrated history of Collinsville, see Lucille M. Stehman, *Collinsville, Illinois: A Pictorial History* (St. Louis: G. Bradley Publishing Inc., 1992).

4. Department of Mines and Minerals, *Twenty-ninth Annual Coal Report of Illinois* (Springfield: Department of Mines and Minerals, 1910), 382–83, 402–3.

5. U.S. Bureau of the Census, *Thirteenth Census of the United States Taken in the Year 1910: Statistics for Illinois* (Washington, D.C.: GPO, 1913), 589; U.S. Bureau of the Census, *Fourteenth Census of the United States Taken in the Year 1920: Statistics for Illinois* (Washington, D.C.: GPO, 1920), 198.

6. Heilig, "Community Torn Apart," 7.

7. Ibid., 33–34.

8. Ibid., 44–46.

9. For an informative look at Belleville in the mid-nineteenth century, see Kay J. Carr, *Belleville, Ottawa, and Galesburg: Community and Democracy on the Illinois Frontier* (Carbondale and Edwardsville: Southern Illinois University Press, 1996).

10. These percentages are based on census figures in Stephanie Booth, "The Relationship Between Radicalism and Ethnicity in Southern Illinois Coal Fields, 1870–1940" (Ph.D. diss., Illinois State University, 1983), 248–51, 256–57, 260–62, 268, 270, 280.

11. Heilig, "Community Torn Apart," 44–46.

12. Ibid., 7.

13. Department of Mines and Minerals, *Thirty-fifth Annual Coal Report of Illinois*, 224–25. A number of former St. Louis and O'Fallon employees claimed in interviews that Busch owned that coal company and a railroad of the same name, which carried the coal to St. Louis, although the interviewer, Delta Masterson, was unable to corroborate their claims. See, for example, Arthur and Mary Belleville Oral History and Alois A. Erwin Oral History in Delta Barber Masterson Coal Mining Oral History Collection, Research Collections, Lovejoy Library, Southern Illinois University Edwardsville. An item in the industry journal *Coal Age*, however, does support their claim. A "Personals" note informs readers that "William Cotter, of New York, has been elected president of the St. Louis & O'Fallon Ry., the coal road controlled by the Busch interests, and also

president of the Manufacturers' Ry., in St. Louis, better known as the Busch line" (*Coal Age* 9 [May 13, 1916]: 862).

14. Illinois Bureau of Labor Statistics, *Eighteenth Annual Coal Report* (Springfield, Ill.: Phillips Bros. State Printers, 1899), 123.

15. United States Immigration Commission, *Immigrants in Industries: Bituminous Coal Mining*, vol. 6 (Washington, D.C.: GPO, 1911), 597.

16. Avinere Toigo Memoir, November 1972–January 1973, Sangamon State University Oral History Collection, Coal Mining and Union Activities Project, Springfield, Illinois.

17. Frank Bertetti, "Benld," in *The Story of Macoupin County, 1829–1979*, by Sesquicentennial Historic Committee (Carlinville: Carlinville and Macoupin County Sesquicentennial, Inc., 1979), 90.

18. Interview with Frances Bauer, Caseyville, Ill., February 27, 1992.

19. Cost of Living Schedule 1-78, Pana, Illinois, Box 67, Record Group 257, Bureau of Labor Statistics, National Archives. In 1918, the U.S. Department of Labor's Bureau of Labor Statistics conducted a series of cost of living surveys in selected cities and towns. One of these was Pana, Illinois, a mining town some forty miles northeast of Mt. Olive on the Illinois Central Railroad. Although falling outside of southwestern Illinois, strictly defined as Macoupin, Madison, and St. Clair Counties, Pana miners shared much with their counterparts farther southwest. Along with miners in Virden and farther south, Pana miners helped establish the eight-hour day in the bitterly fought strike of 1897. By 1904, over one-third of Pana miners were foreign-born, with groups of miners identified as German, Austrian, Hungarian, Russian, Scottish, and Irish.

While Pana resembled southwestern Illinois towns in many respects, the information contained in the surveys must be used carefully. In instructing their agents, the Bureau of Labor Statistics spelled out a series of "requirements" that families needed to meet in order to participate in the survey. Three of these are relevant for our purposes: "The family may not have over three boarders or lodgers either outsiders or children living as such"; "The family must have *kept house* in the locality for the entire year covered" (emphasis in original); and "Do not take slum or charity families or non-English speaking families who have been less than five years in the United States." These three categories comprised a significant number of families in Illinois mining communities like Pana. By employing vague terms like "slum" and "charity" families, the bureau gave its agents broad discretion to choose which families were suitable. By excluding recent immigrant families, the majority from eastern and southern Europe, the survey inevitably painted a distorted picture. As a result, the families actually interviewed were, on the whole, disproportionately better off, less geographically mobile, and small. With these limitations in mind, we can make some careful use of the information.

20. Interview with Pete Perry, Glen Carbon, Ill., May 29, 1991.

21. Department of Mines and Minerals, *Thirty-second Annual Coal Report of Illinois* (Springfield: Department of Mines and Minerals, 1913), 212, 225, 232–33; Department of Mines and Minerals, *Thirty-fourth Annual Coal Report of Illinois* (Springfield: Department of Mines and Minerals, 1915), 188–89, 198–99, 208–9; Department of Mines and Minerals, *Thirty-fifth Annual Coal Report of Illinois*, 200–201, 212–13, 224–25.

22. *Collinsville Herald* (hereafter cited as *CH*), October 4, 1912.

23. *Staunton Star Times* (hereafter cited as *SST*), December 17, 1915.

24. Macoupin County Sesquicentennial, Inc., *The Story of Macoupin County, Illinois, 1829–1879* (Carlinville, Ill.: Macoupin County Sesquicentennial, Inc., 1979), 91.

25. For more on the Czech Slavic Benevolent Society, see Richard Schneirov, "Free Thought and Socialism in the Czech Community in Chicago, 1875–1887," in *"Struggle a Hard Battle": Essays on Working-Class Immigrants,* ed. Dirk Hoerder (DeKalb: Northern Illinois University Press, 1986), 124.

26. *CH,* July 6, 1989. This information appears in an article by Lucille Stehman, a Collinsville resident and local historian. The article is one installment of a weekly column on Collinsville coal miners that Stehman wrote for nearly two years. The series publicized a local campaign to renovate the old Miners' Theatre, which was built in 1918. For fifty dollars, families or friends of those who had worked in the mines during the World War I years could commemorate the miner, whose name appeared on a "Wall of Honor" inside the theater.

27. Interview with Hawley Canterbury, O'Fallon, Ill., February 27, 1992.

28. William H. Turner, of UMWA 848 in Collinsville, Ill., to John H. Walker, August 18, 1916, Box 3, 19-66, John Hunter Walker Papers, Illinois Historical Survey, University of Illinois Library, Urbana (hereafter cited as JHWP).

29. McCartin, *Labor's Great War,* 132.

30. *Belleville City Directory* (Belleville, Ill.: 1904–5).

31. Quoted in Mary Ann Clawson, *Constructing Brotherhood: Class, Gender and Fraternalism* (Princeton, N.J.: Princeton University Press, 1989), 89.

32. Interview with Pete Perry.

33. Clawson, *Constructing Brotherhood,* 131; *CH,* December 17, 1915.

34. Department of Mines and Minerals, *Thirty-fifth Annual Coal Report of Illinois,* 195–99, 207–10, 220–22.

35. Ibid., 48–49, 199. In the summary table of nonfatal accidents, trip riders are listed as a separate category, and they also account for what must be a disproportionate share of accidents—15 of 207, or 7.2 percent. If they are included in the total number of employees listed as drivers for the district—311—then the rate for this combined category is even dramatically higher than I have indicated. If, on the other hand, trip riders are subsumed in the "not classified" category, then the percentage for drivers stands as is. One could get a rough estimate for trip riders in the district by counting up the number of locomotives used in the mines, one trip rider for each motor; this method results in 85. If the trip riders are indeed included in the "not classified" category, then the percentage of trip riders injured during the year would be nearly double that of drivers—17.6 percent.

36. Illinois State Bureau of Labor Statistics, *Sixteenth Annual Report of the State Bureau of Labor Statistics Concerning Coal in Illinois, 1897* (Springfield, 1897), 122–23.

37. Edward A. Wieck, *The American Miners' Association: A Record of the Origin of Coal Miners' Unions in the United States* (New York: Russell Sage Foundation, 1940), 30.

38. For more on pre-UMWA coal mining unionism, with comparative material on the United States, Scotland, and Britain, see Herbert Gutman, "Labor in the Land of

Lincoln: Coal Miners on the Prairie," in *Power and Culture: Essays on the American Working Class* (New York: Pantheon Books, 1987), 117–212; Royden Harrison, *Independent Collier: The Coal Miner as Archetypal Proletarian Reconsidered* (Hassocks, Sussex, Great Britain: Harvester Press, 1978); John H. M. Laslett, *Nature's Noblemen: The Fortunes of the Independent Collier in Scotland and the American Midwest, 1855–1889* (Los Angeles: University of California, Institute of Industrial Relations, 1983); John H. M. Laslett, "British Immigrant Colliers, and the Origins and Early Development of the UMWA, 1870–1912," in *The United Mine Workers of America: A Model of Industrial Solidarity?*, ed. John H. M. Laslett (University Park: Pennsylvania State University Press, 1996), 29–50; and Laslett, *Colliers across the Sea.*

39. *Chicago Daily Tribune,* July 18, 1897, 2. On the Virden battle, see Victor Hicken, "The Virden and Pana Mine Wars of 1898," *Journal of the Illinois State Historical Society* 52 (Summer 1959): 263–78, and John H. Keiser, "The Union Miners Cemetery at Mt. Olive, Illinois: A Spirit-Thread of Labor History," *Journal of the Illinois State Historical Society* 62 (1969): 229–66. For an edited collection of primary documents, see Feurer, *Remember Virden.*

40. Edward A. Wieck, "General Alexander Bradley," *American Mercury* 8 (May 1926): 71

41. Hugh Archbald, *The Four Hour Day in Coal: A Study of the Relation Between the Engineering of the Organization of Work and the Discontent among the Workers in the Coal Mines* (New York: H. W. Wilson Company, 1922), 30.

42. Hicken, "Virden and Pana Mine Wars of 1898," 263–78.

43. John H. Keiser, "Black Strikebreakers and Racism in Illinois, 1865–1900," *Journal of the Illinois State Historical Society* 65 (Autumn 1972): 326. For a provocative and more positive spin on black strikebreaking, see Eric Arnesen, "Specter of the Black Strikebreaker: Race and Labor Activism in the Industrial Era," *Labor History* 44 (Winter 2003): 319–35.

44. Interview with Hawley Canterbury.

45. U.S. Bureau of the Census, *Fourteenth Census of the United States,* 68.

46. Edward A. Wieck to Agnes Burns, March 7, 1918, Agnes Burns Wieck Collection, Box 2, Archives of Labor and Urban Affairs, Wayne State University, Detroit, Mich.

47. David Thoreau Wieck, *Woman from Spillertown: A Memoir of Agnes Burns Wieck* (Carbondale: Southern Illinois University Press, 1992), 71.

48. *Blue Book of the State of Illinois* (Danville: Illinois Printing Company, 1909), 443.

49. *CH,* January 31, 1919.

50. *SST,* April 7, 1916.

51. *Belleville Daily Advocate* (hereafter cited as *BDA*), April 5, 1916; *SST,* April 23, 1915, November 10, 1916.

52. *CH,* April 20, 1917.

53. Ibid., November 11, 1912.

54. Ibid.

55. *SST,* November 10, 1916.

56. *CH*, April 16, 1915, April 20, 1917, March 23, April 6, May 25, June 8, July 20, August 3, 1989; Department of Mines and Minerals, *Thirty-fifth Annual Coal Report of Illinois*, 341.

57. *BDA*, February 1, 1915.

58. Lorin L. Cary, "Adolph Germer: From Labor Agitator to Labor Professional" (Ph.D. diss., University of Wisconsin, 1968), 1.

59. Ibid., 29.

60. *Belleville Semi-Weekly Advocate*, October 13, 1914.

61. Arthur Clark Everling, "Tactics over Strategy in the United Mine Workers of America: Internal Politics and the Question of the Nationalization of the Mines, 1908–1923" (Ph.D. diss., Pennsylvania State University, 1976), 79.

62. Ibid., 86; Cary, "Adolph Germer," 31.

63. Prison record of Robert Powell *[sic]* Prager, Indiana Reformatory, Jeffersonville, transcribed and sent electronically to author on September 23, 2002, by Vicki Casteel, Indiana State Archives, Indianapolis. The transcription of this document lists Prager's age as twenty-one. However, most sources, including Prager's gravestone, list his birthdate as February 28, 1888, making him twenty-four when he was sentenced in December 1912.

64. Stuart Bruce Kaufman, *A Vision of Unity: The History of the Bakery and Confectionery Workers International Union* (Bakery, Confectionery and Tobacco Workers International Union, 1987; distributed by University of Illinois Press), 24, 26.

65. Ibid., 34.

66. Ibid., 75.

2. "Lining Up the People with the Government"

1. Joseph Tumulty to Woodrow Wilson, May 31, 1917, *Papers of Woodrow Wilson* (Princeton, N.J.: Princeton University Press, 1966–) (hereafter cited as *PWW*), 42:427–28 (my emphasis).

2. Annual Message to Congress, December 7, 1915, ibid., 35:307.

3. *CH*, December 10, 1915.

4. UMWA, *Proceedings of the Twenty-fifth Consecutive and Second Biennial Convention of the United Mine Workers of America* (Indianapolis: UMWA, 1916), 2:906–10. One resolution was signed by John Brophy, who urged miners to recognize "that the workers of all countries are their brothers, and the capitalists and the ruling class in general are their natural enemies; and . . . to end forever the robber system of capitalism, the fruitful cause of working class poverty and modern wars." He later changed his mind, as he recounts in his memoirs. See John Brophy, *A Miner's Life* (Madison: University of Wisconsin Press, 1964), 117.

5. UMWA, District 12, *Proceedings of the Twenty-sixth Consecutive and the First Biennial Convention of the United Mine Workers of America, District 12* (Peoria, Ill.: UMWA, 1916), 294–97.

6. George Hicks to John Walker, May 22, 1916, Box 1, 6-95, JHWP. For more on Canton, see Errol W. Stevens, "The Socialist Party of America in Municipal Politics:

Canton, Illinois, 1911–1920," *Journal of the Illinois State Historical Society* 72 (November 1979): 257–72.

7. On Agnes Burns (Wieck), see D. T. Wieck, *Woman from Spillertown.*

8. UMWA, District 12, *Proceedings of the Twenty-sixth Consecutive and the First Biennial Convention,* 330–32.

9. Richard Frost, *The Mooney Case* (Stanford, Calif.: Stanford University Press, 1968), 83–87. Excerpts of the Labor Council resolution are quoted in Philip Foner, *History of the Labor Movement in the United States,* vol. 7, *Labor and World War I, 1914–1918* (New York: International Publishers, 1987), 77.

10. Frost, *Mooney Case,* 1.

11. *BDA,* May 15, 1916. LaFollette introduced his bill in the U.S. Senate on April 30, 1916, calling for a popular vote on war in the event that the United States severed diplomatic relations with any country. On this bill and a similar Socialist Party proposal, see Foner, *History of the Labor Movement,* 7:8–10.

12. *BDA,* November 13, 1915.

13. *Belleville Semi-Weekly Advocate,* August 4, 1914.

14. *CH,* August 20, 1915.

15. UMWA, *Proceedings of the Twenty-fifth Consecutive and Second Biennial Convention of the United Mine Workers of America* (Indianapolis: UMWA, 1916), 2:910–11.

16. *Coal Age* 9 (February 19, 1916): 325.

17. Luebke, *Bonds of Loyalty,* 83–156.

18. *Belleville Semi-Weekly Advocate,* October 16, 1914.

19. *SST,* October 8, 1915.

20. *BDA,* January 22, 1915.

21. *SST,* July 14, 1916.

22. Ibid., September 1, 1916.

23. *BDA,* March 30, 1916.

24. Interview with Jack and Vernon Canterbury, Collinsville, Ill., May 29, 1991.

25. Luebke, *Bonds of Loyalty,* 102.

26. *SST,* August 21, 1914, January 1, September 3, November 12, 1915, September 22, 1916.

27. Ibid., December 10, 1915.

28. Ibid., September 22, 1916.

29. J. W. Donaldson to Postmaster, Chicago, Ill., Division of Second Class Mail, October 2, 1917, Case 47449, RG 28, National Archives.

30. Postmaster, Spring Valley, Ill., to Solicitor, Post Office Department, Washington, D.C., October 8, 1917, ibid.

31. J. W. Donaldson to Solicitor, Post Office Department, Washington, D.C., November 28, 1917, ibid.

32. *La Parola Proletaria,* August 25, 1917, translated by censor (hereafter cited as *LPP*), ibid. One may reasonably assume that some, if not all, of the awkward phrasing is due to poor translation.

33. *LPP,* August 18, 1917, ibid.

34. I. T. Mullen to Inspector in Charge, Post Office Department, Chicago, Ill., November 9, 1917, ibid.

35. *LPP,* September 8, 1917, ibid. The translator's word was "companion," probably from the Italian *compagno,* but "comrade" is a more likely rendition.

36. The *Collinsville City Directory* (1919) indicates that Oberto worked at Donk No. 2. See also the Maryville City Directory for 1916, available at <http://www.iltrails.org/madison/mcmryvl.htm>.

37. *CH,* March 19, 1918. The *Herald* printed the full text of the letter. It appears that Ricca wrote it in English and that the idiosyncrasies of language are his. Ricca's explanation of why Socialists should support the war makes an interesting attempt to place the war in the context of a semi-Marxist history of class society. Just as ancient slavery was necessary to develop the productive forces of agriculture and early industry, Ricca explained, so feudalism and then capitalism were necessary to advance to socialism. Having gotten to the brink of Socialism, the war represented a kind of final cleansing, both moral and physical, in preparation for the next leap forward. As he wrote, "Humanity may be liberated from any kind of violence only when the population of the entire world has reached the physiological perfection or the highest step of human moral or human perfection." The war would do this by eliminating the "right of conquest by force," which was a "dangerous anachronism at the present stage of civilization."

38. Adolph Germer to Henri De Mann, October 8, 1912, reel 1, Adolph Germer Papers, microfilm, Yale University, New Haven, Conn. See also the comments on the Christian German miners unions in UMWA, *Report of Proceedings of International Miners' Congress by United Mine Workers' Delegates* (Indianapolis, n.d. [1913?]), 16–17. For more on German miners unions, see S. H. F. Hickey, *Workers in Imperial Germany: The Miners of the Ruhr* (Oxford: Clarendon Press, 1985).

39. For more on Goldstein, see Henry F. Bedford, *Socialism and the Workers in Massachusetts, 1886–1912* (Amherst: University of Massachusetts Press, 1966).

40. *BDA,* March 31, 1915.

41. Martha Moore Avery and David Goldstein, *Socialism: The Nation of Fatherless Children* (Boston: Union News League, 1903), 162.

42. Martha Moore Avery and David Goldstein, *Bolshevism: Its Cure* (Boston: Boston School of Political Economy, 1919).

43. *SST,* June 4, 1915.

44. At least Saladin's son Henry took his first communion there. *CH,* May 26, 1917.

45. Frank Bertetti Oral History, Gillespie, Ill., April 23, 1973, Sangamon State University Oral History Collection, Coal Mining and Union Activities Project.

46. *United Mine Workers Journal* (hereafter *UMWJ*), February 22, 1917.

47. Ibid.

48. Joseph Bosone to John H. Walker, April 11, 1918, Box 7, 53-7, JHWP. The letter does not indicate where Bosone worked or lived. From his letters, however, it is apparent he was a UMWA member and had campaigned for Walker in the past, probably in the 1916 race for union president.

49. Joseph Bozone to John H. Walker, July 14, 1918, Box 7, 56-17, JHWP. "Bozone" is the spelling of the name in this letter.

50. *SST,* May 4, 1917.

51. *UMWJ,* April 12, 1917.

52. *CH,* February 16, 1918. On World War I–era patriotic songs, see Frederick G. Vogel, *World War I Songs: A History and Dictionary of Popular American Patriotic Tunes, with over 300 Complete Lyrics* (Jefferson, N.C.: McFarland and Company, 1995)

53. "An Address by Governor Frank O. Lowden," March 31, 1917, in *Illinois in the World War,* vol. 6, *War Documents and Addresses,* ed. Marguerite Edith Jenison (Springfield: Illinois State Historical Society, 1923), 16, 19.

54. Quoted in William T. Hutchinson, *Lowden of Illinois: The Life of Frank O. Lowden* (Chicago: University of Chicago, 1957), 1:346.

55. *SST,* August 24, 1917.

56. *St. Louis Labor,* May 5, 1917, Case 47414, RG 28, National Archives.

57. On the Committee for Public Information, see George Creel, *How We Advertised America* (New York: Harper and Bros., 1920), and Stephen Vaughn, *Holding Fast the Inner Lines: Democracy, Nationalism, and the Committee on Public Information* (Chapel Hill: University of North Carolina Press, 1980). For a more critical look at Creel and the CPI, see Stewart Halsey Ross, *Propaganda for War: How the United States Was Conditioned to Fight the Great War of 1914–1918* (Jefferson, N.C.: McFarland and Co., Inc., 1996), 218–51.

58. Creel, *How We Advertised America,* 5.

59. Ibid., 94.

60. This accords with the findings of Christopher Gibbs in his study of war mobilization in neighboring Missouri. See Christopher Gibbs, *The Great Silent Majority: Missouri's Resistance to World War I* (Columbia: University of Missouri Press, 1988), 52–56.

61. C. W. Terry to Harry Herb, September 11, 1917, Four Minute Men, Alton file, and A. C. Gauen to George Jones, August 6, 1918, Committee of Public Information, Four Minute Men Bulletins, Collinsville file, both in RG 517.26, Illinois State Archives, Springfield (hereafter cited as ISA).

62. George Niess to George Jones, November 26, December 4, 1917, Four Minute Men, St. Clair County/Belleville file, ibid.

63. List of towns over population of 1,000 lacking FMM organizations as of July 25, 1918, and state FMM director to John Anderson, chairman of Carlinville FMM, November 13, 1918, Carlinville file, both in ibid.

64. *SST,* April 25, 1918. The film was scheduled to be shown in late April 1918.

65. John H. Clayton to Four Minute Men headquarters, Chicago, August 12, 1918 (my emphasis), 1918 file, Committee on Public Information, Four Minute Men Bulletins, RG 517.26, ISA.

66. For an informative study of this neglected but important organization, see Joan Jensen, *The Price of Vigilance* (Chicago: Rand McNally and Co., 1968). For an APL operative's version of the story, see Emerson Hough, *The Web: A Revelation of Patriotism* (Chicago: Reilly and Lee, 1919).

67. Vaughn, *Holding Fast the Inner Lines,* illustration on 80.

68. Hon. T. W. Gregory, "How the Rear of Our Armies Was Guarded during the World War," Address to North Carolina Bar Association in 1919 (my emphasis), Papers of Thomas Gregory, Library of Congress, Washington, D.C.

69. *CH,* April 13, 1917.

70. Marguerite Jenison, *The War-Time Organization of Illinois* (Springfield: Illinois State Historical Library, 1923), 102–4.

71. UMWA, *Proceedings of the Twenty-sixth Consecutive and Third Biennial Convention of the United Mine Workers of America* (Indianapolis: Bookwalter Ball Printing Co., 1918), 44.

72. In early 1919, Local 264 recorded that 53 out of 518 members were in military service, or slightly over 10 percent. In fact, the overall state figure by this date may well have been higher than the 3.5 percent figure reported for early 1918. Many more men had been drafted by the latter date. UMWA Local 264, Monthly Reports, Box 1, Progressive Mine Workers of America, Local Union #3, Research Collections, Lovejoy Library, Southern Illinois University Edwardsville (hereafter cited as PMW).

73. "Table showing number of members of U.M.W. of A., volunteered, drafted and subject to draft," in UMWA, *Proceedings of the Twenty-sixth Consecutive and Third Biennial Convention,* between 46 and 47.

74. *SST,* November 28, 1918. There were two draft boards in Macoupin County. Figures reported for Staunton in the *Staunton Star-Times* match exactly with the official published figures for Macoupin County No. 2 draft board. This suggests that No. 2 served as the board for the coal towns in the southern portion of the county—Staunton, Mt. Olive, Gillespie, Benld—and that No. 1 covered the northern half, which included the county seat of Carlinville, as well as coal towns like Virden and Girard.

75. Jenison, *War-Time Organization of Illinois,* 97.

76. *SST,* July 18, 1918.

77. See, for example, "Keep Trained Men in the Coal Mines," *Black Diamond* 60 (June 15, 1918): 505, and "Will We Hold the Miners or Lose Production," *Black Diamond* 60 (June 22, 1918): 525.

78. Jenison, *War-Time Organization of Illinois,* 104.

79. *SST,* June 29, 1917.

80. Interview with Pete Perry.

81. *SST,* February 7, 1918.

82. *CH,* October 5, 1917.

83. *SST,* July 6, 1917.

84. Jenison, *War-Time Organization of Illinois,* 70. According to Jenison, there were 301 cases of Selective Service Act violations recorded for the entire southern Illinois district. Seven of eight of these cases were filed under Sections 12 and 13 of the act, which sought to protect areas around training camps from the influence of liquor and "vice." In southwestern Illinois, the only such camp was Scott Field, an airbase outside of Belleville. Only one-eighth of the lawsuits, or roughly forty, alleged that men had evaded the draft in some way.

85. *SST,* June 15, 1917.

86. Ibid., October 5, 1917. For a penetrating examination of working people and World War I conscription in the American south, see Jeanette Keith, "The Politics of Southern Draft Resistance, 1917–1918: Class, Race, and Conscription in the Rural South," *Journal of American History* 87 (March 2001): 1335–61.

87. *CH,* June 8, 1917.

88. Luebke, *Bonds of Loyalty,* 4.

89. Minutes of UMWA Local 826, July 3, 1917, Box 6, PMW.

90. William J. Breen, *Uncle Sam at Home: Civilian Mobilization, Wartime Federalism, and the Council of National Defense, 1917–19* (Westport, Conn.: Greenwood, 1984). One of the few books focusing on the CND, Breen's study is highly informative and includes a wealth of material on Illinois. It is marred, though, by the lack of any critical analysis of the claim that the war was fought for "democracy." Thus Breen is unable to account for the contradiction between the federal government's rhetoric and the savage attacks on working people who opposed the war in any way. He writes, for instance, that "the strength and virulence of the anti-German sentiment in 1917–18 remains puzzling" (79).

91. Donald F. Tingley, *The Structuring of a State: The History of Illinois, 1899 to 1928* (Urbana: University of Illinois, 1980), 199.

92. Breen, *Uncle Sam at Home,* 78–79, 87.

93. Ibid., 89.

94. *SST,* February 14, 1918.

95. Madison County–Neighborhood Council of Defense file, RG 517.38, ISA.

96. Maier Fox, *United We Stand: The United Mine Workers of America* (Washington, D.C.: UMWA, 1990), 181.

97. Edward A. Wieck to John H. Walker, May 21, June 12, 1917, Box 7, 40-16 and 41-27, JHWP.

98. John H. Walker to Edward A. Wieck, June 20, 1917 (my emphasis), Box 7, 42-6, ibid.

99. Jenison, *War-Time Organization of Illinois,* 187–89.

100. *UMWJ,* May 24, 1917.

101. *SST,* September 19, 1918.

102. Ibid., April 18, 1918.

103. Ibid., September 19, 1918.

104. Circular letter, Frank Farrington to Members and Officers of District 12, UMWA, March 25, 1918, John Walker folder, TF 4, Records of the Illinois Federation of Labor, Springfield, Ill. (hereafter cited as IFL). I am indebted to Mike Matejka for helping me get access to these files.

105. Secretary of War to Frank Farrington, July 28, 1918, ibid.

106. Jenison, *War-Time Organization of Illinois,* 200.

107. Liberty Loan Record, RG 517.8, ISA.

108. Jenison, *War-Time Organization of Illinois,* 206. In reference to this figure, Jenison comments that "so imperfect was the system of reporting subscriptions of residents of one county to banks of the same county that the figure cannot be regarded as accurate."

Surely such imperfections affected the reporting of other figures, yet she makes no similar qualification for these. Is it a coincidence that this is the single case that amounts to a clear failure of the government to achieve its goals?

109. *CH*, August 23, October 11, 1918.

110. Affidavit signed by Notary Public Thomas Wilson, Macoupin County, Illinois, 1918 (no date, witnesses' names not given), Box 79, 804, JHWP.

111. *SST*, October 26, 1917.

112. "Subscriptions received to First Liberty Loan from Illinois banks," Liberty Loan Record, RG 517.8, ISA.

113. C. Clavin to Hon. Samuel Insull, November 21, 1917, RG 517.36, ibid.

114. John F. Hutchinson, *Champions of Charity: War and the Rise of the Red Cross* (Boulder, Colo.: Westview Press, 1996), 275.

115. Hough, *The Web*, 128. On the coercive tactics of the Red Cross in Missouri, see Gibbs, *Great Silent Majority*, 79–80.

116. See John F. Hutchinson, "The Nagler Case: A Revealing Moment in Red Cross History," *Canadian Bulletin of Medical History* 9 (1992): 177–90.

117. *SST*, June 20, 1918.

118. Carolyn Dudley Coit, "History of Collinsville, Illinois Chapter of the American Red Cross," signed typescript, no date [1920?], Collinsville Memorial Public Library, Collinsville.

119. Ibid., 11.

120. Coit, "History of Collinsville, Illinois Chapter of the American Red Cross," 15. On women's work in the Red Cross in Europe, see Lettie Gavin, *American Women in World War I: They Also Served* (Niwot: University Press of Colorado, 1997), 183–89.

121. Coit, "History of Collinsville, Illinois Chapter of the American Red Cross," 6–8.

122. Ibid., 6a (there are two successive pages labeled page 6; this is the second one).

123. Ibid., 3.

124. Ibid., 1.

125. *SST*, February 21, 1918.

126. "Record of War Prisoner," Case 9-16-12-3117, Box 275, RG 60, National Archives.

127. E. C. Knotts to Attorney General Thomas Gregory, March 4, 1918, ibid.

128. Henry H. Morgan to John Lord O'Brien, War Emergency Branch, Department of Justice, May 9, 1918, ibid.

129. "Record of War Prisoner"; E. C. Knotts to Attorney General Gregory, July 31, 1919, both in ibid.

3. "To Scab upon This Great National Union"

1. McCartin, *Labor's Great War*, Table 1, 43.

2. UMWA, *Proceedings of the Twenty-sixth Consecutive and Third Biennial Convention*, 471. The figure cited by Frank Farrington was 40,000, but since his figure included the strike over the Washington Agreement, which started October 16, and included an estimated 15,000 Illinois miners, I have estimated 25,000 by October 6.

3. Corbin, *Life, Work, and Rebellion*, 177.

4. Quoted in *Black Diamond* 59 (August 18, 1917): 127.

5. William C. Fitts to Hon. Louis F. Post, May 19, 1917, Classified Subject Files, 16-58, Coal Strike, Virden, Ill., Box 3361, RG 60, National Archives.

6. William B. Wilson to Newton Baker, June 22, 1917, as enclosure in William B. Wilson to Woodrow Wilson, June 22, 1917, *PWW*, 42:563.

7. Annual Message to Congress, December 7, 1915, ibid., 35:307.

8. Foner, *History of the Labor Movement*, 7:55.

9. McCartin, *Labor's Great War*, 60.

10. Foner, *History of the Labor Movement*, 7:52–61.

11. Ibid., 7:61.

12. On Rintelen's activities in regard to the Labor's National Peace Council, see Reinhard R. Doerries, *Imperial Challenge: Ambassador Count Bernstorff and German-American Relations, 1908–1917* (Chapel Hill: University of North Carolina Press, 1989), 183–84. See also Foner, *History of the Labor Movement*, 7:60–62.

13. *CH*, August 3, 1917, reprinted from the *St. Louis Republic*, August 2, 1917.

14. *Belleville Semi-Weekly Advocate*, August 14, 1914.

15. McCartin, *Labor's Great War*, 40.

16. James Walker to John Walker, April 4, 1916, Box 7, 39-2, JHWP.

17. "Amendment to the Agreement of 1916–1918, Entered into by the Interstate Joint Conference, New York, April 17, 1917," in Louis Bloch, *Labor Agreements in Coal Mines* (New York: Russell Sage Foundation, 1931), 356–57.

18. Frank Farrington to Officers and Members of District 12, UMWA, April 28, 1917, United Mine Workers of America, President's Office correspondence with districts, 1898–1973, Box 164, Folder 4. Historical Collections and Labor Archives, Special Collections Library, University Libraries, Pennsylvania State University.

19. *CH*, November 23, 1917.

20. *SST*, August 24, 1917.

21. Report of Special Committee of The [Illinois] State Council of Defense, July 24, 1917, United Mine Workers of America, President's Office correspondence with districts, 1898–1973, Box 164, Folder 4. Historical Collections and Labor Archives, Special Collections Library, University Libraries, Pennsylvania State University.

22. W. T. Hutchinson, *Lowden of Illinois*, 1:335–37.

23. Department of Mines and Minerals, *Thirty-second Annual Coal Report of Illinois*, 217–18.

24. William Graebner, *Coal-Mining Safety in the Progressive Era* (Lexington: University Press of Kentucky, 1976), 57–58, 130.

25. *Coal Age* 13 (March 30, 1918): 593.

26. Interview with Pete Perry.

27. Department of Mines and Minerals, *Thirty-fifth Annual Coal Report of Illinois*, 212–13; Department of Mines and Minerals, *Thirty-sixth Annual Coal Report of Illinois* (Springfield: Department of Mines and Minerals, 1917), 220–21; Department of Mines

and Minerals, *Thirty-seventh Annual Coal Report of Illinois* (Springfield: Department of Mines and Minerals, 1918), 206–7.

28. Ernestine C. Rissi to Woodrow Wilson, November 1, 1919, Box 116, Case File 170\882, Bituminous Coal Strike, RG 280, Washington National Records Center, Suitland, Md.

29. The nonfatal injury rate at No. 2 rose from twenty-one per million miner-hours to thirty per million miner-hours. There was an even more dramatic jump at Lumaghi No. 2 in Collinsville, where the rate more than quadrupled, from twelve per million in 1916–17 to forty-nine per million in 1917–1918. Department of Mines and Minerals, *Thirty-sixth Annual Coal Report of Illinois*, 220–21; Department of Mines and Minerals, *Thirty-seventh Annual Coal Report of Illinois*, 206–7.

30. Corbin, *Life, Work, and Rebellion*, 10.

31. *SST*, December 4, 1914.

32. Quoted in Laslett, "Swan Song or New Social Movement?," 184.

33. *CH*, August 3, 1917.

34. Ibid., April 12, 1918.

35. Ibid., August 17, 1917.

36. *SST*, August 17, 1917.

37. UMWA, *Proceedings of the Twenty-sixth Consecutive and Third Biennial Convention*, 471.

38. *CH*, August 17, 1917.

39. Frank Farrington to Francis Peabody, August 11, 1917, Case 33/620 file, Box 28, RG 280, Washington National Records Center (hereafter cited as 33/620 file).

40. Hugh Kerwin to William B. Wilson, August 13, 1917, ibid.

41. Harry Herb to Woodrow Wilson, August 13, 1917, ibid. The labor secretary received the letter two days later.

42. William B. Wilson to Frank Farrington, August 17, 1917, ibid. In quoting from the telegram, I have omitted the telegraph instruction "stop," which appears at the end of each sentence in this copy.

43. Melvyn Dubofsky, *The State and Labor in Modern America* (Chapel Hill: University of North Carolina Press, 1994), 79. For a more critical theoretical perspective on the contradictory role played by the Department of Labor, see Nancy Di Tomasi, "Class Politics and Public Bureaucracy: The U.S. Department of Labor," in *Classes, Class Conflict, and the State: Empirical Studies in Class Analysis*, ed. Maurice Zeitlin (Cambridge, Mass.: Winthrop Publishers, Inc., 1980).

44. McCartin, *Labor's Great War*, 146.

45. Frank Farrington to William B. Wilson, 21 August 1917, 33/620 file.

46. *CH*, August 24, 1917.

47. For more on the Washington Agreement, see Sylvia Kopald, *Rebellion in Labor Unions* (New York: Boni and Liveright, 1924), 54–57; Montgomery, *Fall of the House of Labor*, 387; and Alexander Bing, *War-Time Strikes and Their Adjustment* (New York: E. P. Dutton and Company, 1921), 96–101.

48. Quoted in Bloch, *Labor Agreements in Coal Mines*, 358.

49. Ibid., 359.

50. Ibid., 399–401.

51. Circular letter, Frank Farrington to Officers and Members of District 12, UMWA, December 24, 1917, Enclosure in Frank Farrington to A. Mitchell Palmer, January 24, 1920, File 16-130-23, "Coal Strike in Illinois," Box 3361, RG 60, National Archives. For more on the "subterfuges" some miners used to get around the penalty clause, see McCartin, *Labor's Great War,* 126.

52. *CH,* October 19, 1917.

53. Ibid.

54. *SST,* October 26, 1917.

55. *CH,* November 2, 1917.

56. For a portrait of the Lead Belt, centered in the towns of Flat River and Bonne Terre, Missouri, see Christopher Gibbs, "The Lead Belt Riot and World War One," *Missouri Historical Review* 71 (July 1977): 396–418.

57. *CH,* December 12, 1913.

58. For an account of the dangers of lead smelting work, see Alice Hamilton, *Exploring the Dangerous Trades: The Autobiography of Alice Hamilton, M.D.* (Boston: Little, Brown and Co., 1943), 143–54.

59. *CH,* December 22, 1916, November 23, 1917.

60. Ibid., April 6, June 2, August 10, 1917.

61. Ibid., August 10, 1917; Minutes of UMWA Local 826, November 13, 1917, Box 6, PMW.

62. *CH,* August 24, 1917.

63. Ibid., November 30, 1917.

64. Ibid., September 28, 1917.

65. Ibid., October 5, 1917.

66. Ibid., October 19, 1917.

67. *SST,* September 14, 1917, quoting coverage in *Illinois State Register* of Springfield. On the Springfield strike, see Kenton Gatyas, "Springfield's General Strike of 1917," *Journal of Illinois History* 1 (Autumn 1998): 43–56; and Montgomery, *Fall of the House of Labor,* 371.

68. The lopsided character of the violence and the collusion of state militia in it suggest that this term is more appropriate than the somewhat amorphous "riot." For a discussion of the East St. Louis attacks as a pogrom, see Herbert Shapiro, *White Violence and Black Response from Reconstruction to Montgomery* (Amherst: University of Massachusetts Press, 1988), 115.

69. Elliott Rudwick, *Race Riot at East St. Louis, July 2, 1917* (Carbondale: Southern Illinois University Press, 1964).

70. *CH,* June 22, July 6, 1917. For a fascinating parallel to East St. Louis, which involves smelter workers scapegoating immigrants instead of blacks in the Missouri Lead Belt south of St. Louis, see Gibbs, "Lead Belt Riot," 396–418.

71. *CH,* October 26, 1917.

72. Ibid., November 2, November 9, 1917.

73. Ibid., November 2, 1917.

74. Ibid.

75. Ibid., November 9, 1917.

76. *Biographical Record: This Volume Contains Biographical Sketches of Leading Citizens of Macoupin County, Illinois* (Chicago: Richmond and Arnold, 1904), 288.

77. *SST,* July 16, 1915.

78. Victor Olander to Samuel Gompers, November 3, 1917, reprinted in *CH,* November 23, 1917 (my emphasis).

79. Irvine Strain to Victor Olander, December 7, 1917, "S" file, TF 4, IFL.

80. Stephen Norwood, *Labor's Flaming Youth: Telephone Operators and Worker Militancy, 1878–1923* (Urbana: University of Illinois Press, 1990).

81. *CH,* February 1, 1918.

82. Ibid., February 15, 1918. The solidarity won by operators in Collinsville is similar to the experience of operators in Fort Smith, Arkansas, another coal mining region with a militant tradition, in the fall of 1918. There, too, local merchants supported the striking operators, as did miners and other organized workers. Solidarity went even further in Fort Smith, as working people carried out a general strike in support of the operators. See Norwood, *Labor's Flaming Youth,* 160–62.

83. *SST,* December 13, 1917.

84. Archbald, *Four Hour Day in Coal,* 107. The incident is identified only by a case number—the location is not specified.

85. McCartin, *Labor's Great War,* 125.

86. UMWA, *Proceedings of the Twenty-sixth Consecutive and Third Biennial Convention,* 399.

87. Ibid., 395.

88. Ibid., 425.

89. The language used by these Illinois miners was remarkably similar to that employed by Kansas miners in 1921 during their fight against the new Industrial Court Law. As James Gray Pope notes, "An abundance of colorful metaphors—chains, shackles, fetters, and lashes—gave testimony to the salience of bodily subjugation. If the miners were to submit to the Industrial Court, they would be 'driven like Uncle Tom'" ("Labor's Constitution of Freedom," *Yale Law Journal* 106 [January 1997]: 979).

90. UMWA, *Proceedings of the Twenty-sixth Consecutive and Third Biennial Convention,* 475.

91. Ibid., 484 (my emphasis).

92. Ibid., 495.

4. "The Spanish Inquisition Has Reached the State of Illinois"

1. Robert H. Ferrell, *Woodrow Wilson and World War I, 1917–1921* (New York: Harper and Row, 1985), 18, 50.

2. Ibid., 65–68.

3. *CH,* February 15, 1918.

4. Ibid., March 8, 1918.

5. Ibid., March 1, 1918.

6. John Keegan, *The Face of Battle* (New York: Viking Press, 1976), 293.

7. "The First Raid," *Saturday Evening Post,* December 29, 1917, 8–9, 42, 45.

8. *CH,* January 4, 1918. See Alfred W. Crosby, *America's Forgotten Pandemic: The Influenza of 1918* (Cambridge: Cambridge University Press, 1989).

9. *CH,* December 6, 1918.

10. Keegan, *Face of Battle,* 255–56, 264–65.

11. *Collinsville City Directory* (1919). Richard, Jim, and their father, Richard Sr., all worked at Donk No. 1.

12. *CH,* March 1, 1918.

13. Thomas Gregory to Hon. R. L. Batts (U.S. Circuit Court of Appeals, New Orleans, La.), March 26, 1918, Papers of Thomas Gregory.

14. Quoted in Paul Murphy, *World War I and the Origin of Civil Liberties in the United States* (New York: W. W. Norton and Co., 1979), 83.

15. *CH,* December 7, 1917.

16. Ibid., January 25, 1918.

17. Ibid., March 1, 1918.

18. Ibid.

19. Flag Day speech, June 14, 1917, *PWW,* 42:499–500.

20. Luebke, *Bonds of Loyalty,* 235.

21. H. C. Peterson, *Propaganda for War: The Campaign Against American Neutrality, 1914–1917* (Norman: University of Oklahoma Press, 1939; Port Washington, N.Y.: Kennikat Press, 1968), 134–58 (page citations are to the reprint edition). For the most extensive and detailed account of German espionage and sabotage operations, see Doerries, *Imperial Challenge.* For one German operative's account, see Franz von Rintelen, *The Dark Invader: Wartime Reminiscences of a German Naval Intelligence Officer* (Portland: International Specialized Book Services, 1998).

22. Quoted in Luebke, *Bonds of Loyalty,* 243.

23. Peterson, *Propaganda for War,* 148–49. On the Black Tom case, see Jules Witcover, *Sabotage at Black Tom: Imperial Germany's Secret War in America: 1914–1917* (Chapel Hill: Algonquin Books, 1989), 308, on damages awarded, and Doerries, *Imperial Challenge,* 188–89. The Black Tom case dragged on for decades; only in 1939 did a joint U.S.-German Mixed Claims Commission award millions of dollars in damages to the plaintiffs. Although the German government never admitted guilt, key documents reviewed by the commission suggest that German agents were likely responsible for the blast. On John Rathom, see Ross, *Propaganda for War,* 206–10.

24. Woodrow Wilson to Thomas Gregory, March 25, 1918, *PWW,* 47:172.

25. Gregory to Wilson, quoted in Wilson to Malcolm Ross McAddoo, March 28, 1918, *PWW,* 47:172–73.

26. "Broken Glass in Foodstuff Not Intentionally Placed, Attorney General Reports," *Official Bulletin* 2 (April 15, 1918): 4.

27. Kaufman, *A Vision of Unity,* 80.

28. *CH,* December 21, December 28, 1917.

29. In fact, it may have been even worse for German-born mine owners. In the Madi-

son County town of Bethalto, John Kowaljik, a German-born owner of a small mine, applied for a license and was refused. Kowaljik had lived in the United States since 1913 and applied for citizenship in 1916, receiving his first papers at that time. According to a press article, after the license was refused, "his case was reported to the Bureau of Mines at Washington" (*Coal Age* 13 [January 12, 1918]: 78).

30. *CH,* March 29, 1918.

31. Ibid., April 5, 1918.

32. *Coal Age* 13 (February 16, 1918): 339.

33. Department of Mines and Minerals, *Thirty-seventh Annual Coal Report of Illinois,* 184–85; *Coal Age* 13 (March 9, 1918): 476.

34. *CH,* March 8, 1918; *Coal Age* 13 (March 9, 1918): 476.

35. The most important of these documents are the following: Josephine Oberdan to President Woodrow Wilson, January 25, 1918, translation from French by author; Edward C. Knotts to U.S. Attorney General Thomas Gregory, December 13, 1917; John L. Metzen to Woodrow Wilson, December 23, 1917; John Metzen to Woodrow Wilson, February 15, 1918, all in 9-19-1739, Box 801, RG 60, National Archives; and Edward Wieck to John Walker, February 14, 1918, John Walker folder, TF 4, IFL.

36. The Oberdan case is briefly discussed in Laslett, "Swan Song or New Social Movement?," 199. The violence in Staunton is treated in D. T. Wieck, *Woman from Spillertown,* 71–72.

37. John Metzen to Woodrow Wilson, February 13, 1918, File 9-19-1739, Box 801, RG 60, National Archives. Metzen's comment offers a bitterly ironic twist on the discussion of patriotic celebrations in Illinois provided by John Bodnar. See his *Remaking America: Public Memory, Commemoration, and Patriotism in the Twentieth Century* (Princeton, N.J.: Princeton University Press, 1991), 119.

38. D. T. Wieck, *Woman from Spillertown,* 72.

39. Edward Wieck to John Walker, February 14, 1918, from St. Louis, Mo., John Walker folder, TF 4, IFL.

40. Severino Oberdan to John Metzen, February 6, 1918, enclosure in John Metzen to Woodrow Wilson, February 15, 1918, File 9-19-1739, Box 801, RG 60, National Archives.

41. On the lynching of Frank Little, see Foner, *History of the Labor Movement,* 7:286–91; Arnon Gutfeld, "The Murder of Frank Little: Radical Labor Agitation in Butte, Montana, 1917," *Labor History* 10 (Spring 1969): 177–92; and Peterson and Fite, *Opponents of War,* 57–60.

42. UMWA, District 12, *Proceedings of the Twenty-seventh Consecutive and the Second Biennial Convention of the United Mine Workers of America, District 12* (Peoria, Ill.: UMWA, 1918), 218–24.

43. *CH,* March 8, 1918.

44. For a study of employers' direct use of vigilantism against unions, see Steven C. Levi, *Committee of Vigilance: The San Francisco Chamber of Commerce Law and Order Committee, 1916–1919: A Case Study in Official Hysteria* (Jefferson, N.C.: McFarland and Company, 1983), and Robert P. Ingalls, "Antiradical Violence in Birmingham during the 1930s," *Journal of Southern History* 47 (November 1981): 521–44.

45. *CH*, March 8, 1918; UMWA, District 12, *Proceedings of the Twenty-seventh Consecutive and the Second Biennial Convention,* 213.

46. Quoted in *SST,* March 14, 1918.

47. *Coal Age* 13 (April 6, 1918): 636.

48. Ibid. (April 20, February 23, 1918).

49. UMWA, District 12, *Proceedings of the Twenty-eighth Consecutive and Third Biennial Convention of the United Mine Workers of America, District No. 12* (Peoria, Ill.: UMWA, 1920), 574–75.

50. *Coal Age* 13 (April 6, 1918): 635.

5. "White-Hot Mass Instinct"

1. "Baker Says R. P. Prager Was Loyal," *East St. Louis Daily Journal,* April 7, 1918, 6.

2. Interview with Albert "Kites" Meyer, Collinsville, Ill., May 28, 1991.

3. Quoted in E. A. Schwartz, "The Lynching of Robert Prager, the United Mine Workers, and the Problems of Patriotism in 1918," unpublished paper, 1995, 24. I am grateful to the author for permission to quote from this paper.

4. Luebke, *Bonds of Loyalty,* 4.

5. Interview with Albert "Kites" Meyer.

6. Quoted in Schwartz, "The Lynching of Robert Prager," 14.

7. Luebke, *Bonds of Loyalty,* 4; D. R. Hickey, "Prager Affair," 117–34.

8. *CH,* May 31, 1918.

9. Ibid., April 5, 1918.

10. Ibid., May 24, 1918.

11. "Was in St. Louis," *Edwardsville Intelligencer,* May 24, 1918.

12. "Baker Says R. P. Prager Was Loyal," 1, 6.

13. Interview with Joe Brabec Sr., White City, Ill., June 3, 1991.

14. "Investigation Waits on Inquest Monday," *New York Times,* April 6, 1918, A15.

15. D. R. Hickey, "Prager Affair," 118.

16. *CH,* April 20, 1917.

17. *St. Louis Republic,* April 8, 1918; *CH,* October 18, 1918.

18. *CH,* April 12, 1918.

19. Ibid., June 13, 1918.

20. Ibid., April 19, 1918.

21. D. R. Hickey, "Prager Affair," 127.

22. Luebke, *Bonds of Loyalty,* 5; D. R. Hickey, "Prager Affair," 118–19. Hickey erroneously dates the first attack on Prager as Thursday, April 4. Luebke's account accurately puts the first attack on Wednesday, April 3, Prager's printed appeal to the miners on Thursday morning, and the subsequent events that culminated in the lynching on Thursday evening and early Friday morning. Peterson and Fite *(Opponents of War)* do not mention the first attack or Prager's subsequent appeal to the miners.

23. "Investigation Waits on Inquest Monday," A15.

24. Luebke, *Bonds of Loyalty,* 5.

25. Text of proclamation quoted in full in Heilig, "Community Torn Apart," 84. To his credit, Heilig is the only scholar to have included the text in his writing.

26. *CH,* April 5, 1918.

27. Heilig, "Community Torn Apart," 85.

28. Luebke, *Bonds of Loyalty,* 6.

29. Department of Mines and Minerals, *Thirty-seventh Annual Coal Report of Illinois,* 207.

30. *CH,* May 28, 1918. This contradicts Luebke's account, which has Mayor Siegel meeting up with the crowd only *after* Prager was in police hands. But Siegel's own testimony, while open to question, is probably accurate. In the aftermath of the lynching, if Siegel had wanted to bend the truth to place himself in a more favorable light, he would probably not have admitted that he saw the antics of the crowd and did nothing. This suggests that his own recollection of the timing of his arrival is probably the correct one.

31. *CH,* May 29, 1918.

32. As a historical document, Riegel's confession has a number of obvious limitations. In addition to the problems of accuracy and precision attending any such eyewitness testimony, it suffers from the fact that Riegel freely admitted to being under the influence of alcohol during the night's events. Moreover, once on trial for murder, Riegel changed his story. Despite these problems, however, there are a number of reasons to consider it a valid source. First, it is not contradicted in any significant way by the testimony of others. Second, in his trial testimony, Riegel did not deny being present during the entire train of events, leading from city hall to the lynching tree. And he did not present an alternate detailed account of the lynching. Rather, he issued a series of flat denials to every question presented to him, suggesting that his original confession may well have been truthfully given. Therefore, in conjunction with other evidence, I will use his confession as a roughly reliable account of the events of April 4–5.

33. *CH,* April 12, 1918.

34. Ibid., May 28, 1918.

35. Luebke, *Bonds of Loyalty,* 7.

36. *CH,* May 31, 1918 (my emphasis).

37. D. R. Hickey, "Prager Affair," 120–21 n. 8.

38. *CH,* May 29, 1918; Luebke, *Bonds of Loyalty,* 8.

39. *CH,* April 27, 1918.

40. Ibid., May 29, 1918.

41. This alleged statement by Prager is the only evidence, aside from Lobenad's claimed conversation with him, that Prager was guilty of anything. But there seems to have been a large degree of vagueness of the meaning of the question and the answer. It was not obvious to Riegel what the question meant. And the subsequent question about relatives suggests that the mob members were not sure that Prager even understood it. If Prager did say such a thing, it is easy to imagine that he made such an admission in the vague hope that it might save his life. In any event, no other witness in the trial or any outside commentator treated this alleged statement as serious evidence of guilt.

42. Luebke, *Bonds of Loyalty*, 9.

43. *CH*, April 5, 1918; translation in Luebke, *Bonds of Loyalty*, 10.

44. Luebke, *Bonds of Loyalty*, 10.

45. "Prager Asked Mob to Wrap Body in Flag," *New York Times*, April 11, 1918, A11.

46. There are twenty-nine individuals who were identified in trial testimony as being present at the lynching. Except in the case of Cecil Larremore, who denied going as far as the lynching tree, the presence of these twenty-nine was not contradicted by any other trial testimony. Their names and, in some cases, ages and occupations are drawn from coverage of the trial in the *Collinsville Herald*. See *CH*, May 28, May 29, May 31, 1918. For a full list of these names, see appendix.

47. D. R. Hickey, "Prager Affair," 121.

48. *CH*, June 1, 1918.

49. Dennis B. Downey and Raymond M. Hyser, *No Crooked Death: Coatesville, Pennsylvania and the Lynching of Zachariah Walker* (Urbana: University of Illinois Press, 1991), 38. In the Wisconsin case, Bertha Olsen was tried and convicted of lynching her husband, though she apparently was not actually present at the scene of the crime. See Jane Pederson, "Gender, Justice, and a Wisconsin Lynching, 1889–1890," *Agricultural History* 67 (Spring 1993): 65–82.

50. See, for example, E. P. Thompson, "The Moral Economy of the English Crowd in the Eighteenth Century," *Past and Present* 50 (1971): 115–18.

51. *CH*, April 12, 1918.

52. For a fascinating study of mob violence in New York City that analyzes a wide range of "rioting" during this earlier period, see Paul Gilje, *The Road to Mobocracy: Popular Disorder in New York City, 1763–1834* (Chapel Hill: University of North Carolina Press, 1987).

53. Richard Maxwell Brown, *Strain of Violence: Historical Studies of American Vigilantism* (New York: Oxford University Press, 1975).

54. James Elbert Cutler, *Lynch-Law: An Investigation into the History of Lynching in the United States* (New York: Longmans, Green, and Co., 1905), 180. On vigilantism in late-nineteenth- and early-twentieth-century Missouri, see David Thelen, *Paths of Resistance: Tradition and Dignity in Industrializing Missouri* (New York: Oxford University Press, 1986), 86–99. On a mid-nineteenth-century lynching of a white man for murder, see John A. Lupton, "'In View of the Uncertainty of Life': A Coles County Lynching," *Illinois Historical Journal* 89 (Autumn 1996): 134–46. On the lynching of an Illinois African American later in the nineteenth century, see Sundiata Cha-Jua, "'Join Hands and Hearts with Law and Order': The 1893 Lynching of Samuel J. Bush and the Response of Decatur's African American Community," *Illinois Historical Journal* 83 (1990): 187–200.

55. See Roberta Senechal, *The Sociogenesis of a Race Riot: Springfield, Illinois, in 1908* (Urbana: University of Illinois Press, 1990).

56. W. Fitzhugh Brundage, *Lynching in the New South: Georgia and Virginia, 1880–1930* (Urbana: University of Illinois Press, 1993), 36–41.

57. Suzanne Desan, "Crowds, Community, and Ritual in the Work of E. P. Thomp-

son and Natalie Davis," in *The New Cultural History,* ed. Lynn Hunt (Berkeley: University of California Press, 1989), 67–68.

58. For a thoughtful discussion of the scholarship, see Brundage, *Lynching in the New South,* 1–16.

59. George Creel, *Rebel at Large: Recollections of Fifty Crowded Years* (New York: G. P. Putnam's Sons, 1947), 196, 199.

60. *New York Times,* April 6, 1918, 15; Gregory quoted in *Chicago Daily Tribune,* April 6, 1918, 4.

61. Liberty Loan Address, Baltimore, Md., April 6, 1918, *PWW,* 47:270.

62. *New York Times,* April 8, 1918, A14.

63. Hon. J. D. Perkins to Thomas Gregory, April 6, 1918, Department of Justice, RG 60, Straight Numerical File 191395, Box 2760, National Archives (hereafter cited as Box 2760).

64. Lee Beaty to Hon. Dan Garrett, April 6, 1918, ibid.

65. Helmer M. Feroe to Thomas Gregory, April 8, 1918, ibid.

66. Walter Lancaster Lingenfelder to Thomas Gregory, May 17, 1918, ibid.

67. George Creel, "Unite and Win," *Independent* 94 (April 6, 1918): 5–6.

68. *St. Louis Republic,* April 7, 1918, 2.

69. *CH,* April 26, 1918.

70. Ibid., April 7, 1918.

71. *Chicago Daily Tribune,* April 7, 1918, 7. For more incidents, see Luebke, *Bonds of Loyalty,* 14–15.

72. *St. Louis Republic,* April 8, 1918.

73. *CH,* April 26, 1918 (emphasis in original). It is not clear from the text of the ad who placed it. It is the style of CPI material, but it is not so identified. Possibly it was done by a group like the National Security League.

74. *CH,* May 28, 1918.

75. Quoted in Tingley, *Structuring of a State,* 206.

76. Luebke, *Bonds of Loyalty,* 16.

77. *CH,* April 19, 1918.

78. *Chicago Daily Tribune,* April 6, 1918, 8.

79. *CH,* April 19, 1918.

80. *St. Louis Republic,* April 6, 1918.

81. *St. Louis Globe-Democrat,* April 5, 1918.

82. *Chicago Daily Tribune,* April 7, 1918, 1. Lowden's speech is reprinted in Jenison, *Illinois in the World War,* 6:350–52.

83. *Congressional Record,* 65th Cong., 2d sess., 1918, pt. 5:4633.

84. Ibid., 4645.

85. Ibid., 4769.

86. D. R. Hickey, "Prager Affair," 124.

87. *Chicago Daily Tribune,* April 8, 1918, 17.

88. Adolph Germer to Woodrow Wilson, April 8, 1918, Box 2760.

89. Jean Y. Tussey, ed., *Eugene Debs Speaks* (New York: Pathfinder Press, 1972), 251, 258–59.

90. Ibid., 276. Thanks to the late Meyer Weinberg for calling my attention to this reference.

91. Minutes of Joint Conference of National Executive Committee and State Secretaries, August 10–12, 1918, Chicago, Ill., reel 95, Papers of the Socialist Party of America, microfilm, Yale University.

92. *New York Times,* April 12, 1918, A10.

93. John Lord O'Brien to Frank Polk, April 13, 1918, quoted in O'Brien to Polk, September 17, 1918, Box 2760.

94. Quoted in *New York Times,* May 8, 1918, A7.

95. *New York Times,* May 9, 1918, A12.

96. James Walker to John Walker, May 11, 1918, Box 7, 54-10, JHWP.

97. *CH,* January 11, 1990.

98. Ibid., April 5, 1918.

99. "Resolution of Hormonie Lodge 353 I.O.O.F.," dated April 9, 1918, St. Louis, Mo., Box 2760.

100. *CH,* May 24, 1918.

101. Minute Books of Madison Lodge #43, I.O.O.F., 1918. I am grateful to Odd Fellow Richard Hays, secretary of Madison Lodge #43, who allowed me access to these records.

102. "Lynched Man Is Interred in U.S. Flag," *St. Louis Globe-Democrat,* April 11, 1918, 1, <http://www.staff.uiuc.edu/~rcunning/stlgd4.htm> (July 16, 1999).

103. Ott, "The Anti-German Hysteria," 341. For maps with directions to St. Matthew's Cemetery and the Prager gravesite, see 324–25.

104. *CH,* April 12, 1918. Some words are illegible due to the poor quality of the microfilm.

105. "Collinsville Mob Leaders Expected to Be Put on Trial," *St. Louis Globe-Democrat,* April 6, 1918, 1, <http://www.staff.uiuc.edu/~rcunning/stlgd2.htm> (May 17, 2001).

106. *CH,* March 15, 1990.

107. Nancy MacLean, "The Leo Frank Case Reconsidered: Gender and Sexual Politics in the Making of Reactionary Populism," *Journal of American History* 78 (December 1991): 917–48. For other studies that make a similar connection, see Jacquelyn Dowd Hall, "Disorderly Women: Gender and Labor Militancy in the Appalachian South," *Journal of American History* 73 (September 1986): 354–82, and Kathy Peiss, *Cheap Amusements: Working Women and Leisure in Turn-of-the-Century New York* (Philadelphia: Temple University Press, 1986).

108. Quoted in Ruth Rosen, *The Lost Sisterhood: Prostitution in America, 1900–1918* (Baltimore: Johns Hopkins University Press, 1982), 113.

109. Ibid., 118 (for conviction figures), 133.

110. *East St. Louis Daily Journal,* April 14, 1918.

111. Mark Thomas Connelly, *The Response to Prostitution in the Progressive Era* (Chapel Hill: University of North Carolina Press, 1980), 6, 47. See also Rosen, *Lost Sisterhood;* Peiss, *Cheap Amusements;* and Joanne Meyerowitz, *Women Adrift: Independent Wage-Earners in Chicago, 1880–1930* (Chicago: University of Chicago Press, 1988).

112. *CH*, May 8, 1914.

113. Ibid., September 5, 1913, January 16, March 27, 1914.

114. James McGovern, *Anatomy of a Lynching: The Killing of Claude Neal* (Baton Rouge: Louisiana State University Press, 1982), x.

115. Quoted in D. R. Hickey, "Prager Affair," 128.

116. *CH*, April 27, 1918; *New York Times*, April 12, 1918, 10.

117. *CH*, April 12, 1918.

118. D. R. Hickey, "Prager Affair," 129.

119. *CH*, May 28, 1918.

120. Luebke, *Bonds of Loyalty*, 23.

121. *CH*, May 31, 1918 (my emphasis).

122. Foreign Office (German) to Swiss Legation, June 10, 1918, translation, Box 2760.

123. *Proceedings of the Reichstag*, 172d sess., June 11, 1918, 5375–76. I am indebted to Manuela Thurner for translating this passage from the original German.

124. *New York Times*, June 13, 1918, 12.

125. Robert Zangrando, *The NAACP Crusade Against Lynching, 1909–1950* (Philadelphia: Temple University Press, 1980). On attempts to move antilynching legislation through Congress, see Claudine L. Ferrell, *Nightmare and Dream: Antilynching in Congress, 1917–1922* (New York: Garland Publishing, Inc., 1986).

126. Leslie Pinckney Hill to Thomas Gregory, April 6, 1918, Box 2760.

127. Attorney General Gregory to Alfred Bettman, April 16, 1918, ibid.

128. Algie Simons, "A Reply to the 'Labour Leader,'" *London Justice*, July 25, 1918, reel 95, Papers of the Socialist Party of America.

129. Statement to the American People, *PWW*, 49:98–99.

130. Robert Russa Moton to Woodrow Wilson, July 27, 1918, *PWW*, 49:113–14.

131. Shapiro, *White Violence and Black Response*, 145. For a discussion of how Dwight Eisenhower's presidential administration handled a later prominent lynching case, see Stephen Whitfield, *A Death in the Delta: The Story of Emmett Till* (New York: Free Press, 1988), 71–84.

132. Gerstle, *Working-Class Americanism*, 309.

133. McCartin, *Labor's Great War*, 42.

134. Yvette Huginnie, "Wobblies, War and Repression: The Politics of Race and Radicalism in the Arizona Strikes of 1917–1919," unpublished paper, 1993, in possession of author. For another insightful study that emphasizes the contradictions of Wilson administration policy in regard to vigilantism, see Christopher Capozzola, "The Only Badge Needed Is Your Patriotic Fervor: Vigilance, Coercion, and the Law in World War I America," *Journal of American History* 88 (March 2002): 1354–82.

6. "The Great Class War"

1. Quoted in *New Majority* (hereafter cited as *NM*), March 1, 1919, 10.

2. Quoted in Jeremy Brecher, *Strike!* (Boston: South End Press, 1972), 101.

3. UMWA, District 12, *Proceedings of the Twenty-eighth Consecutive and Third Biennial Convention*, 119–20.

4. *CH,* November 11, 1918.

5. *SST,* November 28, 1918; UMWA, District 12, *Proceedings of the Twenty-eighth Consecutive and Third Biennial Convention,* 428.

6. *CH,* November 29, 1918.

7. Crosby, *America's Forgotten Pandemic,* xiv, 5, 206.

8. Ibid., 11.

9. Joseph R. Buckles Memoir, Sangamon State University Oral History Collection, Coal Mining and Union Activities Project.

10. UMWA, District 12, *Proceedings of the Twenty-eighth Consecutive and Third Biennial Convention,* 338–438.

11. *CH,* December 12, 1918.

12. Ibid., October 18, 1918.

13. Crosby, *America's Forgotten Pandemic,* 86, 323.

14. UMWA, *Proceedings of the Twenty-seventh Consecutive and Fourth Biennial Convention of the United Mine Workers of America,* 3 vols. (Indianapolis: UMWA, 1919), 102.

15. UMWA, District 12, *Proceedings of the Twenty-eighth Consecutive and Third Biennial Convention,* 90–91.

16. John R. Bowman, *Capitalist Collective Action: Competition, Cooperation, and Conflict in the Coal Industry* (Cambridge: Cambridge University Press, 1989), 98–99.

17. Ernestine C. Rissi to Woodrow Wilson, November 1, 1919, Case File 170/882, "Bituminous Coal Strike," Box 116, RG 280, National Archives.

18. UMWA, *Proceedings of the Twenty-seventh Consecutive and Fourth Biennial Convention,* 128.

19. Quoted in *NM,* March 1, 1919, 10.

20. Minutes of UMWA Local 826, May 1, 1917, Box 6, PMW.

21. Financial Statement of the International Workers Defense League [for 1918], Mooney File, TF 3, IFL.

22. Foner, *History of the Labor Movement in the United States,* 7:78–95. For a detailed examination of the evidence by the Mooney defense campaign, see Robert Minor, *Justice Raped in California* (San Francisco: Tom Mooney Molders Defense Committee, n.d.), File 278, Box 6, RG 28, National Archives.

23. *NM,* January 25, 1919.

24. Laslett, "Swan Song or New Social Movement?," 183.

25. *NM,* January 25, 1919.

26. John B. Lennon to Hugh L. Kerwin, File 16/510-F, Box 52, RG 174, National Archives.

27. UMWA, District 12, *Proceedings of the Twenty-eighth Consecutive and Third Biennial Convention,* 485.

28. Ibid., 511.

29. Ibid., 585.

30. International Executive Board Minutes, May 5–6, 1919, United Mine Workers of America, International Executive Board Records, 1900–1989, Box 32, Folder 4. Historical

Collections and Labor Archives, Special Collections Library, University Libraries, Pennsylvania State University.

31. International Workers Defense League, "The Right to Strike for Liberty," March 20, 1919, Mooney File, TF 3, IFL.

32. Laslett, "Swan Song or New Social Movement?," 183–84.

33. Tellers' Report of Mooney Strike Referendum Vote of Sub-District No. 7, U.M.W.A., Belleville, Ill., May 21, 1919, and International Workers Defense League Record of Votes on Mooney Strike, both in Mooney File, TF 3, IFL. There are three locals in Subdistrict 7 for which no vote is recorded in the UMWA report, but a tally does appear in the IWDL record. Their combined vote was 419–28 for the strike. It is entirely possible that the figures appear in the IWDL record by mistake or were even fabricated. On the other hand, given the controversy within the UMWA about the vote and the strike, it is also conceivable that a vote took place and was not recorded in official records. I have hesitantly included these locals (Pocahontas, Rentchler, Freeburg, and Mascoutah) in the total.

34. The Maryville vote is recorded in International Workers Defense League Record of Votes on Mooney Strike, Mooney File, TF 3, IFL. For the breakdown of the UMWA Illinois subdistricts, as of 1918, see Frank Farrington to Officers and Members, District 12, UMWA, March 14, 1918, United Mine Workers of America, President's Office correspondence with districts, 1898–1973, Box 164, Folder 6. Historical Collections and Labor Archives, Special Collections Library, University Libraries, Pennsylvania State University.

35. *CH*, March 14, 1919.

36. Southern Illinois Mooney Defense League, "Proclamation," June 29, 1919, Case 16/510-F, Box 52, Case of Thomas Mooney, RG 174, National Archives.

37. UMWA, *Proceedings of the Twenty-seventh Consecutive and Fourth Biennial Convention*, 599.

38. Philip Foner, *History of the Labor Movement in the United States,* vol. 8, *Postwar Struggles, 1918–1920* (New York: International Publishers, 1988), 257–61. For more on John Fitzpatrick, see John H. Keiser, "John Fitzpatrick and Progressive Unionism" (Ph.D. diss., Northwestern University, 1965), and Eugene Staley, *History of the Illinois State Federation of Labor* (Chicago: University of Chicago Press, 1930).

39. *NM*, January 4, 1919, 15. On the CFL's program, see Elizabeth McKillen, *Chicago Labor and the Quest for a Democratic Diplomacy, 1914–1924* (Ithaca: Cornell University Press, 1995), and Andrew Strouthous, *U.S. Labor and Political Action, 1918–24: A Comparison of Independent Political Action in New York, Chicago, and Seattle* (New York: St. Martin's Press, 2000).

40. Return sheets on vote on proposal to organize the Illinois State Labor Party, Affiliated Organizations file, TF 5, IFL.

41. *CH*, April 15, 1919.

42. John McGowan to Frank Esper, April 22, 1919, Labor Party–1919 file, TF 5, IFL.

43. *CH*, April 18, 1919.

44. *NM*, March 29, 1919.

45. Ibid., January 25, 1919.

46. Ibid., August 2, 1919, 12.

47. *CH,* April 18, 1919.

48. Ibid., April 18, May 2, 1919.

49. *NM,* May 3, 1919, 8–9.

50. Ibid., April 19, 1919, 8; *CH,* April 18, 1919.

51. *NM,* March 15, April 12, 1919.

52. "The Bolsheviki Movement in America, at St Louis, Madison, Ill., West Frankfort, Frankfort Heights, Orient, Ill. and Vicinity, November 1920," in *U.S. Military Intelligence Reports: Surveillance of Radicals in the United States, 1917–1941* (microfilm), reel 19, frame 411-453, Yale University. This report was prepared by an agent of the Bureau of Investigation of the U.S. Justice Department.

53. *CH,* June 27, 1919.

54. Ben Dinsmore to William B. Wilson, October 26, 1919, Case 170/882, Box 116, RG 280, Washington National Records Center.

55. James P. Johnson, *The Politics of Soft Coal: The Bituminous Industry from World War I Through the New Deal* (Urbana: University of Illinois Press, 1979), 102.

56. For existing accounts of the activities of the Illinois miners in 1919, see Kopald, *Rebellion in Labor Unions,* 50–123; Brecher, *Strike!* 130–35; Laslett, "Swan Song or New Social Movement?," 167–214; and Montgomery, *Fall of the House of Labor,* 389–92.

57. *CH,* August 29, September 5, 1919.

58. Frank Farrington to the Officers and Members, District 12, UMWA, September 8, 1919, File 16-130-23, "Coal Strike in Illinois," Box 3361, RG 60, National Archives.

59. UMWA, District 12, *Proceedings of the Twenty-eighth Consecutive and Third Biennial Convention,* 591.

60. Kopald, *Rebellion in Labor Unions,* 74–5.

61. UMWA, District 12, *Proceedings of the Twenty-eighth Consecutive and Third Biennial Convention,* 552–53.

62. UMWA, *Proceedings of the Twenty-seventh Consecutive and Fourth Biennial Convention,* 87, 153, 173, 209–10, 230–33, 455, 488–89, 661.

63. Frank Farrington to the Officers and Members, District 12, UMWA, September 8, 1919, File 16-130-23, "Coal Strike in Illinois," Box 3361, RG 60, National Archives.

64. *CH,* September 5, 1919.

65. UMWA, *Proceedings of the Twenty-seventh Consecutive and Fourth Biennial Convention,* 484–85 (my emphasis).

66. UMWA, District 12, *Proceedings of the Twenty-eighth Consecutive and Third Biennial Convention,* 462, 468.

67. *CH,* August 15, 1919.

68. UMWA, District 12, *Proceedings of the Twenty-eighth Consecutive and Third Biennial Convention,* 600.

69. *CH,* September 19, 1919.

70. UMWA, *Proceedings of the Twenty-seventh Consecutive and Fourth Biennial Convention,* 498.

71. Belleville District Miners Defense League, Appeal for support, United Mine Workers

of America, President's Office correspondence with districts, 1898–1973, Box 164, Folder 6. Historical Collections and Labor Archives, Special Collections Library, University Libraries, Pennsylvania State University.

72. *CH,* September 19, September 26, 1919; *SST,* September 18, 1919.

73. *SST,* September 4, 1919; Kopald, *Rebellion in Labor Unions,* 108–9. The persistent appeal of the American flag as a potential symbol of working-class solidarity is suggested by an incident two years later, when Kansas coal miners were waging a militant strike against the legislation establishing the "corporatist" Industrial Court. When the strike started to weaken, women took the lead. They held a mass meeting from which men were excluded and soon were roaming from mine to mine, exhorting working miners to join the strike. As they confronted strikebreakers on the street,

> [t]he women demanded not only that working miners rejoin the strike, but also that they seal their promises by kissing the flag. Joining other working class Americans, the marchers had their own interpretation of the flag. After a group of marchers asked mine foreman Bob Murray to kiss the flag, a bewildered reporter commented that the "reason for this was not clear as Murry is known as a thoroughly patriotic American." A marcher explained that "Mr. Murray knew he had been bossing so we had to make him over." To the marchers, the American flag was the "flag of liberty," and the marching was designed to secure "our democracy that we was to receive after the World War." (Pope, "Labor's Constitution of Freedom," 1008)

On the women's participation in the strike, see Ann Schofield, "The Women's March: Miners, Family, and Community in Pittsburg, Kansas, 1921–22," *Kansas History* 7 (Summer 1984): 159–68.

74. UMWA, *Proceedings of the Twenty-seventh Consecutive and Fourth Biennial Convention,* 851–52.

75. UMWA, District 12, *Proceedings of the Twenty-eighth Consecutive and Third Biennial Convention,* 573–74.

76. Kopald, *Rebellion in Labor Unions,* 123.

77. See UMWA District 12, "Report of Secretary-Treasurer Walter Nesbit Relative to the $27,000.00 Expenditure," United Mine Workers of America, President's Office correspondence with districts, 1898–1973, Box 164, Folder 10. Historical Collections and Labor Archives, Special Collections Library, University Libraries, Pennsylvania State University.

78. *CH,* September 19, 1919.

79. Melvyn Dubofsky and Warren Van Tine, *John L. Lewis: A Biography* (New York: Quadrangle/The New York Times Book Co., 1977), 52–53.

80. Robert K. Murray, *Red Scare: A Study in National Hysteria, 1919–1920* (Minneapolis: University of Minnesota Press, 1955), 155.

81. *New York Times,* October 31, 1919, A12.

82. On the cossacks, see David Brody, *Labor in Crisis: The Steel Strike of 1919,* rev. ed. (Urbana: University of Illinois Press, 1987), 149.

83. *CH,* October 3, 1919.

84. Text of President's Statement Relative Coal Situation, Case 170/882, Dispute Case Files, Box 115, RG 280, Washington National Records Center.

85. Mrs. J. A. Faulkner to Woodrow Wilson, October 27, 1919, ibid.

86. *SST,* October 30, 1919.

87. *CH,* October 17, 1919.

88. Ibid., November 7, 1919.

89. Dubofsky and Van Tine, *John L. Lewis,* 55.

90. Ibid., 57.

91. Minutes of UMWA Local 264, November 10, 1919, Box 5, PMW.

92. *SST,* November 13, 1919; Dubofsky and Van Tine, *John L. Lewis,* 57.

93. *CH,* November 14, 1919.

94. Resolutions Committee of UMWA Local 730, Benld, Ill., to John L. Lewis, c/o William B. Wilson, U.S. Department of Labor, Case 170/882, Dispute Case Files, Box 115, RG 280, Washington National Records Center.

95. Minutes of UMWA Local 264, November 24, 1919, Box 5, PMW.

96. *CH,* November 14, 1919.

97. "To the Public of Carterville and the U.S.A. in General," Case 170/882-1, RG 280, Washington National Records Center.

98. Fred C. Williams to [Attorney General Palmer], December 2, 1919, File 16-130-23, Box 3361, RG 60, National Archives.

99. Belleville [Ill.] Manufacturers Association to A. Mitchell Palmer, December 5, 1919, ibid.

100. Dubofsky and Van Tine, *John L. Lewis,* 59.

101. Ibid., 59–60.

102. "Walker Attacks Judge Anderson," *Illinois State Journal,* November 7, 1919, and U.S. Attorney E. C. Knotts to A. Mitchell Palmer, December 3, 1919, both in File 16-130-23, Box 3361, RG 60, National Archives; Minutes of UMWA Local 264, December 8, 1919, Box 5, PMW.

103. *SST,* December 18, 1919, January 1, 1920.

104. UMWA, District 12, *Proceedings of the Twenty-eighth Consecutive and Third Biennial Convention,* 465–66.

105. "Why Illinois Miners Don't Trust the U.S.," *Chicago Daily News,* November 19, 1919, in File 170/882-B, Box 116, RG 280, National Archives.

106. U.S. Marshal Dallman to A. Mitchell Palmer, December 7, 1919, File 16-130-23, Box 3361, RG 60, National Archives.

107. Frank Farrington to A. Mitchell Palmer, January 24, 1920, ibid.

108. Marx and Engels, *The Communist Manifesto,* 21.

Epilogue

1. Leon Trotsky, *The History of the Russian Revolution* (New York: Pathfinder, 1980).

2. David Montgomery, "New Tendencies in Union Struggles and Strategies in Europe and the United States, 1916–1922," in *Work, Community and Power*, ed. James Cronin and Carmen Sirianni (Philadelphia: Temple University Press, 1983), 112.

3. On Agnes Burns Wieck and the Progressive Mine Workers of America Women's Auxiliary, see D. T. Wieck, *Woman from Spillertown*. On the PMWA, see Harriet Hudson, *The Progressive Mine Workers of America: A Study in Rival Unionism* (Urbana: University of Illinois, Bureau of Economic and Business Research, 1952).

4. Melvyn Dubofsky and Warren Van Tine, *John L. Lewis: A Biography* (Urbana: University of Illinois Press, 1986; abridged edition), 302–22; Art Preis, *Labor's Giant Step*, 2d ed. (New York: Pathfinder Press, 1972), 227–54.

5. Heilig, "Community Torn Apart," 95.

6. *CH*, January 17, 1919.

7. Heilig, "Community Torn Apart," 96.

8. Ibid.

9. Frederick Engels to Friedrich Adolph Sorge in Hoboken, N.J., from London, December 31, 1892, in Karl Marx and Frederick Engels, *Selected Correspondence, 1844–1895* (Moscow: Progress Publishers, 1955), 426.

10. Neather, "Labor Republicanism, Race, and Popular Patriotism," 100.

11. James Weinstein, *The Decline of Socialism in America, 1912–1925* (New York: Monthly Review Press, 1967), 339.

12. R. Dan Neely and Carla G. Heister, comps., *The Natural Resources of Illinois* (Champaign: Illinois Natural History Survey, 1989), 189, 191; Illinois Clean Coal Institute, "Facts about Coal in Illinois," <http://www.icci.org/fact.html> (August 2, 1999).

13. *Militant*, October 26, 1998.

14. *St. Louis Post-Dispatch*, November 18, 1998, A1.

15. *Militant*, November 30, 1998.

INDEX

Carl R. Weinberg is a native of Chicago, Illinois. He received his PhD in history from Yale University in 1995. His research interests include labor history and the controversy over evolutionary science. He currently teaches about history and politics at Indiana University.